MAR 2019

Android® Phones & Tablets

by Dan Gookin

A Wiley Brand

Android® Phones & Tablets For Dummies®

Published by: **John Wiley & Sons, Inc.**, 111 River Street, Hoboken, NJ 07030-5774, www.wiley.com

Copyright © 2018 by John Wiley & Sons, Inc., Hoboken, New Jersey

Published simultaneously in Canada

No part of this publication may be reproduced, stored in a retrieval system or transmitted in any form or by any means, electronic, mechanical, photocopying, recording, scanning or otherwise, except as permitted under Sections 107 or 108 of the 1976 United States Copyright Act, without the prior written permission of the Publisher. Requests to the Publisher for permission should be addressed to the Permissions Department, John Wiley & Sons, Inc., 111 River Street, Hoboken, NJ 07030, (201) 748-6011, fax (201) 748-6008, or online at http://www.wiley.com/go/permissions.

Trademarks: Wiley, For Dummies, the Dummies Man logo, Dummies.com, Making Everything Easier, and related trade dress are trademarks or registered trademarks of John Wiley & Sons, Inc. and may not be used without written permission. Android is a trademark of Google, Inc. All other trademarks are the property of their respective owners. John Wiley & Sons, Inc. is not associated with any product or vendor mentioned in this book.

For general information on our other products and services, please contact our Customer Care Department within the U.S. at 877-762-2974, outside the U.S. at 317-572-3993, or fax 317-572-4002. For technical support, please visit https://hub.wiley.com/community/support/dummies.

Wiley publishes in a variety of print and electronic formats and by print-on-demand. Some material included with standard print versions of this book may not be included in e-books or in print-on-demand. If this book refers to media such as a CD or DVD that is not included in the version you purchased, you may download this material at http://booksupport.wiley.com. For more information about Wiley products, visit www.wiley.com.

Library of Congress Control Number: 2017959978

ISBN: 978-1-119-45385-7; 978-1-119-45392-5 (ebk); 978-1-119-45390-1 (ebk)

Manufactured in the United States of America

C10004503_091118

Contents at a Glance

Table of Contents

Introduction

You know it's intimidating when they call it a "smartphone." Worse, the supersize smartphone, the tablet, supposedly does everything your computer does but without a keyboard — or very many knobs or switches. Still, if you own one of these devices, don't you want to get all the features you paid for?

This book makes the complex subject of Android phones and tablets understandable. It's done with avuncular care and gentle handholding. The information is friendly and informative, without being intimidating. And yes, ample humor is sprinkled throughout the text to keep the mood light. New technology can be frustrating enough without a touch of levity.

About This Book

Please don't read this book from cover to cover. This book is a reference. It's designed to be used as you need it. Look up a topic in the table of contents or the index. Find something about your Android mobile gizmo that vexes you or something you're curious about. Look up the answer, and get on with your life.

Every chapter is written as its own, self-contained unit, covering a specific Android topic. The chapters are further divided into sections representing tasks you perform with the device or explaining how to get something done. Sample sections in this book include

- » Typing without lifting your finger
- » Making a conference call
- » Dealing with a missed call
- » Adding more email accounts
- » Uploading a picture or video to Facebook

>> Helping others find your location

>> Recording video

>> Creating a mobile hotspot

>> Flying with an Android

>> Extending battery life

You have nothing to memorize, no sacred utterances or animal sacrifices, and definitely no PowerPoint presentations. Instead, every section explains a topic as though it's the first thing you've read in this book. Nothing is assumed, and everything is cross-referenced. Technical terms and topics, when they come up, are neatly shoved to the side, where they're easily avoided. The idea here isn't to learn anything. This book's philosophy is to help you look it up, figure it out, and move on.

How to Use This Book

This book follows a few conventions for using your Android phone or tablet, so pay attention!

First of all, no matter what name your phone or tablet has, whether it's a manufacturer's name or a pet name you've devised on your own, this book refers to it as an *Android phone* or *Android tablet*. Sometimes the terms *phone* or *tablet* are used, and also *device* or, rarely, *gizmo*.

Because Samsung modifies the Android operating system, and the company's gizmos sell more than other phones and tablets, its devices are often called out in the text — specifically when a Samsung galactic gizmo does something different than a typical Android gizmo.

The main way to interact with an Android mobile device is to use its *touchscreen*, which is the glassy part of the device as it's facing you. The physical buttons on the device are called *keys*. These items are discussed and explained in Part 1 of this book.

The various ways to touch the screen are explained and named in Chapter 3.

Chapter 4 covers text input, which involves using an onscreen keyboard. When you tire of typing, you can dictate your text. It's all explained in Chapter 4.

This book directs you to do things by following numbered steps. Each step involves a specific activity, such as touching something on the screen; for example:

3. Tap the Apps icon.

This step directs you to tap or touch the graphical Apps icon on the screen. When a button is shown as text, the command reads:

3. Tap the DOWNLOAD button.

You might also be directed to choose an item, which means to tap it on the screen.

 Various settings can be turned off or on, as indicated by a master control, which looks like the on–off toggle. Tap the master control to enable or disable the feature, or slide its button to the right or left. When the feature is enabled, the Master Control icon appears in color, as shown in the margin.

Foolish Assumptions

Though this book is written with the gentle handholding required by anyone who is just starting out, or who is easily intimidated, I've made a few assumptions.

I'm assuming that you're still reading the introduction. That's great. It's much better than getting a snack right now or checking to ensure that the cat isn't chewing through the TV cable again.

My biggest assumption: You have or desire to own a phone or tablet that uses Google's Android operating system.

Your phone can be any Android phone from any manufacturer supported by any popular cellular service provider in the United States. Because Android is an operating system, the methods of doing things on one Android phone are similar, if not identical, to doing things on another Android phone. Therefore, one book can pretty much cover the gamut of Android phones.

If you have an Android tablet instead, it could be a Wi-Fi-only tablet or an LTE tablet that uses the same mobile data network as an Android phone. This book covers both models.

Any differences between an Android phone and tablet are noted in the text. For the most part, the devices work similarly because they run the same Android operating system.

The Android operating system itself comes in versions, or flavors. This book covers all current Android versions 5.0 through 8.0. These versions are known by the flavors Lollipop, Marshmallow, Nougat, and Oreo. To confirm which Android version your gizmo uses, follow these steps:

1. **At the Home screen, tap the Apps icon.**

   Refer to Chapter 3 for a description of the Apps icon. On some devices without an Apps icon, swipe up the Home screen from bottom-to-top.

2. **Tap to open the Settings app.**

3. **Choose System and then About Phone or About Tablet.**

   If you see the About Phone or About Tablet item on the main Settings app screen, choose it. This item might be named About Device.

4. **Look at the item titled Android Version.**

   The number that's shown indicates the Android operating system version.

Don't fret if these steps confuse you: Review Part 1 of this book, and then come back here. (I'll wait.)

More assumptions:

You don't need to own a computer to use your Android mobile thingy. If you have a computer, great. Your phone or tablet works well with both PC and Mac. When directions are specific to a PC or Mac, the book says so.

Programs that run on your Android are *apps*, which is short for *applications*. A single program is an *app*.

Finally, this book assumes that you have a Google account, but if you don't, Chapter 2 explains how to configure one. Do so. Having a Google account opens up a slew of useful features, information, and programs that make using your Android more productive.

Icons Used in This Book

This icon flags useful, helpful tips or shortcuts.

TIP

This icon marks a friendly reminder to do something.

REMEMBER

WARNING

This icon marks a friendly reminder not to do something.

TECHNICAL STUFF

This icon alerts you to overly nerdy information and technical discussions of the topic at hand. Reading the information is optional, though it may win you the Daily Double on *Jeopardy!*

Contacting the Author

My email address is dgookin@wambooli.com. Yes, that's my real address. I reply to every email I receive, and more quickly when you keep your question short and specific to this book. Although I enjoy saying Hi, I cannot answer technical support questions, resolve billing issues, or help you troubleshoot your phone or tablet. Thanks for understanding.

My website is `wambooli.com`. This book has its own page on that site, which you can check for updates, new information, and all sorts of fun stuff. Visit often:

`wambooli.com/help/android`

Beyond the Book

Thank you for reading the introduction. Few people do, and it would save a lot of time and bother if they did. Consider yourself fortunate. No, consider yourself handsome, well-read, and worthy of praise, though you probably knew that.

Beyond my own website (see the preceding section), my beloved publisher also offers its own helpful site, which contains official updates and bonus information I'm forbidden by law to offer to you. Visit the publisher's official support page at `www.dummies.com`, though that's not the right page. You must search for *Android Phones & Tablets For Dummies* — the whole thing! After you find the proper search result, click it and then open the Download tab on this book's dedicated page. I'd offer more specific information, but I don't have it. The publisher told me that the actual address of the online material is held in one of 20 briefcases and that if I choose the right one, I get paid — something like that.

Your task now: Start reading the rest of the book — but not the whole thing, and especially not with the chapters in order. Observe the table of contents and find something that interests you. Or look up your puzzle in the index. When these suggestions don't cut it, just start reading Chapter 1.

Enjoy this book and your Android mobile gizmo!

1

Your Own Android

IN THIS PART . . .

Get started with your Android gizmo.

Work through configuration and setup.

Learn basic techniques and procedures.

Force yourself to enjoy the onscreen keyboard.

Chapter **1**

An Out-of-the-Box Experience

You begin your Android adventure by removing the device from its box. Yes, I know: You've already completed that task. I don't blame you; I removed my new Android from the box before I wrote this chapter. Yet you may consider a few helpful tips and suggestions before that out-of-the-box experience becomes a distant memory.

Liberation

Like most electronics, your new Android phone or tablet works fastest when you remove it from its box. Savor the moment. Breathe deep the scent of industrial glue used to seal the box. Gingerly lift out the packaging. Marvel as you peel back the plastic sheeting.

Array before you the contents of the box. These useful items include

>> **The device itself:** Tablets come fully assembled, but some phones require that you insert the battery and then snap on the back of the case. Directions are found inside the box.

- » **USB cable:** You can use it to connect the phone or tablet to a computer or a wall charger. Some tablets may come with a charger cord only.

- » **Power adapter:** Use this thing (and the USB cable) to charge the Android's battery. The adapter may come in two pieces, both of which must be assembled.

- » **Earbud headset:** This item might be a simple headset, or you might find a microphone/controller gizmo on one of the earbud leads.

- » **Useless pamphlets:** It's odd that the safety and warranty information is far more extensive than the flimsy setup guide. That shows the priority our culture places on lawyers over technology writers.

- » **The SIM card and removal tool:** For cellular Androids, you may find the card holder used to install the device's SIM card. If you purchased your device at a phone store, someone there may have tossed the SIM card holder into the box as well. You can throw it out, though I recommend keeping the SIM card removal tool.

The important thing to do is confirm that nothing is missing or damaged. Ensure that you have all the parts you paid for, including any optional accessories. If anything is missing or appears to be damaged, immediately contact the folks who sold you the phone or tablet.

TIP

I recommend keeping the packaging and its contents as long as you own the Android: The box makes an excellent storage place for that stuff — as well as for anything else you don't plan to use right away.

ANDROID BUYING TIPS

The major things to look for when purchasing an Android phone or tablet are its cellular provider, storage, camera options, screen size, and overall design.

All phones have a cellular connection, but only some tablets use this feature. Most tablets use only the Wi-Fi connection for Internet access, which is fine. For cellular devices, the key issue is coverage. The only way to ensure that a cellular provider has the coverage you need is to ask your friends and associates who use that same provider. Does the signal work everywhere?

Some phones and tablets feature removable storage in the form of a microSD card. This feature allows you to expand the device's storage and more easily share files with a computer, though using removable storage isn't without its issues. See Chapter 19.

The device's camera has a maximum resolution measured in megapixels (MP). The higher the value, the better the camera. Ensure that an Android tablet has both a front and rear camera. And confirm that the rear camera has a flash. It's not an important feature, but it's best to find out before you buy the device.

Both screen size and design play together, specifically with how the device feels in your hand. Some large-format phones, often called *phablets* (for *phone/tablets*) are too big for some people. Tablets come in two sizes: a smaller format, about the size of a paperback book, and a larger format, better suited for watching videos. The best way to know which size works best for you is to try out a few devices at the store.

Beyond these basic items, Android phones and tablets have only subtle software differences. Do ensure, however, that your device can access and use Google Play, the online store for the Android operating system. Some low-price, bargain phones and tablets restrict your purchases to the manufacturer's own app store. I would avoid those gizmos.

Device Assembly

Most Android phones come fully assembled. If yours didn't, the folks at the phone store will put everything together for you. When you're on your own, you must perform this task. This process might involve installing the SIM card, though you might also need to install the phone's battery and, optionally, insert a microSD card. To assist you, specific directions come with the phone.

Don't worry about the assembly process being overly complex: If you're good with LEGOs, you can put together an Android phone.

Many of the topics in this section also apply to Android tablets, though they all come fully assembled.

Peeling off the plastic sheeting

The phone or tablet ships with a clingy plastic sheeting over its screen, back, or sides. The sheeting might tell you where to find various features, so look it over before you peel it off. And, yes, you must remove the sheeting; it's for shipping protection, not for long-term protection.

TIP

>> Check the device's rear camera to confirm that you've removed the plastic sheeting from its lens.

>> Feel free to throw away the plastic sheeting.

Installing the SIM card

A *SIM card* identifies an Android phone or tablet to the digital cellular network. Before you can use the device on that network, the SIM card must be installed.

Most of the time, the kind people at the phone store install the SIM card. They pretend like it's a task that requires a Ph.D. in quantum mechanics, though the task is LEGO-brick simple.

If you've purchased your phone or LTE tablet outside the realm of the phone store and you have a SIM card to install (and you know how to obtain service for it and all that), follow these steps when the device is turned off:

1. **Pop the SIM card out of the credit-card-size holder.**

   Push the card with your thumb and it pops out. Don't use scissors or you may damage the card.

2. **Locate the SIM card cover on the device's outer edge.**

   The cover features a dimple or hole on one end.

3. **Firmly insert the SIM card removal tool into the hole on the SIM card cover, and remove the SIM card tray.**

   The SIM card cover pops up or the SIM card tray slides out.

4. **Set the SIM card into the SIM card tray or otherwise insert it into the SIM card slot.**

   The SIM card is shaped in such a way that it's impossible to insert improperly. If the card doesn't slide into the slot, reorient the card and try again.

5. **Insert the SIM card tray back into the slot or close the SIM card cover.**

   You're done.

The good news is that you seldom, if ever, need to remove or replace a SIM card.

» On some phones, the SIM card is inserted internally. In that case, remove the phone's back cover and, if necessary, remove the battery to access the SIM card slot.

» SIM stands for *subscriber identity module*. SIM cards are required for GSM cellular networks as well as for 4G LTE networks.

TECHNICAL STUFF

Installing a microSD card

A few phones and tablets offer removable storage in the form of a microSD card slot. This storage is in addition to internal storage that comes with every Android device.

A microSD card provides your device with more storage, plus the capability to easily transfer storage between devices. More details on using the card are offered in Chapter 19. Here are the directions for inserting the card:

1. **Locate the microSD card slot.**

The slot is labeled as illustrated in Figure 1-1. It is not the same as the SIM card slot.

microSD card hatch or cover

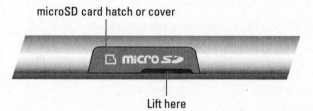

FIGURE 1-1:
Opening the
microSD card
hatch.

Lift here

2. **Flip open the teensy hatch on the microSD card slot.**

Insert your thumbnail into the tiny slot and flip the hatch outward. It's attached on one end, so it may not completely pop off.

3. **Insert the microSD card into the slot.**

The card goes in only one way. If you're fortunate, a little outline of the card illustrates the proper orientation. If you're even more fortunate, your eyes will be good enough to see the tiny outline.

TIP

You may hear a faint clicking sound when the card is fully inserted. If not, use the end of a paper clip or your fingernail to fully insert the card.

>> You must purchase a microSD card separately from your phone or tablet.

>> It's okay to insert the microSD card while the device is on. If so, a notification appears, detailing information about the card.

>> Refer to Chapter 19 if the notification indicates that the card must be formatted.

>> The Android works with or without a microSD card installed.

>> Storage capacity for microSD cards is measured in gigabytes (GB). Common capacities are 8GB, 16GB, 32GB, and higher. The maximum size allowed depends on the phone or tablet's design. The side of the box lists compatible capacities.

Removing the microSD card

To remove the microSD card, follow these steps:

1. Turn off the phone or tablet.

It's possible to remove the card while the gizmo is on, and directions are offered in Chapter 19. For now, ensure that the device is off. Specific power-off directions are found in Chapter 2.

2. Open the little hatch covering the microSD card slot.

Refer to the preceding section.

3. Using your fingernail or a bent paper clip, gently press the microSD card inward a tad.

The microSD card is spring-loaded, so pressing it in pops it outward.

4. Pinch the microSD card between your fingers and remove it completely.

After you've removed the card, you can continue using the phone or tablet. It works just fine without a microSD card.

The microSD card is too tiny to leave lying around. Put it into a microSD card adapter or its original plastic container. Don't lose it!

WARNING

Charge the Battery

Manufacturers give your new phone or tablet enough charge to survive the setup process, but little more. Therefore, one of your first duties, and eventually a routine task, is to charge the Android's battery. You can wait in an old castle for a lightning storm or just abide by these steps:

1. If necessary, assemble the charging cord.

Connect the charger head (the wall adapter) to the USB cable that comes with the Android.

2. Plug the charger head and cable into a wall socket.

3. **Connect the Android to the USB cable.**

The charger cord plugs into the micro-USB connector, found at the device's bottom.

As the device charges, you may see a Charging Battery graphic on the touchscreen, or a notification lamp may glow. Such activity is normal.

When the device is fully charged, the icon is "full" or you see 100% on the battery indicator. At that point, you can remove the charging cord, though leaving the Android plugged in doesn't damage the device.

>> The phone or tablet may turn on when you plug it in for a charge. That's okay, but read Chapter 2 to find out what to do the first time the Android turns on.

>> Some tablets use their own charging cord, not the USB cable.

>> I recommend fully charging the gizmo. You can use it while it's charging, but give it a full charge before you disconnect the cord.

>> Older Androids feature a micro-A USB connector, which plugs in only one way. If the cable doesn't fit, flip it over and try again.

>> Newer USB Type-C cables and connectors plug in any-which-way.

>> Some Androids can charge wirelessly, but only when you purchase a special wireless charger: Lie the phone or tablet on its charging pad or set it in the charging cradle.

>> If the battery charge is too low, the phone or tablet won't turn on. This is normal behavior. Let the device charge a while before you turn it on.

>> The Android also charges itself whenever it's connected to a computer's USB port. The computer must be on for charging to work. The device may charge only when plugged into a powered USB port, such as one of those found directly on the computer console.

>> Androids charge more quickly when plugged into the wall than into a computer's USB port or a car adapter.

>> Unlike with the old NiCad batteries, you don't need to worry about fully discharging the battery before recharging it. If the phone or tablet needs a charge, even when the battery is just a little low, feel free to do so.

>> Some Androids can be charged wirelessly. See the later section "Adding accessories."

>> Also see Chapter 24 for battery and power management information.

Android Exploration

No one told the first person to ride a horse which way to sit. That's because some things just come naturally. If using your Android phone or tablet doesn't come naturally, refer to this section for help finding important items on the device and learning what those doodads are called.

Discovering what's what and where

Take a gander at Figure 1-2, which illustrates common items found on the front and back of a typical Android phone. Figure 1-3 provides the same details, but for a typical Android tablet.

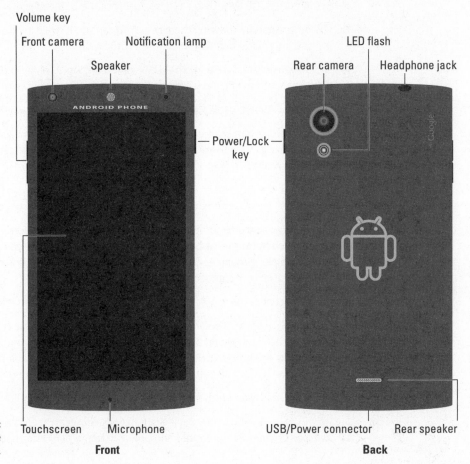

FIGURE 1-2: Your phone's face and rump.

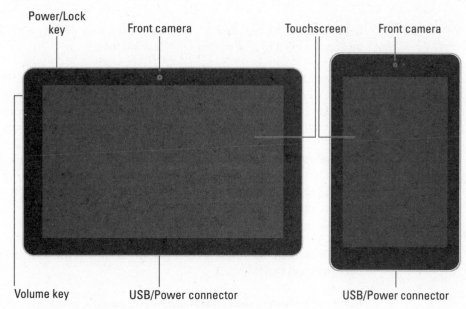

Power/Lock key   Front camera   Touchscreen   Front camera

Volume key   USB/Power connector   USB/Power connector

Not every item shown in the figures may be in the exact same spot on your phone or tablet. For example, the Power/Lock key might be found on top of the device, not on the side.

The items illustrated in Figures 1-2 and 1-3 use terms found throughout this book and in whatever scant Android documentation exists. Here are the highlights:

Power/Lock key: This button, or key, turns the device on or off or locks or unlocks the device. Directions for performing these activities are found in Chapter 2.

Volume key: The volume control is two buttons in one. Press one side of the key to set the volume higher, or the other side to set the volume lower.

Touchscreen: The biggest part of an Android gizmo is its touchscreen display, which occupies almost all the territory on the front of the device. The touchscreen is a look-touch gizmo: You look at it but also touch it with your fingers to control the Android.

Front camera: The front-facing camera, found above the touchscreen, is used for taking self-portraits as well as for video chat. Small-format Android tablets feature the front camera above the touchscreen as the device is held vertically; larger tablets put the front camera above the touchscreen as the device is held horizontally.

Rear camera: The rear camera is found on the back of the phone or tablet. It may be accompanied by one or two LED flash gizmos.

Speaker(s): The primary phone speaker is located top-center, above the touch-screen. One or more additional speakers might also be found on the phone's bottom edge or backside. Tablets feature stereo speakers on either side of the device, though some smaller tablets may have their speakers on the back.

Microphone: Somewhere below the touchscreen, you'll find the phone's microphone. It's tiny, about the diameter of a pin. Don't stick anything into the hole! A second, noise-canceling microphone might also be found on the back of the phone. Android tablets put the microphone along the edge, typically on the bottom.

Headphone jack: Somewhere on the device's edge is the hole where you can connect standard headphones.

Removable storage slot: Into this slot you insert a microSD card, which expands the device's storage. Not every Android features this expansion option.

SIM card cover: This spot is where you access a cellular device's SIM card, as covered earlier in this chapter.

USB/Power connector: This slot is where you connect the USB cable, which is used both to charge the battery and to connect your Android to a computer.

Take a moment to locate all the items mentioned in this section, as well as shown in Figures 1-2 and 1-3. It's important that you know where these items are.

>> As you might expect, some devices feature extra doodads beyond the basics here. For example, you may find a row of navigation icons along the bottom of the touchscreen. Older Samsung devices feature a physical Home button. Newer Samsung devices have a Bixby button, used to summon Samsung's digital assistant.

>> A common feature found on the back of many phones is a fingerprint reader. This gizmo is used to unlock the device. Refer to Chapter 22.

>> The Galaxy Note line of Androids features a pointing device, in the form of a digital stylus called an S Pen. It docks at the device's bottom edge.

>> It's common for some phones to feature controls on the back. You may find the power button (near the top-center on the back of the phone), a volume key, or a fingerprint reader.

Using earphones

You can use your Android without earphones, but they're nice things to have. If you didn't find a set of earbuds in the box with the phone or tablet, I recommend that you buy a pair: The earbud-style earphone sets directly into your ear. The sharp, pointy end of the earphones, which you don't want to stick into your ear, plugs into the device's headphone jack.

Between the earbuds and the sharp, pointy thing, you might find a doodle button. The button is used to answer a call on an Android phone, mute the mic, or, on both a phone and tablet, start or stop the playback of music.

A teensy hole on the doodle serves as a microphone. The mic allows you to wear the earbuds and talk on the phone while keeping your hands free. If you gesture while you speak, you'll find this feature invaluable.

REMEMBER

TIP

>> The earphones must be inserted fully into the jack. If not, you won't hear anything.

>> You can also use a Bluetooth headset with your phone, to listen to a call or some music. See Chapter 18 for more information on Bluetooth.

>> Fold the earphones when you put them away, as opposed to wrapping them in a loop. Put the earbuds and connector in one hand, and then pull the wire straight out with the other hand. Fold the wire in half and then in half again. You can then put the earphones in your pocket or on a tabletop. By folding the wires, you avoid creating something that looks like a wire ball of Christmas tree lights.

Adding accessories

Beyond earphones, you can find an entire phone store full of accessories and baubles that you can obtain for your Android phone or tablet. The variety is seemingly endless, and the prices, well, they ain't cheap. Here are some of your choices:

Phone case: Protect your phone by getting it a jacket, one that further expresses your individuality.

Pouches, sleeves, and keyboard covers: Android tablets have larger-format cases, almost like folios. Special pouches double as tablet stands. The fanciest tablet accessory is a keyboard cover, which features a wireless (Bluetooth) keyboard.

Keyboard: Speaking of keyboards, even if it isn't part of the case, a Bluetooth keyboard is a handy Android tablet accessory.

Screen protector: This clear, plastic sheet adheres to the touchscreen, protecting it from scratches, finger smudges, and sneeze globs while still allowing you to use the touchscreen. Ensure that you get a screen protector designed specifically for your phone or tablet.

Belt clip: To sate your envy of Batman's utility belt, consider getting a fine leatherette or Naugahyde phone case that you can quickly attach to your belt.

Vehicle charger: Use the vehicle charger to provide power to your phone or tablet for a long trip. This accessory is a must for older vehicles that lack USB ports.

Car mount: This device holds your Android phone so that you can easily see it while driving. It makes for easier access, although these things are forbidden in some states.

microSD Card: When your Android supports this type of removable storage, consider buying this memory card. See the earlier section "Installing a microSD card."

Wireless charger: Not every phone can be charged wirelessly, but if yours can, definitely get a wireless charger. Set your phone on the pad or prop it up in the dock. The phone's battery starts magically recharging.

Screencasting dongle: This accessory connects to an HDTV or computer monitor. Once configured, it allows you to cast the Android's screen onto the larger-screen device. It's ideal for watching movies or Netflix or YouTube videos, or for enjoying music. Google's Chromecast is an example of a screencasting gizmo. See Chapter 19 for more information on screencasting.

Other exciting and nifty accessories might be available for your phone or tablet. Check frequently for new garnishes and frills at the location where you bought your Android. Your credit card company will love you.

>> Android devices generally don't recognize more than one button on the earphone doodle. For example, if you use earphones that feature a Volume button or Mute button, pressing that extra button does nothing.

>> Another useful accessory to get is a microfiber cloth to help clean the touchscreen, plus a special cleaning-solution wipe. See Chapter 24 for more information about cleaning an Android's screen.

Where to Keep Your Digital Pal

The good news is that an Android combines multiple devices. So instead of keeping track of a clock, camera, phone, video recorder, game machine, tiny TV, or other gizmos, you need to mind only one device. Of course, the panic is still there when you misplace the phone or tablet. This section offers hints on how to avoid that situation.

Toting an Android phone

The compactness of the modern smartphone makes it perfect for a pocket or even the teensiest of party purses. And its well-thought-out design means you can carry your phone in your pocket or handbag without fearing that something will accidentally turn it on, dial Mongolia, and run up a heck of a cell phone bill.

>> Most phones feature a proximity sensor. It keeps the touchscreen locked, which prevents a phone in a pocket or purse from waking up and making a call.

>> See Chapter 22 for details on the On Body Detection feature used to keep the phone from locking while you're moving.

WARNING

>> Don't forget that you've placed the phone in your pocket, especially in your coat or jacket. You might accidentally sit on the phone, or it can fly out when you peel off your coat. The worst fate for any smartphone is to take a trip through the wash. I'm sure your phone has nightmares about it.

Taking an Android tablet with you

The ideal place for an Android tablet is in a specially designed pouch or sleeve. The pouch keeps the device from being dinged, scratched, or even unexpectedly turned on while it's in your backpack, purse, or carry-on luggage or wherever you put the tablet when you're not using it.

Also see Chapter 23 for information on using an Android tablet on the road.

Making a home for the Android

It's best to keep your phone or tablet in the same place when you're not actively using it, especially a tablet. I prefer to keep my gizmos by my computer, where I can charge them and also refer to them as I work.

Another ideal location is on a nightstand. Especially if you get a dock for the phone or tablet, you can use it as your alarm clock. Ensure that you connect the Android to a power source so that it charges overnight.

Above all, keep the phone or tablet in the same spot. That's the key to not losing it. Always set it back in the same place. (This advice applies to anything you're prone to losing, not just a phone or tablet.)

>> Phones and tablets on coffee tables get buried under magazines and are often squished when rude people put their feet on the furniture.

>> Avoid putting your phone or tablet in direct sunlight; heat is bad news for any electronic gizmo.

Chapter **2**

The On-Off Chapter

The bestselling *Pencils For Dummies* has no chapter describing how to activate a pencil. *Pens For Dummies* does have the chapter "Enabling the Pen to Write," but that's not really an on–off thing. No, a phone or tablet is far more complex than a pen or a pencil. It requires more instruction for something even as basic as turning it on or off.

Greetings, Android

It would be delightful if your phone or tablet were smart enough to pop out of the box, say "Hello," and immediately know everything about you. The real world is far more disappointing. Therefore, turning on an Android is more complex than just flipping a switch.

TIP

» The Android setup process works best when you already have a Google (Gmail) account. If you lack one, you're prompted to create an account during the setup process.

» The phone or tablet will not start unless the battery is charged. See Chapter 1.

Turning on the device for the first time

The very first time you turn on an Android gizmo is a special occasion. That's when you're required to work through the setup-and-configuration process. This ordeal needs to be endured only once, and it's not terribly complex. In fact, you can merrily skip many of the options and complete them later, though I recommend that you get it out of the way now.

The specifics of the setup and configuration differ subtly, depending on the device's manufacturer and cellular provider. If the people at the phone store helped you through the process, great! If not, first read the generic steps presented in this section and then go back and work the steps with your phone or tablet:

1. **Press and hold the Power/Lock key.**

You may have to press the key longer than you think; when you see the brand logo appear on the screen, release the key.

TIP

It's okay to turn on the device while it's plugged in and charging.

2. **Answer the questions presented.**

The prompts you see include the following:

- Select your language
- Activate the device on the mobile data network
- Connect to a Wi-Fi network
- Set the time zone
- Accept terms and conditions
- Sign in to your Google account
- Restore data from another Android mobile device or your Google account
- Add other online accounts
- Set location information
- Grant permissions

When in doubt, accept the choice presented. Even if you don't tap the SKIP button, you can use the Android to make or change a setting later. Details are offered throughout this book.

To fill in text fields, use the device's onscreen keyboard. See Chapter 4 for keyboard information.

3. **After each choice, tap the NEXT or SKIP button.**

The NEXT button might be labeled with the text or an icon, as shown in the margin. The SKIP button is always text, though it's sometimes difficult to locate on the screen.

4. **Tap the FINISH button.**

The FINISH button appears on the last screen of the setup procedure.

From this point on, starting the phone or tablet works as described in the next section.

After the initial setup, you're taken to the Home screen. Chapter 3 offers details on using the Home screen, which you probably should read right away, before the temptation to play with your new phone or tablet becomes unbearable.

>> During setup as well as immediately after and as you explore your Android, you see prompts to try out or understand various phone or tablet features. Some of those prompts are helpful, but it's okay to skip them. To do so, tap the GOT IT or OK button. If it's present, select the Do Not Show Again check box so that you won't be bothered again.

>> Additional information on connecting your Android to a Wi-Fi network is found in Chapter 18.

TIP

>> If you're upgrading from an older phone or you already have an Android tablet, the restore operation ensures that your new device has all your old apps and other details from that other device. This is one of the beauties of the Android operating system: Moving to a new device isn't that painful.

>> Apps must ask permission to use certain features or device hardware. I recommend that you tap the ALLOW button for now. You can review app permissions later, which is a topic covered in Chapter 22.

>> Some apps request use of the device's GPS technology to obtain your location. As with other permissions, I recommend that you allow the apps to proceed. That way, you get the most from your phone or tablet.

>> It's not necessary to use any specific software provided by the device's manufacturer or your cellular provider. For example, if you don't want a Samsung account, you don't need to sign up for one; skip that step.

>> Your Google account provides for coordination between your Android and your Gmail messages, contacts, Google Calendar appointments, and information and data from other Google Internet applications.

>> See the later sidebar "Who is this Android person?" for more information about the Android operating system.

Turning on the phone or tablet

To turn on your Android, press and hold the Power/Lock key. After a few seconds, you feel the device vibrate slightly and the start-up logo appears. You can release the Power/Lock key and enjoy the hypnotic animation and perhaps start-up music.

Eventually, you see the lock screen. See the later section "Working a screen lock" for information on what to do next.

» You may be prompted to work a screen lock before the device fully starts. This could be an option you set when the Android was first configured or because internal storage is encrypted. See Chapter 22 for details.

» An Android won't turn on when the battery charge is too low, even if you connect it to a power source. In this situation, wait for the battery to charge.

Unlocking the device

Most of the time, you don't turn your phone or tablet off and on. Instead, you lock and unlock it. To unlock and use the device, press the Power/Lock key. A quick press is all that's needed. The touchscreen comes to life and you see the lock screen, similar to what's illustrated in Figure 2-1.

To begin using the Android, swipe the screen as illustrated in the figure. If you have the screen lock applied, work the lock; see the next section for details. For gizmos with a fingerprint reader, tap your finger to the reader to unlock.

Eventually you find yourself at the Home screen, where you can begin to use and interact with your phone or tablet.

» Samsung devices with a Home key are unlocked when you press that key. The key is centered below the touchscreen.

» On Samsung Galaxy Note gizmos, remove the S Pen to unlock the device.

» Opening the cover on an Android tablet unlocks the device.

» You can answer an Android phone, or decline an incoming call, without having to unlock the device. See Chapter 5 for more information.

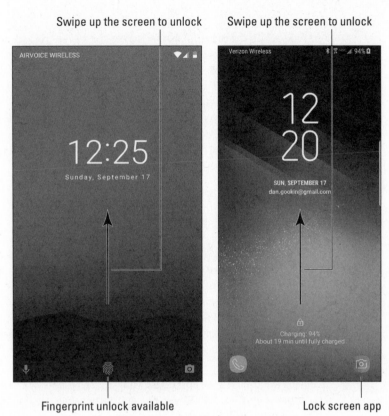

Swipe up the screen to unlock

Swipe up the screen to unlock

Swipe up the screen to unlock

FIGURE 2-1:
The lock screen.

Fingerprint unlock available

Lock screen app

Working a screen lock

The point of the lock screen is to prevent the Home screen from appearing imme-diately after you press the Power/Lock key: Swipe the screen to unlock the phone or tablet. Yet, the swipe lock isn't that difficult to pick.

If you've added more security to your phone or tablet, you must work a screen lock after you swipe the lock screen. The common types of screen lock include:

Pattern: Trace a preset pattern over dots on the screen.

PIN: Use the onscreen keyboard to type a number to unlock the device.

Password: Type a password, which can include letters, numbers, and symbols.

One of these screen locks appears after you swipe the screen and before you can access the Home screen. To apply these locks, see Chapter 22.

>> The swipe lock is considered the standard Android screen lock: Swipe the screen as directed in the preceding section.

>> If you've applied the dreadful "None" screen lock, even the lock screen doesn't appear: Press the Power/Lock key to immediately see the Home screen. I do not recommend this type of screen lock.

>> For the fingerprint lock, tap the reader with your finger.

>> Other wacky screen locks are available on some devices, including the signature unlock found on Galaxy Note phones and tablets. These all work the same: Press the Power/Lock key, and then work the screen lock to gain access to your Android.

Unlocking and running an app

Your phone or tablet's lock screen may feature app icons, such as the Camera icon, illustrated earlier, in Figure 2-1. To unlock the screen and run that app, drag its icon across the touchscreen.

For example, to place a quick phone call, swipe the phone icon up the screen. The phone unlocks and the Phone app appears. Similarly, you can swipe the Camera app icon to snap a quick photo.

>> Unlocking and running an app doesn't fully unlock the device when a secure screen lock is applied. If you try to use apps other than the one you swiped, the device prompts you for the screen lock.

>> Some devices let you customize lock screen apps. Look for a Lock Screen item in the Settings app, where you can add or remove lock screen apps.

TECHNICAL STUFF

WHO IS THIS ANDROID PERSON?

Just like a computer, your Android phone or tablet has an operating system. It's the main program in charge of all the software (apps) inside the device. Unlike a computer, however, Android is a mobile device operating system, designed primarily for use in smartphones and tablets.

Android is based on the Linux operating system, which is also a computer operating system, though it's much more stable and bug-free than Windows, so it's not as popular. Google owns, maintains, and develops Android, which is why your online Google information is synced with your phone or tablet.

The Android mascot, shown here, often appears on Android apps or hardware. He has no official name, though most folks call him Andy.

Add More Accounts

Your Android serves as home to your various online incarnations. This list includes your email accounts, online services, social networking, subscriptions, and other digital personas. I recommended adding those accounts to your mobile gizmo to continue the setup-and-configuration process.

With your phone or tablet on and unlocked, follow these steps:

1. **Tap the Apps icon.**

The Apps icon is found at the bottom of the Home screen. It looks similar to the icon shown in the margin, although it has many variations. For devices that lack an Apps icon, swipe up the Home screen. Also refer to Chapter 3 for details on the Apps icon varieties and techniques.

The goal of tapping the Apps icon is to access the Apps drawer, where all the device's apps are listed.

2. **Open the Settings app.**

You may have to swipe the Apps drawer screen a few times, paging through the various icons, to find the Settings app.

After you tap the Settings icon, the Settings app runs. It's used to configure various features on your device.

3. **Choose the Users & Accounts category.**

The category may be titled Accounts or Accounts and Sync.

Upon success, you see all existing accounts on your Android, such as email accounts, social networking, cloud storage, and whatever else you may have already set up.

If you don't see any accounts, look for an Accounts item and choose it.

4. **Tap Add Account.**

   You see a list of account types you can add. More or fewer items appear on the list, which is generated based on installed apps and settings made by the device manufacturer.

5. **Choose an account type from the list.**

   For example, to add a Facebook account, choose Facebook.

   Don't worry if you don't see the exact type of account you want to add. You may have to add a specific app before an account appears. Chapter 17 covers adding apps.

6. **Follow the directions to sign in to your account.**

   The steps that follow depend on the account. Generally speaking, you sign in using your existing username and password.

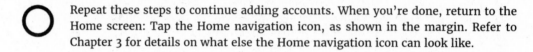 Repeat these steps to continue adding accounts. When you're done, return to the Home screen: Tap the Home navigation icon, as shown in the margin. Refer to Chapter 3 for details on what else the Home navigation icon can look like.

>> See Chapter 9 for specific information on adding email accounts to your Android.

>> Chapter 11 covers social networking on your Android and offers advice on adding those types of accounts.

Farewell, Android

You can dismiss your Android in several ways, only two of which involve using a steamroller or raging elephant. The other methods are documented in this section.

Locking the device

Locking the gizmo is cinchy: Press and release the Power/Lock key. The display goes dark; your phone or tablet is locked.

>> The phone or tablet spends most of its time locked.

>> Some Androids may not turn off the display while they're locked. You may see the current time and notifications displayed, albeit on a very dim screen. This feature doesn't impact the device's battery life, and in many cases this setting can be changed if you don't like the always-on touchscreen. See Chapter 21 for details.

>> Your phone or tablet spends most of its time locked. The gizmo still works while locked; email comes in, music continues to play, alerts bleep, and alarms clang. Phone calls arrive. Yet, while the device is locked, it doesn't use as much power as it does when the display on.

>> Press and release the Power/Lock key to lock an Android phone during a call. The call stays connected, but the touchscreen display is disabled.

>> Locking doesn't turn off your Android.

>> The phone or tablet locks automatically after a period of inactivity, usually 30 seconds. You can set another timeout value, if you like. Refer to Chapter 21.

REMEMBER

Turning off your Android

To turn off your mobile device, heed these steps:

1. Press and hold the Power/Lock key.

The Device Options card appears.

2. Release the Power/Lock key.

The Device Options card may contain only one item, Power Off, as shown in Figure 2-2. Also shown is the Power Options card, with more options,

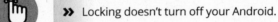

If you chicken out and don't want to turn off your Android, tap the Back navigation icon to dismiss the Device Options card.

3. Tap the Power Off item.

If a confirmation message appears, tap the OK button. The Android shuts itself off.

The Android doesn't run when it's off. You aren't reminded about appointments. Email stays on the server. Alarms don't trigger. Phone calls are missed. The device isn't angry with you for turning it off, though you may sense some resentment when you turn it on again.

>> Calls received while an Android phone is off are routed instead to voice mail.

>> You can charge your phone or tablet while it's off.

>> The Device Options card might sport more options than what's shown in Figure 2-2. The bare minimum is the Power Off item. Other items might include Restart, Sleep, Kid Mode, as well as volume and vibration settings.

>> Keep your Android in a safe place while it's turned off. Chapter 1 offers some suggestions.

REMEMBER

Stock Android Device Options card   Samsung Device Options buttons

FIGURE 2-2:
The Device
Options card.

Back navigation icon
(stock Android style)

Back navigation icon
(Samsung style)

Chapter **3**

Android Tour

t used to be that you could judge how advanced something was by how many buttons it had. Starting with the dress shirt and progressing to the first computer, more buttons imply sophistication. Your Android phone or tablet tosses that rule right out the window. Beyond the Power/Lock key and the volume key, the device is shamefully low on buttons.

As an alternative to the button-festooned modern marvel, your phone or tablet features a touchscreen as its main input device. A touchscreen can do all sorts of wondrous and useful things. Knowing how to use it is important.

Basic Operations

Your Android's capability to frustrate you is only as powerful as your fear of the touchscreen and how it works. After you clear that hurdle, as well as understand some other basic operations, you'll be on your way toward mobile device contentment.

Manipulating the touchscreen

The touchscreen works in combination with one or two of your fingers. You can choose which fingers to use, or whether to be adventurous and try using the tip of your nose, but touch the screen you must. Here are some of the many ways you manipulate your Android's touchscreen:

Tap: The basic touchscreen technique is to touch it. You tap an object, an icon, a control, a menu item, a doodad, and so on. The tap operation is similar to a mouse click on a computer. It may also be referred to as a *touch* or a *press*.

Double-tap: Tap the screen twice in the same location. A double-tap can be used to zoom in on an image or a map, but it can also zoom out. Because of the double-tap's dual nature, I recommend using the pinch and spread operations to zoom.

Long-press: Tap part of the screen and keep your finger down. Depending on what you're doing, a pop-up or card may appear, or the item you're long-pressing may get "picked up" so that you can drag (move) it around. Long-press might also be referred to as *tap and hold*.

Swipe: To swipe, tap your finger on one spot and then move your finger to another spot. Swipes can go up, down, left, or right; the touchscreen content moves in the direction in which you swipe your finger, similar to the way scrolling works on a computer. A swipe can be fast or slow. It's also called a *flick* or *slide*.

Drag: A combination of long-press and then swipe, the drag operation moves items on the screen. Start with the long press, and then keep your finger on the screen to swipe. Lift your finger to complete the action.

Pinch: A pinch involves two fingers, which start out separated and then are brought together. The effect is used to zoom out, to reduce the size of an image or see more of a map. This move may also be called a *pinch close*.

Spread: In the opposite of pinch, you start out with your fingers together and then spread them. The spread is used to zoom in, to enlarge an image or see more detail on a map. It's also known as a *pinch open*.

Rotate: Use two fingers to twist around a central point on the touchscreen, which has the effect of rotating an object on the screen. If you have trouble with this operation, pretend that you're turning the dial on a safe.

Variations on these techniques are available in several apps. For example, you swipe down from the top of the screen using two fingers to access the quick set-tings drawer. A short swipe from the top-center of the screen downward refreshes a web page as well as the contents of other apps.

You can't manipulate the touchscreen while wearing gloves unless the gloves are specially designed for using electronic touchscreens, such as the gloves that Batman wears.

Selecting a group of items

A common touchscreen technique that might be new to you is the way a group of items is selected. On a computer, you drag the mouse over the items. On a touch-screen, you perform these steps:

1. **Long-press the first item, such as a photo thumbnail in an album or another item in a list.**

The item is selected. It appears highlighted, is adorned with a tiny check mark, or features a filled-in circle. An action bar appears atop the screen, like the one shown in Figure 3-1. It lists icons such as Share, Delete, and so on, which manipulate the group of selected items.

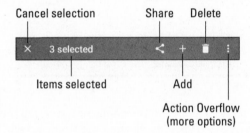

Cancel selection Share Delete

Items selected Add

Action Overflow
(more options)

FIGURE 3-1:
A typical
Action Bar.

2. **Tap additional items to select them.**

The action bar lists the total number of selected items, as illustrated in Figure 3-1.

3. **Do something with the group.**

Choose an icon from the action bar.

To cancel the selection, tap the Cancel (X) icon on the action bar, which deselects all items. You can also tap the Back navigation icon to back out of Group-Selection mode.

Using the navigation icons

Below the touchscreen dwell three navigation icons. They can appear as part of the touchscreen itself, they may be part of the bezel, or they can be physical buttons. These icons serve consistent functions throughout the Android operating system.

The navigation icons are Home, Back, and Recent. Table 3-1 illustrates how the navigation icons appear for the current and recent releases of the Android operating system, as well the variation found on Samsung devices.

TABLE 3-1   ## Navigation Icon Varieties

Icon	Android 5.0 and Later	Earlier Releases	Samsung Variation
Home	○	⌂	⎕
Back	◁	↰	←
Recent	☐	⧉	⅃

Home: No matter what you're doing on the phone or tablet, tap this icon to display the Home screen. When you're already viewing the Home screen, tap this icon to view the main or center Home screen page.

Back: The Back icon serves several purposes, all of which fit neatly under the concept of "back." Tap the icon once to return to a previous page, dismiss an onscreen menu, close a card, and so on.

When text or voice input is active, the Back icon changes its orientation as shown in the margin. Tap this icon to hide the onscreen keyboard, dismiss dictation, or perform other actions.

Recent: Tap the Recent icon to display the Overview, a list of recently opened or currently running apps. See the later section "Switching between running apps" for more information on the Overview.

The navigation icons hide themselves when certain apps run. To access the icons, tap the screen. For some full-screen apps and games, swipe the screen from top to bottom to access the navigation icons.

>> Some apps feature a left-pointing arrow in the upper left corner of the screen. This icon represents the Back action in addition to the Back navigation icon.

>> The Home, Back, and Recent icons may be hollow, as shown in Table 3-1, or filled-in. The shapes are consistent, though.

>> Samsung departs from the stock Android navigation icon shapes, as shown in Table 3-1. On some Samsung devices, a setting determines whether the navigation buttons appear. When they're hidden, swipe up at the bottom of the screen to see them.

>> Older Samsung devices feature a physical Home button or key, which performs the same duties as the Home navigation icon. The key may double as a fingerprint reader.

>> Android 5.0 and later includes the Android operating system nicknames Lollipop, Marshmallow, Nougat, and Oreo.

>> Android version 4.4, codename KitKat, uses the examples shown on the right in Table 3-1.

TECHNICAL
STUFF

Setting the volume

The volume key is located on the edge of your phone or tablet. Press the top part of the key to raise the volume. Press the bottom of the key to lower the volume. When the volume key is located on the top edge of an Android tablet, press the left part to increase volume and the right part to decrease volume.

As you press the volume key, a card appears on the touchscreen, to illustrate the relative volume level, as shown in Figure 3-2. You can continue pressing the volume key, or use your finger to adjust the onscreen slider and set the volume.

Not every volume card looks like the one shown in Figure 3-2, though they all feature a slider control. Additional controls let you set specific volumes; tap an icon on the card to view details. If a Settings icon appears on the card, tap it to make more specific adjustments.

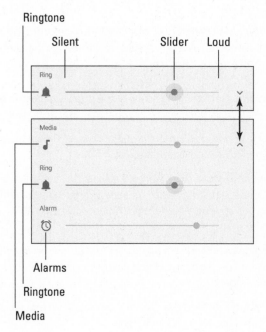

FIGURE 3-2: Setting the volume.

TIP

>> The volume key controls whatever noise the phone or tablet is making when you use it: If you're on a call, the volume key sets the call level. When you're listening to music or watching a video, the volume key adjusts those sounds.

>> When the volume is set all the way down, the speaker is muted.

>> The volume key works even when the touchscreen is locked. That means you don't need to unlock the device if you're playing music and you only need to adjust the volume.

>> Some Androids may enter Vibration mode when the volume is muted. All Android phones have Vibration mode, though not every tablet has this feature.

>> Refer to Chapter 21 for more details on volume controls.

"Silence your phone!"

How many times have you heard the admonition "Please silence your cell phone"? The quick way to obey this command with an Android phone is to unlock the touchscreen and keep pressing the bottom part of the volume key until the phone vibrates. You're good to go.

TIP

>> Some phones feature a Mute action on the Device Options card: Press and hold the Power/Lock key and then choose Mute or Vibrate.

>> When the phone is silenced or in Vibration mode, an appropriate status icon appears on the status bar. The stock Android status icon is shown in the margin.

>> You make the phone noisy again by reversing the directions in this section. Most commonly, press the "louder" end of the volume key to restore the phone's sound.

Changing the orientation

Your Android features a gizmo called an *accelerometer*. It determines in which direction the device is pointed as when its orientation has changed from horizontal to vertical – or even upside down. That way, the information displayed on the touchscreen always appears upright, no matter how you hold it.

To demonstrate how the phone or tablet orients itself, rotate the gizmo to the left or right. Most apps, such as the web browser app, change their presentation between horizontal and vertical to match the device's orientation.

>> The rotation feature may not work for all apps or even the Home screen. Specifically, most games present themselves in one format only.

>> The onscreen keyboard is more usable when the device is in its horizontal orientation. Chapter 4 covers using the onscreen keyboard.

TIP

>> You can lock the orientation if the rotating screen bothers you. See Chapter 21.

>> A great app that demonstrates the device's accelerometer is the game Labyrinth. You can purchase it at Google Play or download the free version, Labyrinth Lite. See Chapter 17 for more information about Google Play.

Home Screen Chores

The *Home screen* is where you start your Android day. It's the location from which you start an app and perform other duties. Knowing about the Home screen is an important part of understanding your Android phone or tablet.

To view the Home screen at any time, tap the Home navigation icon, found at the bottom of the touchscreen.

Exploring the Home screen

Typical Android Home screens are illustrated in Figure 3-3 — a phone on the left and a tablet on the right. Several fun and interesting things appear on the Home screen. Find these items on your own device's Home screen:

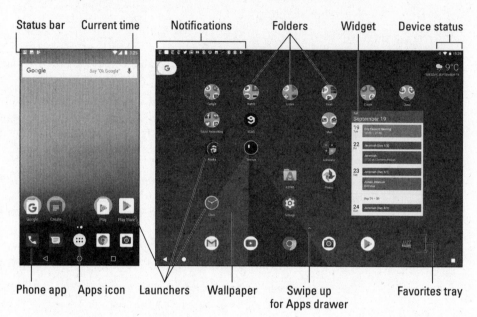

FIGURE 3-3:
The Home screen
(phone left,
tablet right).

Status bar: The top of the Home screen shows the status bar. It contains notification icons, status icons, and the current time. If the status bar disappears, a quick swipe from the top of the screen downward redisplays it.

Notifications: These icons come and go, depending on what happens in your digital life. For example, a new notification icon appears whenever you receive a new email message or for a pending appointment. See the later section "Reviewing notifications."

Device Status: Icons on the right end of the status bar represent the Android's current condition, such as the type of network connection, signal strength, Wi-Fi status, and battery charge, as well as other items.

Launchers: Tap a launcher to run, or "launch," the associated app.

Widgets: Widgets display information or let you control the phone or tablet, manipulate a feature, access an app, or do something purely amusing.

Folders: Multiple launchers can be stored in a folder. Tap the folder to open it and view the launchers inside.

Wallpaper: The Home screen background image is the wallpaper, which can be changed.

Favorites Tray: The bottom of the screen is reserved for popular launchers. The favorites tray shows the same launchers at the bottom of every Home screen page.

Phone app: You use the Phone app to make calls on an Android phone. It's kind of a big deal.

Apps icon: Tap this icon to view the Apps drawer, a collection of all apps available on your Android. Not every device has an Apps icon. For example, to access the Apps drawer from the tablet shown on the right in Figure 3-3, you swipe up the screen. See the later section "Finding an app in the Apps drawer."

REMEMBER

Ensure that you recognize the names of the various parts of the Home screen. These terms are used throughout this book and in whatever other scant Android documentation exists.

>> The Home screen is entirely customizable. You can place launchers, create folders, add widgets, and change the wallpaper. See Chapter 21 for information.

>> Touching a part of the Home screen that doesn't feature an icon or a control does nothing. That is, unless you're using the live wallpaper feature. In that case, touching the screen changes the wallpaper in some way, depending on the wallpaper that's selected. You can read more about live wallpaper in Chapter 21.

>> You may see numbers affixed to certain Home screen icons. Those numbers are notifications for pending actions, such as unread email messages, as shown in the margin.

Switching Home screen pages

The Home screen is more than what you see. It's actually an entire street of Home screens, with only one Home screen page visible at a time.

To switch from one panel to another, swipe the Home screen left or right. On some devices, a Home screen page index appears above the favorites tray. You can tap an icon on the index to zoom to a specific Home screen page.

>> When you tap the Home navigation icon, you return to the last Home screen page you viewed. To return to the main Home screen panel, tap the Home icon a second time.

» On some devices, the main Home screen page is shown by a House icon on the Home screen page index.

» The far right Home screen page might be occupied by a full-screen app, such as the Google app or Google Assistant. On Samsung devices, the Bixby assistant appears on the far right page.

» The number of available Home screen pages depends on the device. See Chapter 21 for directions on adding or removing Home screen pages.

Reviewing notifications

Notifications appear as icons on the left side of the status bar atop the Home screen, as illustrated earlier, in Figure 3-3. To review them, or to pull down the notifications drawer, you drag your finger from the top of the screen downward. The notifications drawer is illustrated in Figure 3-4.

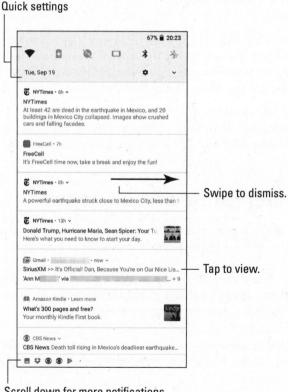

Quick settings

Swipe to dismiss.

Tap to view.

FIGURE 3-4:
The notifications
drawer. Scroll down for more notifications.

Swipe the list of notifications up or down to peruse them. To deal with a specific notification, tap it. What happens next depends on the notification or the app that generated it. Typically, the app runs and shows more details.

To dismiss an individual notification, swipe it left or right. To dismiss all notifications, tap the CLEAR ALL button. This button dwells at the end of the list, so you may have to swipe the notification drawer all the way to the bottom to see it.

To hide the notifications drawer, tap the Back icon, swipe the screen upward, or tap anywhere else on the Home screen.

>> Notifications can stack up if you don't deal with them!

>> When more notifications are present than can appear on the status bar, a More Notifications icon appears, similar to what's shown in the margin.

>> Dismissing some notifications doesn't prevent them from appearing again in the future. For example, notifications to update your apps continue to appear, as do calendar reminders.

>> The bottom of the notifications list may contain ongoing items, such as details about traffic, weather, or status information such as when the phone or tablet is charging, Wi-Fi and Bluetooth connections, and so on. These notifications cannot be dismissed.

>> Older Android devices used a Clear Notifications icon, shown in the margin, to dismiss notifications. This icon dwells at the bottom of the notifications drawer.

>> Some apps, such as Facebook and Twitter, don't display notifications unless you're signed in to the service.

>> New notifications are heralded by a notification ringtone. Chapter 21 provides information on changing the sound.

>> Notifications may also appear on the Android's lock screen. Controlling which types of notifications appear is covered in Chapter 22.

Accessing the quick settings

The quick settings appear as large buttons or icons atop the notifications drawer. These buttons let you access popular features or turn options on or off, such as Bluetooth, Wi-Fi, Airplane mode, Auto Rotate, and more.

To access the quick settings, use two fingers to swipe the touchscreen from the top downward. The quick settings appear as illustrated in Figure 3-5, though many devices have variations on the quantity and presentation of buttons and icons.

Quick settings

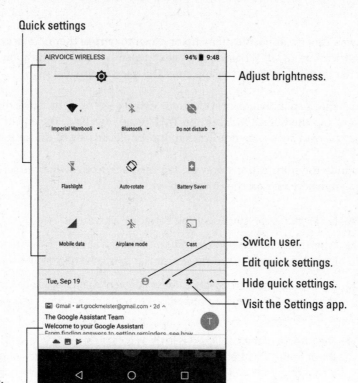

Adjust brightness.

Switch user.

Edit quick settings.

Hide quick settings.

Visit the Settings app.

FIGURE 3-5:
The Quick
Settings drawer.

Notifications

To use a quick setting, tap its icon. Some icons represent on–off features, such as Flashlight and Airplane mode, shown in Figure 3-5. Other buttons feature menus that let you select options, such as Wi-Fi and Bluetooth. Tap the menu to peruse additional options.

To dismiss the quick settings drawer, tap either the Back or Home navigation icons.

TIP

>> Tap the Settings icon on the Quick Settings drawer to quickly open the useful Settings app.

>> The Edit (pencil) icon, shown in Figure 3-5, lets you add or remove items from the Quick Settings drawer.

>> The notification drawer appears below the quick access drawer. Swipe up the screen, or tap the Hide chevron (refer to Figure 3-5) to view pending notifications.

>> Some Samsung devices present the quick settings as a left-right scrolling list.

>> Many of the features accessed from the quick settings drawer are covered elsewhere in this book.

The World of Apps

The Android operating system can pack thrill-a-minute excitement, but it's probably not the only reason you purchased the device. No, Android's success lies with the available apps. Knowing how to deal with apps is vital to becoming a successful, happy phone or tablet user.

Starting an app

To start an app, tap its launcher icon. The app starts.

Apps are started from the Home screen: Tap a launcher to start its associated app. Apps can be started also from the Apps drawer, as described in the later section "Finding an app in the Apps drawer."

You can also start an app found in a Home screen folder: Tap to open the folder, and then tap a launcher to start that app.

Quitting an app

Unlike on a computer, you don't need to quit apps on your Android. To leave an app, tap the Home navigation icon to return to the Home screen. You can keep tapping the Back navigation icon to back out of an app. Or you can tap the Recent navigation icon to switch to another running app.

>> Some apps feature a Quit or Exit command, but for the most part you don't quit an app like you quit a program on a computer.

>> If necessary, the Android operating system shuts down apps you haven't used in a while. You can directly stop apps run amok, which is described in Chapter 20.

TECHNICAL STUFF

Finding an app in the Apps drawer

The launchers you see on the Home screen don't represent all the apps in your Android. To view all installed apps, visit the Apps drawer: Tap the Apps icon on the Home screen. Variations on the Apps icon are shown in Figure 3-6. This icon appears on the favorites tray, at the bottom of every Home screen.

FIGURE 3-6:
Apps icon
varieties.

If you don't see the Apps icon, swipe up the Home screen. You may see a small chevron about the favorites tray, indicating the swipe-up action. Some devices might even let you swipe down the touchscreen to access the Apps drawer.

The Apps drawer lists all installed apps on your phone or tablet. You may see a long list, or the apps may be presented on pages you swipe left and right. Atop the list you might find a row of apps you use most frequently.

 The Apps drawer features a search bar, which helps you quickly locate a specific app: Tap the search box and type the app name. This tool is handy for locating a specific app in a highly populated Apps drawer.

To run an app, tap its icon. The app starts, taking over the screen and doing whatever magical thing that app does.

» Apps you add to your phone or tablet appear in the Apps drawer as well as on the Home screen. See Chapter 17 for information on adding new apps.

» Some Androids let you create folders in the Apps drawer. These folders contain multiple apps, which helps keep things organized. To access apps in the folder, tap the Folder icon.

» The stock Android Apps drawer displays apps alphabetically. Some devices let you change the order and edit the Apps drawer. Look for an Edit (pencil) or Action Overflow icon on the Apps drawer to edit the pages.

Switching between running apps

The apps you run on your phone or tablet don't quit when you dismiss them from the screen. For the most part, they stay running. To switch between running apps, or to access any app you've recently opened, tap the Recent navigation icon. You see the Overview, similar to what's shown in Figure 3-7.

Swipe

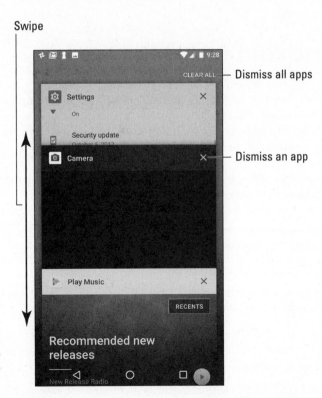

Dismiss all apps

Dismiss an app

FIGURE 3-7: The Overview shows recently used apps.

Swipe the list to view all the apps, though the presentation differs on some devices. For example, you may see a grid of thumbnails on an Android tablet. Tap the app's card to switch to that app.

To exit from the Overview, tap the Back navigation icon.

>> To remove an app from the Overview, swipe it off the list or tap the Close (X) icon, as illustrated in Figure 3-7.

>> Removing an app from the Overview is pretty much the same thing as quitting an app.

>> For older Androids that lack the Recent navigation icon, long-press the Home navigation icon to see the Overview.

>> Samsung gizmos use the Recent navigation icon, shown in the margin.

>> The Android operating system may shut down apps that haven't received attention for a while. Don't be surprised if you can't find a recent app on the Overview. If so, just start it up again as you normally would.

REMEMBER

Common Android Icons

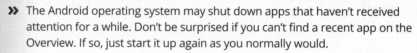

In additional to the navigation icons, the Android operating system features a consistent armada of other, helpful icons. These icons serve common and consistent functions in apps as well as in the Android operating system. Table 3-2 lists the most common of these icons and their functions.

Various sections throughout this book give examples of using these icons. Their images appear in the book's margins where relevant.

>> Other common symbols are used on icons in various apps. For example, the standard Play and Pause icons are used as well.

>> The Chevron icon might also appear as a solid triangle.

>> The Share icon shown in Table 3-2 has an evil twin, shown in the margin. Both icons represent the Share action.

>> Some Samsung galaxy gizmos use a MORE button in place of the Action Overflow icon. In fact, you often see text buttons such as SAVE or DONE instead of icons on Samsung phones and tablets.

>> Another variation on the Settings icon is shown in the margin. It serves the same purpose as the Gear icon, shown in Table 3-2. Though this older Settings icon is being phased out, it still appears in some apps.

TABLE 3-2

Common Icons

Icon	Name	What It Does
	Action Overflow	Displays a list of actions, similar to a menu.
	Add	Adds or creates an item. The plus symbol (+) may be used in combination with other symbols, depending on the app.
	Chevron	Points in various directions; tap this icon to expand or collapse a card, a menu, or another item.
	Close	Dismisses a card, clears text from an input field, or removes an item from a list.
	Delete	Removes one or more items from a list or deletes a message.
	Dictation	Activates voice input.
	Done	Dismisses the action bar or confirms and saves edits.
	Edit	Lets you edit an item, add text, or fill in fields.
	Favorite	Flags a favorite item, such as a contact or a web page.
	Refresh	Fetches new information or reloads.
	Search	Searches the screen, the device, or the Internet for a tidbit of information.
	Settings	Adjusts options for an app.
	Share	Shares information via a specific app, such as Gmail or Facebook.
	Side Menu	Also called the *hamburger,* tap this icon to view the navigation drawer available in most Android apps.

Chapter **4**

Type to Type, Text to Edit

seriously doubt that anyone would consider using their Android to write the Great American Novel. The gizmo lacks a real keyboard! Even so, typing is something you do on a phone or tablet, thanks to something called the onscreen keyboard. You can also dictate to generate text. No matter how it gets in there, your Android is ready to accept, process, and even edit text.

Onscreen Keyboard Mania

The onscreen keyboard reveals itself on the bottom half of the touchscreen whenever text input is required. The stock Android keyboard is called the *Gboard* ("jee-board"), for Google Keyboard. The phone version of the Gboard is shown in Figure 4-1. The tablet version is wider and has additional keys.

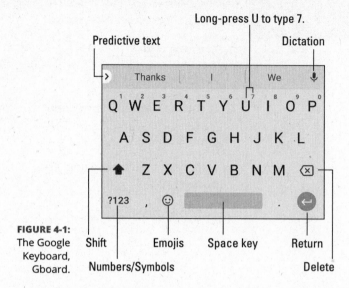

FIGURE 4-1:
The Google
Keyboard,
Gboard.

Long-press U to type 7.

Predictive text

Dictation

Shift

Numbers/Symbols

Emojis

Space key

Return

Delete

Samsung gizmos use the Samsung keyboard, illustrated in Figure 4-2. It works like the Gboard, but offers its own special features, primarily a row of number keys, as shown in the figure.

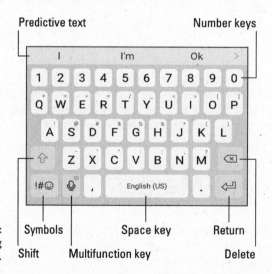

FIGURE 4-2:
The Samsung
Keyboard.

Predictive text

Number keys

Symbols

Space key

Return

Shift

Multifunction key

Delete

No matter how the keyboard looks, all onscreen keyboards are based on the traditional QWERTY layout: You see keys from A through Z, albeit not in that order. You also see the Shift key for changing the letter case, and the Delete key, which backspaces and erases.

The Return key changes its look and function depending on what you're typing. Your keyboard may show these variations graphically or by labeling the key with text. The stock Android symbols are illustrated in Figure 4-3. Here's what each one does:

Return: Just like the Return or Enter key on a computer keyboard, this key ends a paragraph of text. It's used mostly when filling in long stretches of text or when multiline input is needed.

Search: You see this key appear when you're searching for something. Tap the key to start the search.

Go: This key directs the app to proceed with a search, accept input, or perform another action.

Next: This key appears when you type information into multiple fields. Tap this key to switch from one field to the next, such as when typing a username and password.

Done: This key appears whenever you've finished typing text in the final field and you're ready to submit input.

The large key at the bottom-center of the onscreen keyboard is the Space key. It's flanked left and right by other keys that may change, depending on the context of what you're typing. For example, a / (slash) key or .com key may appear in order to assist in typing a web page or email address. These keys may change, but the basic alphabetic keys remain the same.

>> To display the onscreen keyboard, tap any text field or spot on the screen where typing is permitted.

>> To dismiss the onscreen keyboard, tap the Back navigation icon. It may appear as shown in the margin.

>> Some onscreen keyboard variations feature a multifunction key, as shown in Figure 4-2. It may be labeled with the Settings (gear) icon, a Microphone icon, an emoji, or some other icon. Long-press the multifunction key to view its options.

>> The keyboard changes its width when you reorient the phone or tablet. The keyboard's horizontal presentation is wider and easier for typing.

>> If you pine for a real keyboard, one that exists in the fourth dimension, consider getting a Bluetooth keyboard. Such a wireless keyboard also doubles as a docking stand or portfolio cover for an Android tablet. You can read more about Bluetooth in Chapter 18.

Everybody Was Touchscreen Typing

Typing is a necessary skill, something they now call "keyboarding" in school. That necessity extends to your Android mobile device, though typing on a touch-screen keyboard isn't anyone's favorite activity. That's because if you're the world's fastest touch-typist, you can only hunt-and-peck on your phone or tab-let. It's a limitation everyone must face. Yes, it's the old hunt-and-peck all over again.

Typing one character at a time

The onscreen keyboard is cinchy to figure out: Tap a letter key to produce the character. As you type, the key you touch is highlighted. The Android may provide a wee bit of feedback in the form of a faint click sound or vibration.

>> A blinking cursor on the touchscreen shows where new text appears, which is how typing text works on a computer.

>> When you make a mistake, tap the Delete key to back up and erase.

>> When you type a password, the character you type appears briefly, but for security reasons, it's then replaced by a black dot.

>> To type in all caps, tap the Shift key twice. The Shift key may appear high-lighted, and the shift symbol may change color, which indicates that Shift Lock is on. Tap the Shift key again to deactivate Shift Lock.

>> People generally accept the concept that composing text on a phone or tablet isn't perfect. Don't sweat it if you make a few mistakes as you type text messages or email, though you should expect some curious replies about unintended typos.

>> Above all, it helps to type slowly until you become familiar with the onscreen keyboard.

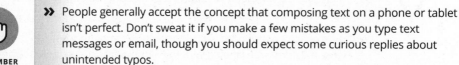
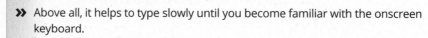

Accessing other keyboards

You're not limited to typing only the characters shown on the alphabetic keyboard. On the Gboard, tap the ?123 key to access the Symbols keyboard. Also available are the emoji and keypad keyboards, as illustrated in Figure 4-4. You can cycle between them.

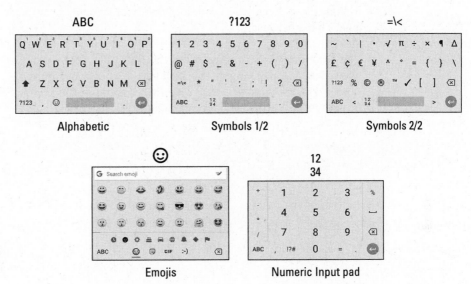

ABC — Alphabetic

?123 — Symbols 1/2

=\< — Symbols 2/2

Emojis

12 34 — Numeric Input pad

On the Symbols keyboard, tap the =\< key to access the second Symbols keyboard. The !?# key found on the Numeric Input Pad keyboard also accesses the first Symbols keyboard (refer to Figure 4-4).

Tap the 1234 key to access the numeric input pad. A similar keyboard is available in the Phone or Dialer app, though it's called the *dial pad.*

Tap the ☺ key to view the emoji keyboard. This keyboard features several tabs (along the bottom) as well as a scrolling list of categories. Also, use the search bar to look up specific emojis by their meaning, such as "celebration" and "angry cat."

Tap the ABC key to return to the alphabetic keyboard.

On the Samsung keyboard, tap the !#☺ key to access the symbols keyboards. Use the 1/2 and 2/2 keys to page between the two keyboard sets.

Typing accented characters

You can access some special characters, such as foreign or accented characters, without having to switch keyboard layouts. Both techniques involve long-pressing a key.

The first trick is to look for a tiny symbol next to a key, such as the 7 above the U in Figure 4-1. Even when you don't see that symbol, a character might be available. That's because:

The second trick is to long-press the letter key that looks like the symbol you want. For example, long-press the A key, as shown in Figure 4-5, to access variations on that character. Drag your finger through the pop-up palette. Lift your finger to select a specific, accented character.

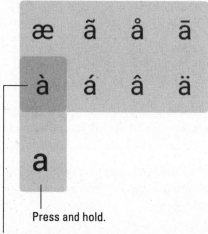

FIGURE 4-5:
Special-symbol
pop-up
palette-thing.

Press and hold.

Drag your finger over a character to select it.

>> Most keys on the onscreen keyboard feature special characters, though they're not that obvious.

>> If you choose the wrong character, tap the Delete key on the onscreen keyboard to erase the mistyped symbol.

Using predictive text to type quickly

As you type, you see a selection of word suggestions just above the keyboard (refer to Figure 4-1). That's the onscreen keyboard's predictive text feature. Choose a word from the list to greatly accelerate your typing; the word you tap is inserted into the text.

If the desired word doesn't appear, continue typing: The predictive text feature makes suggestions based on what you've typed so far.

TIP

>> If predictive text replaces your correctly typed word with something else, tap the Delete key. The replaced word is restored.

>> With some versions of the onscreen keyboard, you can long-press a word to see similar words.

>> The predictive text feature is unavailable for typing passwords or when filling in forms.

>> If the predictive text feature is inactive, see Chapter 21 for information on activating it.

Typing without lifting your finger

If you're really after typing speed, consider using glide typing. It allows you to swipe your finger over the onscreen keyboard to type words. It's like mad scribbling but with a positive result.

To use glide typing, drag a finger over letters on the onscreen keyboard. Figure 4-6 illustrates how the word *taco* would be typed in this manner.

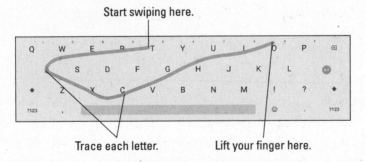

FIGURE 4-6: Using gesture typing to type *taco*.

Gesture typing is disabled when typing a password or an email address or for other specific typing duties. When it doesn't work, tap one letter at a time.

>> The glide typing feature was once called *gesture* typing.

>> Refer to Chapter 21 for glide typing settings.

Google Voice Typing

Your Android mobile gizmo has the amazing capability to interpret your utterances as text. It works almost as well as computer dictation in science fiction movies, though I can't seem to find the command to locate intelligent life.

» The dictation feature is available whenever you see the Dictation (microphone) icon. This icon appears on the keyboard as well as in other locations, such as search boxes.

» On Samsung keyboards, the Microphone icon appears on a multifunction key. Long-press that key to choose its dictation function.

Dictating text

Talking to your phone or tablet works quite well, providing that you tap the Dictation icon and you don't mumble.

After you tap the Dictation icon on the Gboard, text appears saying that the device is "listening," as shown in Figure 4-7 on the left. Samsung gizmos may display a card that covers the onscreen keyboard, as shown on the right in Figure 4-7.

Stock Android   Samsung

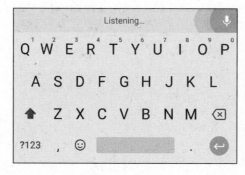

FIGURE 4-7:
Google Voice
Typing.

Dismiss dictation.

To pause, tap the Dictation icon again or tap the text *Tap to Pause.*

On a Samsung phone or tablet, tap the Cancel (X) icon in the upper right corner of the card to dismiss dictation.

>> The first time you try voice input, you might see a description displayed. Tap the OK or GOT IT button to continue.

>> Tap misinterpreted words to view a pop-up list of alternatives. Choose an alternative to replace the text.

>> Speak the punctuation in your text. For example, you would say, "I'm sorry comma and it won't happen again" to produce the text *I'm sorry, and it won't happen again* or something close to that.

>> Common punctuation you can dictate includes the *comma, period, exclamation point, question mark, colon,* and *new line.*

>> If keys are visible on the onscreen keyboard, you can type them as you dictate. This feature makes it easier to add punctuation, which is a weak spot in the Android dictation feature.

>> You cannot dictate capital letters. If you're a stickler for such things, you must go back and edit the text.

>> Dictation may not work without an Internet connection.

Uttering s**** words

The Android dictation has a voice censor. It replaces those naughty words you might utter; the first letter appears on the screen, followed by the appropriate number of asterisks.

For example, if *spatula* were a blue word and you uttered "spatula" when dictating text, the dictation feature would place s****** on the screen rather than the word *spatula.*

Yeah, I know: silly. Or, should I say, "s****."

>> The phone or tablet knows a lot of naughty words, including George Carlin's infamous "Seven Words You Can Never Say on Television," but apparently the terms *crap* and *damn* are fine. Don't ask me how much time I spent researching this topic.

>> See Chapter 25 if you'd like to disable the dictation censor.

Text Editing

You'll probably do more text editing on your phone or tablet than you anticipated. That editing includes the basic stuff, such as spiffing up typos and adding a period here or there as well as complex editing involving cut, copy, and paste. The concepts are the same as you find on a computer, but the process can be daunting without a physical keyboard and a mouse.

Moving the cursor

The first part of editing text is moving the cursor to the right spot. The cursor is that blinking, vertical line that marks the location where new text appears, edited text changes, or cut/copied text is pasted.

 To set the cursor's location, tap the text. To help your accuracy, a tab appears below the cursor, as shown in the margin. Drag that tab to precisely locate the cursor.

After you move the cursor, you can continue to type, tap the Delete key to back up and erase, or paste text copied from elsewhere.

>> You may see the PASTE COMMAND button appear above the cursor tab. Use this button to paste in text, as described in the later section "Cutting, copying, and pasting text."

>> Samsung keyboards may feature cursor movement keys. Use those keys to move the cursor as well as the stab-your-finger-on-the-screen method.

Selecting text

Selecting text on an Android phone or tablet works just like selecting text in a word processor: You mark the start and end of a block. That chunk of text appears highlighted on the screen. How you get there, however, can be a mystery — until now!

To select text, long–press a word. Upon success, you see a chunk of selected text, as shown in Figure 4–8.

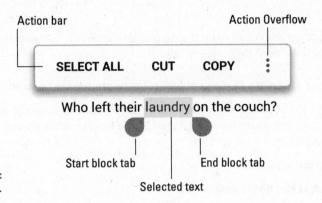

Drag the start and end markers around the touchscreen to define the block of selected text. Use the action bar to choose what to do with the text, as shown in Figure 4-8. Tap the Action Overflow to view additional commands.

What can you do with selected text? Just like on a computer, tap the DELETE button to remove the block. Type new text to replace. You can also copy, cut, and paste, as covered in the following section.

To cancel text selection, tap elsewhere in the text.

TIP

» On some devices, the action bar may appear a top the touchscreen. Icons might be used instead of the text buttons illustrated in Figure 4-8.

» Selecting text on a web page works the same as selecting text in any other app. The difference is that text can only be copied from the web page, not cut or deleted.

» Seeing the onscreen keyboard is a good indication that you can edit and select text.

» The SELECT ALL action marks all text as a single block.

Cutting, copying, and pasting text

Selected text is primed for cutting or copying, which works just like it does in your favorite word processor. After you select the text, choose the proper action: COPY to copy text or CUT to cut the text.

Text cut or copied is stored on the Android's clipboard. To paste any previously cut or copied text, heed these directions:

1. **Move the cursor to the spot where you want the text pasted.**

   Refer to the earlier section "Moving the cursor." The location can also be in another app where text is accepted (and where the onscreen keyboard appears).

2. **Tap the cursor tab.**

3. **Choose the PASTE action.**

   The text appears at the cursor's location, or if any text was selected, the pasted text replaces it.

Some Androids feature a Clipboard app, which lets you peruse, review, and select previously cut or copied text or images. If you see a Clipboard action icon when you go to paste text, tap it to access the Clipboard app.

Dealing with speling errrs

As you plunk away on the onscreen keyboard, your Android highlights misspelled words. A vicious red underline appears beneath the suspect spelling, drawing attention to the problem and general embarrassment to the typist.

Tap the red-underlined word. Choose a replacement from the predictive text part of the onscreen keyboard, or from a list that's displayed. If the word is correctly spelled but unknown to the Android, choose to add the word to a personal dictionary.

>> Words may be autocorrected as you type them. To undo an autocorrection, tap the word again. Choose a replacement word from the predictive text list, or tap the original word to keep it.

>> Yes! Your Android has a personal dictionary. See Chapter 25 for details.

2
Stay Connected

Chapter **5**

Telephone Stuff

n 1876, Alexander Graham Bell beat a host of competitors to the patent office and has since been credited with the invention of the telephone. Other great dates in phone history are: 1878, when the busy signal was invented; 1896, when the Clayton household added a second line for their teenage daughter; and 1902, when the extension cord was patented to allow for simultaneous talking and pacing.

In the modern world, a phone call is only a minor feature of the device known as an Android phone. Yet the namesake feature offers a host of handy calling tools, all fully patented or in current legal battles, that telephone users from the last century could only dream of.

» The information in this chapter is exclusive to Android phones.

» To fake a phone call on an Android tablet, you can use the Google Hangouts or Skype apps. See Chapter 11.

Reach Out and Touch Someone

Making a phone call is the second most popular way you can use your Android phone to connect with another human. Number one is texting. In fact, phone calls are kind of quaint, but still necessary, sort of like the turn signal on a BMW.

Placing a phone call

To place a call on your phone, heed these steps:

1. **Open the Phone app.**

   The Phone app's launcher is found on the Home screen, on the favorites tray. The app's icon features a Phone Handset icon, similar to the one shown in the margin.

2. **If necessary, display the dialpad.**

   If you don't see the dialpad, illustrated in Figure 5-1, tap the Dialpad icon, similar to what's shown in the margin.

3. **Type a phone number.**

   You may hear the traditional touch-tone sounds as you punch in the number.

   If you make a mistake, tap the Delete icon, labeled in Figure 5-1, to back up and erase.

TIP

   The phone displays matching contacts as you type. Choose a contact to instantly input that person's number.

4. **Tap the Dial icon to place the call.**

   While a call is active, the screen changes to show contact information, or a contact image when one is available, similar to Figure 5-2.

5. **Place the phone to your ear and wait.**

6. **When the person answers the phone, talk.**

   What you say is up to you, though it's good not to just blurt out unexpected news, like: "Twenty people are showing up for dinner" or "Your lawn is on fire."

   Use the phone's volume key to adjust the volume during the call.

7. **Tap the End Call icon to end the call.**

   The phone disconnects. You hear a soft beep, which is the phone's signal that the call has ended.

Matching contacts Signal strength

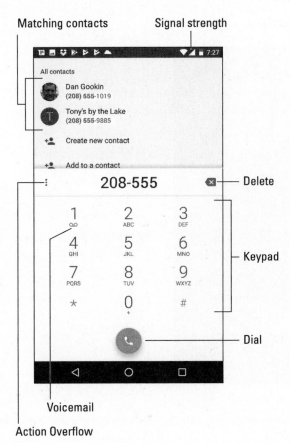

FIGURE 5-1:
The Phone app's
dialpad.

Delete

Keypad

Dial

Voicemail

Action Overflow

TIP

You can do other things while you're making a call: Tap the Home navigation icon to run an app, read old email, check an appointment, or do whatever. Activities such as these don't disconnect you, although your cellular carrier may not allow you to do other things with the phone while you're on a call.

To return to a call after doing something else, choose the Call in Progress notification icon, similar to the one shown in the margin.

>> The Phone app might be titled Dialer on some devices.

>> Some manufacturers may spruce up the Phone app beyond what you see in Figures 5-1 and 5-2. For example, Samsung offers video calling between two Samsung devices, and a Camera icon appears to activate this feature.

>> Don't worry about the phone's microphone being too far away from your mouth; it picks up your voice just fine.

Active call notification

Contact image

Dan Gookin

00:15 — Call duration

Mute   Keypad   Speaker

Various controls

Add call   Hold

Hang Up/End Call

FIGURE 5-2:
A successful call.

>> For hands-free operation, use earbuds with a microphone doodle, as discussed in Chapter 1.

>> You can connect or remove the earphones at any time during a call.

>> Use a Bluetooth headset to go hands-free. If a Bluetooth icon doesn't appear on the screen, tap the Speaker icon (refer to Figure 5-2) to ensure that the Bluetooth headset is active. See Chapter 18 for information on Bluetooth.

>> If you're going hands-free, press the phone's Power/Lock key during the call to lock the phone. Locking the phone doesn't disconnect the call, but it does prevent you from accidentally hanging up or muting the call.

>> To mute a call, tap the Mute icon, shown earlier in Figure 5-2. A Mute status icon, similar to the one shown in the margin, appears atop the touchscreen.

>> You can't accidentally mute or end a call when the phone is placed against your face; the device's proximity sensor prevents that from happening.

>> Tap the Speaker icon and hold the phone at a distance to listen and talk, which helps facilitate the common cell-phone-as-a-slice-of-pizza method of communications. The speaker also allows you to let others listen and share in the conversation. You see a Speaker status icon while the speaker is active.

>> Don't hold the phone right at your ear while the speaker is active.

>> If you're wading through one of those nasty voicemail systems, tap the Dialpad icon, labeled in Figure 5-2, so that you can "Press 1 for English" when necessary.

>> See the later section "Multi-Call Mania," for information on using the Hold and Add Call icons.

>> You hear an audio alert whenever the call is dropped or the other party hangs up. The disconnection can be confirmed by looking at the phone, which shows that the call has ended.

>> You cannot place a phone call when the phone has no service; check the signal strength (refer to Figure 5-1). Also see the nearby sidebar, "Signal strength."

>> You cannot place a phone call when the phone is in Airplane mode. See Chapter 23.

>> Also see Chapter 23 for details on international calling.

Dialing a contact

To access your phone's address book, start the Phone app and tap the Contacts tab, which might be titled All Contacts or feature an icon such as the one shown in the margin. Browse the list for someone to call; tap their entry and then tap their phone number or Phone icon to place the call.

SIGNAL STRENGTH

One of your Android phone's most important status icons is Signal Strength. It appears in the top-right corner of the screen, next to the Battery status icon and the time.

The Signal Strength icon features the familiar bars, rising from left to right. The more bars, the better the signal. An extremely low signal is indicated by zero bars. When no signal is available, you may see a red circle with a line through it (the International No symbol) over the bars.

When the phone is out of its service area but still receiving a signal, you see the Roaming icon, which typically includes an R near or over the bars. See Chapter 23 for more information on roaming. Also see Chapter 18 for information on the mobile data network status icon.

>> You can also use the phone's address book app directly to find and phone a contact. See Chapter 7.

>> A special contact category in the phone's address book is Favorites. To quickly access your favorites, tap the Favorites tab in the Phone app. This tab may feature the Favorites (star) icon, shown in the margin.

>> Some variations on the Phone app place the favorite contacts on the main screen or on the Speed Dial screen. See the next section.

Using speed dial

To speed dial a number, long-press one of the digits on the Phone app's dialpad. The phone number associated with that key is dialed instantly. For example, if your bookie is on speed dial 2, long-press the 2 key to instantly dial his number.

To assign a speed dial number, or just review the current settings, heed these steps when using the Phone app:

1. Display the dialpad.

2. Tap the Action Overflow icon.

On some Samsung phones, tap the MORE button.

3. Choose Speed Dial or Speed Dial Setup.

If you don't see that these are similar actions, the Phone app most likely lacks a speed dial feature.

Most carriers configure number 1 as the voicemail system's number. The remaining numbers, 2 through 9, are available to program.

4. Tap an item on the list, or tap the Add icon.

The item may say Add Speed Dial or Not Assigned as opposed to being blank.

5. Choose a contact or type a number.

The number should really be a contact in your phone's address book, so read Chapter 7 for details on adding a contact.

6. Repeat Steps 4 and 5 to assign more speed dial contacts.

When you're done adding numbers, tap the Back navigation icon to exit the speed dial screen.

To remove a speed dial entry, long–press it and choose the Delete or Remove action. Or, in some cases, tap the Minus (remove) icon to the right of the speed dial entry.

Adding pauses when dialing a number

When you tap the Phone icon to dial a number, the number is instantly spewed into the phone system, like water out of a hose. If you need to pause the number as it's dialed, you need to know how to insert secret pause characters. Two are available:

>> The comma (,) adds a 2-second pause.

>> The semicolon (;) adds a wait prompt.

To insert the pause or wait characters into a phone number, obey these directions:

1. **Type the number to dial.**

2. **At the point that the pause or wait character is needed, tap the Action Overflow icon.**

   The Action Overflow icon is illustrated in Figure 5-1. On some phones, tap the MORE button.

3. **Choose the action Add 2-Sec Pause or Add Wait.**

4. **Continue composing the rest of the phone number.**

When the number is dialed and the comma (,) is encountered, the phone pauses two seconds and then dials the rest of the number.

When the semicolon (;) is encountered, the phone prompts you to continue. Tap the YES or OK button to continue dialing the rest of the number.

>> The comma (,) and semicolon (;) can also be inserted into the phone numbers you assign to contacts in the phone's address book. See Chapter 7.

>> Alas, you cannot program an interactive phone number, such as one that pauses and lets you provide input and then continues to dial. You must perform such a task manually on an Android phone.

It's for You!

Who doesn't enjoy getting a phone call? It's an event! Never mind that it's the company that keeps calling you about lowering the interest rate on your credit cards. The point is that someone cares enough to call. Truly, your Android phone ringing can be good news, bad news, or mediocre news, but it always provides a little drama to spice up an otherwise mundane day.

Receiving a call

Several things can happen when you receive a phone call on your Android phone:

>> The phone sounds a ringtone, signaling an incoming call.

>> The phone vibrates.

>> The touchscreen reveals information about the call, as shown in Figure 5-3.

>> The car in front of you explodes in a loud fireball as your passenger screams something inappropriately funny.

That last item happens only in Bruce Willis movies. The other three possibilities, or a combination thereof, are signals that you have an incoming call.

To answer the call, swipe the Answer icon up or to the right, as indicated on the touchscreen. If you're using a Bluetooth headset, tap the button or otherwise work the gizmo to use that device for listening and speaking.

When you're done jabbering, tap the End Call icon to hang up: Move the phone away from your face to activate the touchscreen, then tap the icon. If the other party hangs up first, the call ends automatically.

>> You don't have to work a screen lock to answer a call. The phone remains locked, however, so if you want to do other things while you're on the call, you must work the screen lock.

>> Other options may appear on the incoming calls screen, including sending the call immediately to voicemail, responding with a text message, and others. Directions on the touchscreen explain your choices.

>> When the phone is unlocked, incoming calls are heralded by a card that appears atop the screen. Tap the ANSWER button to receive the call; tap DECLINE to dismiss it.

>> The contact's picture appears only when you've assigned a picture to the contact. Otherwise, a generic contact image appears.

Incoming call info

FIGURE 5-3:
You have an
incoming call.

Answer button   Swipe right to answer   Swipe left to decline

Swipe for text message reply   Swipe up for text message reply

>> The sound you hear for an incoming call is termed the ringtone. You can configure your phone's ringtone depending on who is calling, or you can set a universal ringtone. Ringtones are covered in Chapter 21.

Rejecting a call

Several options are available when you don't want to answer an incoming call.

Let the phone ring: Just do something else or pretend that you're dead. To silence the ringer, press the phone's volume key.

Dismiss the call: Swipe the Answer button in the direction of the call rejection option. Or, if available, swipe the Decline button, shown in the right in Figure 5-3.

Reply with a text message: Choose the text message rejection option, which dismisses the call and sends the caller a preset text message.

In all cases, unanswered calls are sent to voicemail. See Chapter 6 for information on voicemail. Chapter 6 also covers the call log, which shows a list of recent calls, incoming, missed, and rejected.

Rejecting a call with a text message

A thoughtful way to dismiss a call is to send an instant text message reply. Upon receiving an incoming call you are unable or unwilling to answer, follow these steps:

1. **Select the text message rejection option from the incoming call screen.**

   Swipe the text message rejection item up or to the center of the screen.

2. **Choose a preset text message from the list.**

   For example, "Can't talk now. I'll call you later."

The call is dismissed and, in a few cellular seconds, the person who called receives the message.

REMEMBER

>> Not every phone offers the text message rejection feature.

>> Only a cell phone receives the text message rejection. If the doctor's office is calling, they won't see your quick response message.

>> The method for adding, removing, or editing the call rejection messages differs from phone to phone. Generally, tap the Action Overflow icon or MORE button while using the Phone app. Choose Settings. Look for a Quick Responses or Call Rejection action.

>> See Chapter 8 for more information on text messaging.

Multi-Call Mania

As a human being, your brain limits your ability to hold more than one conversation at a time. Your phone's brain, however, lacks such a limitation. It's entirely possible for an Android phone to handle more than one call at a time.

Putting someone on hold

It's easy to place a call on hold — as long as your cellular provider hasn't disabled that feature. Tap the Hold icon, shown in the margin.

To take the call out of hold, tap the Hold icon again. The icon may change its look, for example, from a Pause symbol to a Play symbol.

Fret not if your phone's call-in-progress screen lacks the Hold icon. Rather than hold the call, mute it: Tap the Mute icon. That way, you can sneeze, scream at the wall, or flush the toilet and the other person will never know.

Receiving a new call when you're on the phone

You're on the phone, chatting it up. Suddenly, someone else calls you. What happens next?

Your phone alerts you to the new call, perhaps by vibrating or making a sound. Look at the touchscreen to see who's calling and determine what to do next. You have three options:

>> **Answer the call.** Slide the Answer icon just as you would answer any incoming call. The current call is placed on hold.

>> **Send the call directly to voicemail.** Dismiss the call as you would any incoming phone call.

>> **Do nothing.** The call eventually goes into voicemail.

When you choose to answer the second call, additional options become available to manage both calls. Use special icons on the call-in-progress screen to perform special, multi-call tricks:

Swap/Switch Calls: To switch between callers, tap the Swap or Switch Calls icon on the touchscreen. You might instead see a card at the bottom of the screen; tap the card to switch to that caller. The current person is placed on hold when you switch calls.

Merge Calls: To combine all calls so that everyone is talking (three people total), tap the Merge Calls icon. This icon may not be available if the merge feature is suppressed by your cellular provider.

End Call: To end a call, tap the End Call icon, just as you normally do. You're switched back to the other caller.

To end the final call, tap the End Call or Hang Up icon, just as you normally would.

>> The Merge Calls icon might also appear as shown in the margin.

» The Swap/Switch Calls icon might be the standard Refresh icon, shown in the margin.

» The number of different calls your phone can handle depends on your carrier. For most subscribers in the United States, your phone can handle only two calls at a time. In that case, another person who calls either hears a busy signal or is sent directly to voicemail.

» If the person on hold hangs up, you may hear a sound or feel the phone vibrate when the call is dropped.

» When you end a second call on the Verizon network, both calls may appear to have been disconnected. That's not the case: In a few moments, the call you didn't disconnect "rings" as though the person is calling you back. No one is calling you back, though: you're returning to that ongoing conversation.

Making a conference call

You can call two different people by using your Android phone's merge calls feature. To start, connect with the first person and then add a second call. Soon, everyone is talking. Here are the details:

1. **Phone the first person.**

2. **After the call connects and you complete a few pleasantries, tap the Add Call icon.**

    The Add Call icon may appear as shown in the margin. If not, look for a generic Add (+) icon. After you tap that icon, the first person is placed on hold.

3. **Dial the second person.**

    You can use the dialpad or choose the second person from the phone's address book or the call history.

    Say your pleasantries and inform the party that the call is about to be merged.

4. **Tap the Merge or Merge Calls icon.**

    The two calls are now joined: Everyone you've dialed can talk to and hear everyone else.

5. **Tap the End Call icon to end the conference call.**

    All calls are disconnected.

REMEMBER

When several people are in a room and want to participate in a call, you can always put the phone in Speaker mode: Tap the Speaker icon on the ongoing call screen.

Your Android phone may feature the Manage icon while you're in a conference call. Tap this icon to list the various calls, to mute one, or to select a call to disconnect.

Chapter **6**

Forward Calls, Missed Calls, and Voicemail

G one are the days when you could say you were "out" and missed a call. That's because your Android phone goes with you everywhere. The quantity of excuses for not taking a call is weak and limited. You can blame call forwarding. You can confirm a missed call on the call log. And you can always resort to voicemail, which is becoming more accepted — especially when the message is sincere.

» As in Chapter 5, most of the information here is specific to Android phones.

» Your Android tablet can use the Google Voice app, covered later in this chapter. You may not receive a call on your tablet, but you can check your voicemail.

Forward Calls Elsewhere

Call forwarding is traditionally a trick you used from your old landline phone to a cell phone. It's odd to think of it used another way, but the tool still exists. In fact, voicemail itself is a form of call forwarding in action.

Forwarding phone calls

The Android operating system offers call forwarding options, though your cellular provider might control that feature instead. To determine which is which, follow these steps to configure call forwarding:

1. **Open the Phone app.**

2. **Tap the Action Overflow icon.**

3. **Choose Settings or Call Settings.**

4. **Choose Calls.**

   If you don't see this item, skip to Step 5.

5. **Choose Call Forwarding.**

6. **Select a call forwarding option.**

   Sometimes only one option is available: a phone number to use for forwarding all incoming calls. You might instead see separate options, such as these:

   - *Always Forward:* All incoming calls are sent to the number you specify; your phone doesn't even ring. This option overrides all other forwarding options.

   - *When Busy:* Calls are forwarded when you're on the phone and choose not to answer. This option normally sends a missed call to voicemail.

   - *When Unanswered:* Missed calls are forwarded. Normally, the call is forwarded to voicemail.

   - *When Unreachable:* Calls are forwarded when the phone is turned off, out of range, or in Airplane mode. As with the two previous settings, this option normally forwards calls to voicemail.

7. **Set the forwarding number or edit an existing number.**

   For example, you can type your home landline number for the Forward When Unreached option so that your cell calls are redirected to your home number when you're out of range.

   To disable the option, tap the TURN OFF button.

8. Tap the UPDATE button to confirm the new forwarding number.

If your phone lacks Call Forwarding settings, you must rely upon the cellular carrier to set up and forward your calls. For example, Verizon in the United States uses the call forwarding options described in Table 6-1.

TABLE 6-1 ## Verizon Call Forwarding Commands

To Do This	Input First Number	Input Second Number
Forward unanswered incoming calls	*71	Forwarding number
Forward all incoming calls	*72	Forwarding number
Cancel call forwarding	*73	None

So, to forward all calls to (714) 555-4565, open the Phone app and dial the number ***727145554565**. You hear only a brief tone after dialing, and then the call ends. After that, any call coming into your phone rings at the other number.

REMEMBER

You must disable call forwarding to return to normal cell phone operations: Dial ***73**.

Call forwarding may affect your phone's voicemail service. See the later section "Using Google Voice for voicemail" for details.

Blocking calls

To stifle those calls that bug you repeatedly, block the phone number before it rings. Obey these steps:

1. Open the Phone app.

2. Tap the Action Overflow icon or the MORE button.

3. Choose Settings.

4. Choose Call Blocking or Block Numbers.

On some phones, you then choose Block List; otherwise, you see a list of numbers or contacts currently blocked.

5. Tap the ADD A NUMBER button or just type a number to block.

6. Tap the BLOCK button or DONE button to confirm.

Repeat Steps 5 and 6 to add more numbers.

An easier way to block calls is to use the call log or history list, which is covered in the next section. From the list, long-press an entry and choose the Block action.

To remove a number from the Blocked Numbers list, follow Steps 1 through 4 to view blocked numbers. Tap the X or minus (–) icon next to a number, and then tap the UNBLOCK button to confirm.

Who Called Who When?

All phone calls made on your Android phone are noted: to whom, from whom, date, time, duration, and whether the call was incoming, outgoing, missed, or dismissed. I call this feature the *call log*, although on your phone it may be referenced as Recent Calls or Call History. The place to look is in the Phone app.

Dealing with a missed call

When you miss a call, a Missed Call notification icon appears atop the touchscreen. This icon, similar to the one in the margin, specifically applies to a call you didn't pick up; it doesn't appear for calls you dismiss or calls missed because the phone was turned off or in Airplane mode.

Choose the Missed Call notification to view the Phone app's call log, illustrated in Figure 6-1. There you see details about who called and when. Choose an item from the call log to view more details and return the call.

REMEMBER

>> Some Android phones show more details on the Missed Call notification, including icons that let you return the call, text, and so on.

>> The phone doesn't consider a call you've dismissed as being missed.

Reviewing the call log

Your Android phone tracks all calls in a list or *call log.* It's found in the Phone app: Tap the Call History tab, which might be titled Recent or Logs. Refer to Figure 6-1 to see what a call log might look like.

Swipe through the list to examine recent calls. The list is sorted so that the most recent calls appear at the top. Information is associated with each call, such as the date and time, call duration, and whether the call was incoming, outgoing, missed, or ignored.

Missed-call notification

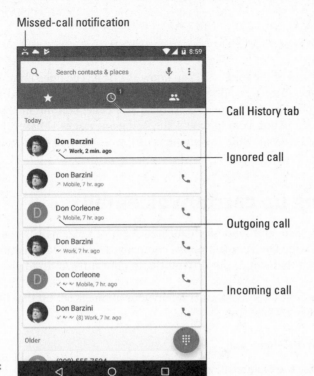

Call History tab

Ignored call

Outgoing call

Incoming call

FIGURE 6-1:
The call log.

To see more details about the call, tap an item in the list. You see a call history specific to that number or contact, options to block the call, or an action to display the contact's information.

TIP

» On Samsung phones, swipe an entry in the RECENTS (call history) list right-to-left to redial that number or contact. Swipe the entry left-to-right to send a text message.

» The call log provides a quick way to create new contacts: Tap a phone number in the list, one that lacks contact information. Choose the action Create New Contact or Add to Contacts. See Chapter 7 for more information about contacts.

» To remove an item from the call log, get more information on the item: Tap it and choose INFO. On the next screen, tap the Delete (trash) icon. On Samsung phones, long-press items in the RECENTS list to select them, and then tap the DELETE button to purge.

Voicemail

"At the sound of the tone . . ." You know the drill. The once humble tape recorder that connected to a landline, or "answering machine," gained the fancy term *voicemail* back in the 1990s. The service is a collection bin at the bottom of the rejection chute for your phone's incoming messages. Missed calls, dismissed calls, calls received while the phone is offline — they all go to voicemail for later retrieval.

Setting up carrier voicemail

The most basic and least sophisticated form of voicemail is the free voicemail service provided by your cell phone company. This standard feature has few frills and nothing that stands out differently for your nifty Android phone.

One of the first duties you must do on your phone is set up that boring voicemail service. Obey these steps:

1. **Open the Phone app.**

2. **Display the dialpad, if necessary.**

3. **Long-press the 1 key.**

   The 1 key is preset to speed-dial your carrier's voicemail service. It's adorned with the standard Voicemail icon, shown in the margin.

4. **Pull the phone away from your head and activate the speaker and dialpad.**

   Tap the speaker and dialpad icons so that you can listen and type as you configure the carrier's voicemail service.

5. **Heed the directions as dictated.**

   Obey the robot to set up the voicemail service.

REMEMBER

Your callers cannot leave messages until you configure carrier voicemail. Even when you plan on using another voicemail service, I recommend that you set up carrier voicemail.

>> An example of another voicemail service is Google Voice, covered later in this chapter.

>> Your phone may also feature a Voicemail app, which you can use to collect and review your messages.

>> The most important step for voicemail setup is to create a customized greeting. If you don't do so, you may not receive voicemail messages, or people may believe that they've dialed the wrong number.

Picking up carrier voicemail messages

Carrier voicemail collects missed calls as well as calls you thrust into voicemail. The standard Voicemail notification icon appears, looking like the one shown in the margin, whenever a new message is pending. You can choose this notification to dial into your carrier's voicemail system, listen to your calls, and use the phone's dialpad to manage the carrier voicemail system.

Most carrier voicemail systems work the same: You dial in, type your PIN, and then use the dialpad to review and delete messages. Therefore, it's best to look at the phone and display the dialpad and then activate the speaker as you hear the prompts and listen to the messages.

To help you remember the prompts, write them down here:

Press _____ to listen to the first message.

Press _____ to delete the message.

Press _____ to skip a message.

Press _____ to hear the menu options.

Press _____ to hang up.

While you're at it, write your voicemail PIN: _____

Using Google Voice for voicemail

Perhaps the best option I've found for working with voicemail is Google Voice. It's more than just a voicemail system: You can use the service to make phone calls in the United States, place cheap international calls, and perform other amazing feats, though I use it primarily for voicemail.

To configure your Android phone for use with Google Voice, you must do two things: First, create a Google Voice account. Second, obtain the Google Voice app.

Start your adventure by visiting the Google Voice home page at:

```
https://voice.google.com
```

I recommend using a computer to complete these steps: Follow the directions on the screen. Log in to your Google account, if necessary, and agree to the terms of service.

Click the Action Overflow icon on the web page to link your Android's phone number with the Google Voice service. You must set up a Google Voice number for your account, so choose a number if one isn't already available.

Second, visit Google Play to get the Google Voice app. Specific directions for using Google Play are offered in Chapter 17.

After you install the app, open it to complete configuration. Follow the steps on the screen to associate your Android's phone number with Google Voice. Accept the confirmation code. You're done. Now you just have to wait to miss a call to see how the service works.

> » Even when you choose to use Google Voice, I still recommend setting up and configuring the boring carrier voicemail, as covered earlier in this chapter.
>
> » Your phone's call forwarding feature disables Google Voice. If you forward calls, you must reset Google Voice after you're done. That's because Google Voice relies upon call forwarding to deal with unanswered or dismissed calls.

WARNING

Checking your Google Voice messages

Google Voice transcribes your voicemail messages, turning the audio from the voicemail into a text message you can read. The messages show up eventually in the Google Voice app and in your Gmail inbox, if you've configured that option on the Google Voice website.

When a new Google Voice message arrives, a notification icon appears, like the one shown in the margin. Choose the notification to open the Google Voice app and listen to your message. The app's main interface looks like, and works similarly to, an email program and is illustrated in Figure 6-2.

Tap the Play icon to listen to your message, or just read the transcript.

The text *Transcript Not Available* appears whenever Google Voice is unable to create a text message from your voicemail or whenever the Google Voice service is temporarily unavailable.

Contact info (if available)

Voicemail tab

Message text translation

Play message.

FIGURE 6-2:
Voicemail with
the Google
Voice app.

Turn on speaker.

Reviewing voicemail settings

Your Android phone contains internal settings that further configure the voice-mail service. If everything is working well with voicemail, don't mess with the settings. Otherwise, work through these steps to see what's going on:

1. **Open the Phone app.**

2. **Tap the Action Overflow icon.**

   On some phones, tap the MORE button.

3. **Choose Settings.**

4. **Choose the Voicemail action, which may be titled Voicemail Services. Or Voicemail Settings.**

   On some phones, you must choose the Calls or Call Settings item first and then locate the Voicemail action.

5. **Choose Service.**

   If you don't see this item, choose Advanced or Advanced Settings.

6. **Select the voicemail service.**

   The options are Carrier (or Your Carrier) and Google Voice, though only one option might be available.

When the Carrier option is chosen, the phone number used for voicemail is the carrier's voicemail service. You can confirm that number by choosing the Setup or Voicemail Settings item on the Voicemail screen.

REMEMBER

The voicemail service might be configured by using call forwarding options, as described earlier in this chapter. For Verizon phones, that's how it's done, especially with Google Voice: Unanswered calls are forwarded to your Google Voice number and then processed as voicemail.

Chapter **7**

The Address Book

Way back when, humans were required to memorize phone numbers. Think of it! Not everyone's number was committed to memory — just a few key contacts. So kids stranded at the bowling alley could phone Mom's workplace, Grandpa, or even a neighbor lady to ask for a lift. The human brain has marvelous power.

Memorizing a phone number isn't a requirement for being human today. That's because Android devices, both phones and tablets, are capable of storing incredibly detailed information about people, including phone numbers, email addresses, physical world addresses, and just about everything else you can imagine, all in a single app.

The People You Know

The address book app is central to many operations in an Android phone — less so on a tablet, but still necessary. It's used by Gmail, Email, Hangouts, and (most obviously) the Phone app.

» The address book app is named Contacts. Older Androids may call the app People, which is the same thing. For the sake of consistency, this chapter refers to the app as Contacts.

» The address book is probably full of people already; your Gmail contacts are instantly synchronized, as are social networking contacts and any contacts associated with other accounts and apps you've added to the device.

Accessing the address book

To open the Contacts app, look for its launcher on the Home screen. It might be in the Google folder. And if it's not available on the Home screen, look for it in the Apps drawer.

Figure 7-1 shows how the Contacts app might look, though its appearance differs from device to device. Specifically, some apps list favorites at the top, followed by frequently contacted entries. A full index might also appear on the side of the list.

Index

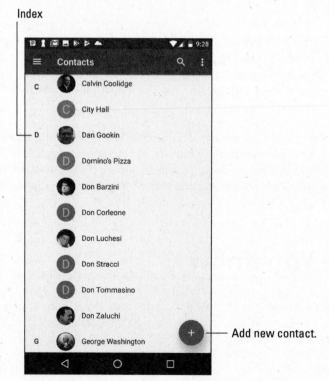

Add new contact.

FIGURE 7-1:
The Contacts list.

By default, the Contacts app shows all contacts presented alphabetically by first name. Swipe your finger on the touchscreen to scroll the list.

To see more details about a contact, tap the entry. The details screen varies, depending on the Contacts app, but it looks similar to what's shown in Figure 7-2.

Send email.

Call phone.

Favorite

Text message.

Get directions.

Edit contact.

FIGURE 7-2:
More details
about a contact.

Locate in the Maps app.

The number of things you can do with a contact depends on the information shown and the apps installed on your phone or tablet. Here are some common activities:

Place a phone call. To call a contact on an Android phone, tap one of the phone entries. This activity works on an Android tablet as well, providing you have a phone-dialer app installed, such as the Hangouts Dialer or Skype.

Send a text message. Tap the Text Message icon (refer to Figure 7-2) to open the text messaging app (phones only) and send the contact a message. See Chapter 8 for information about text messaging.

Send email. Tap the contact's email address to compose an email message. When the contact has more than one email address, you can choose to which one you want to send the message. Chapter 9 covers email.

View a social networking status. Some address book apps display social networking information on the contact's screen, such as a tweet or Facebook status update. See Chapter 11 for more information on social networking.

Locate the contact's address. When the contact's information shows a home or business address, tap that item to summon the Maps app and view the location. Refer to Chapter 12 to see all the fun stuff you can do with Maps.

Some tidbits of information that show up for a contact have no associated actions. For example, the Android doesn't sing "Happy Birthday" whenever you tap a contact's birthday information.

» You can also access the list of contacts from within the Phone app: Tap the Contacts tab to view the list.

» Not every contact has a picture, and the picture can come from many sources (Gmail or Facebook, for example). See the later section "Adding a contact picture" for more information.

» Many Androids feature an account named Me. It shows your personal information as known by the device. The Me account may be in addition to your other accounts shown in the address book.

» Some cellular providers add accounts to an Android's address book. You may see entries such as BAL, MIN, or Warranty Center. Those aren't real people; they're shortcuts to various services. For example, the BAL contact is used on Verizon phones to get a text message detailing your current account balance.

» Also see the later section "Managing contacts" for information on how to deal with duplicate entries for the same person.

Sorting the address book

Your Android gizmo's address book displays contacts in a certain order. By default, that order is alphabetically by first name. You can change this order if the existing arrangement drives you nuts. Follow these steps when using the Contacts app:

1. **Tap the Side Menu icon.**

2. **Choose Settings.**

   In some Contacts apps, tap the Action Overflow icon and then choose Settings. Some Samsung devices use the MORE button instead of the Action Overflow icon.

3. **Choose Sort By.**

4. **Select First Name or Last Name, depending on how you want the contacts sorted.**

5. **Choose Name Format.**

6. **Choose First Name First or Last Name First.**

   This command specifies how the contacts appear in the list: first name first or last name first.

The list of contacts is updated, displayed per your preferences.

Searching contacts

The Contacts app doesn't provide a running total for all your contacts. Either you have very few friends, or a lot of people owe you money. When it's the latter, you can choose to endlessly scroll the list of contacts, or you can employ the powerful Search command to quickly find a contact:

1. **Tap the Search icon.**

   Some versions of the Contacts app may always show the Search text box at the top of the screen. If so, tap in the box.

2. **Start typing a contact name.**

   As you type, a list of matching contacts appears. The list narrows the more you type.

3. **Once you see the matching person, tap that entry.**

To clear a search, tap the X at the right side of the Search text box. To exit the search screen, tap the Back navigation icon.

No, there's no correlation between the number of contacts you have and how popular you are in real life.

REMEMBER

Making New Friends

Having friends is great. Having more friends is better. Keeping all those friends as entries in the Contacts app is best.

>> Contacts are associated with your various online accounts and services. For example, your Google account plays host to all your Gmail contacts as well as new contacts you create.

>> If you use Yahoo! as your primary email account, create new contacts and associate them with that account. The next section offers details.

Creating a new contact from scratch

Sometimes it's necessary to create a contact when you actually meet another human being in the real world. Or maybe you finally got around to transferring information from your old datebook. In either instance, you have information to input, and it starts like this:

1. **Tap the Add Contact icon in the Contacts app.**

   The ADD button is illustrated in the margin, as well as shown earlier, in Figure 7-1. The icon may appear in a festively colored circle.

2. **Ensure that your Google account is associated with the new contact.**

   You may see your Google (or Gmail) account listed on the Create Contact card. If not, choose that account from a list. Or, if you primarily use another email service, such as Yahoo!, choose that account instead.

   TIP

   I recommend choosing your Google account because this account is synchronized with the Internet and any other Android gizmos you may own.

   WARNING

   Do not choose the Device account, which might also be labeled Phone or Tablet. When you do, the contact information is saved only on your Android. It won't be synchronized with the Internet or any other devices.

3. **Fill in the contact's information as best you can.**

   Type text in the various boxes with the information you know. The more information you provide, the better. At minimum, the contact needs a name.

   Tap the chevron to the right of a field to set more details, such as whether a phone number is Mobile, Home, Work, or so on.

   To add a second phone number, email, or location, tap the ADD NEW button, which may look like a large Plus icon.

TIP

Always type a phone number with the area code.

At the bottom of the Add New Contact screen, you'll find the button MORE FIELDS or ADD ANOTHER FIELD. Use that button when you can add more details for the contact, such as a birthday or website address.

4. **Tap the SAVE button to complete editing and add the new contact.**

The new contact is created. As a bonus, it's also automatically synced with your Google account on the Internet, or with whichever account you chose in Step 3.

Adding a contact from the call log

A quick and easy way to build up the address book on an Android phone is to add people as they call. To do so, check the call log:

1. **Open the Phone app.**

2. **Display the call log.**

   Tap the History or Recent tab. See Chapter 6 for specific directions.

   Unknown phone numbers appear by themselves, without a contact picture, name, or other details.

3. **Display details about the phone number for an incoming call.**

   If the details aren't presented right away, long-press the entry or tap the DETAILS button.

4. **Choose the option to create a new contact.**

   Two options present themselves: one to update an existing contact and a second to create a new contact.

5. **Continue adding contact details.**

6. **Save the new contact.**

If you make a mistake and create a new contact for an entry already in the address book, you can merge the contacts later. See the later section "Managing contacts."

Creating a contact from an email message

You can use email messages to help build the address book, by either creating a new account based on a message or adding someone's email address to an existing account. The good news is that the email message supplies both the contact name and the email address. Follow these steps:

1. **View the email message.**

   You can't add a contact from the inbox; tap the message to view its contents.

2. **Tap the contact's name or the icon by the contact's name.**

   The icon has a letter in it, like the one shown in the margin. This boring icon is a sign that the email address isn't associated with a contact in your Android's address book. After tapping the icon, you see more details.

3. **Tap the Add Contact icon.**

   If you don't see the Add Contact icon (shown in the margin), choose the action View Contact.

4. **Choose an existing contact from the list, or tap the top item, Create Contact.**

   The commands may be shown separately from the entire address book list. For example, you may see two actions: CREATE CONTACT and UPDATE EXISTING.

Choosing an existing contact adds the email address to that contact's information. Otherwise, you see the Create Contact card and can proceed as outlined in the earlier section "Creating a new contact from scratch." Of course, the email address is already supplied.

Manage Your Friends

Sure, some folks just can't leave well enough alone. For example, Tracy may change her phone number. Sandy moves all the time. And Steve finally got rid of his 25-year-old AOL email addresses. When such things occur, you must undertake the task of address book management.

Making basic changes

To make minor touch-ups on any contact, locate and display the contact's information. Tap the Edit icon, similar to the Pencil icon shown in the margin. The button might say EDIT, or you can tap Action Overflow and choose Edit.

To change or add information, tap a field and then edit or add new text.

Some contact information cannot be edited. For example, fields pulled in from social networking sites can be edited only by that account holder on the social networking site.

When you're finished editing, tap the Done icon or the SAVE button.

Adding a contact picture

Contact photos are supplied automatically, depending on the contact's email address. For example, your Android may show the contact's photo from their own Gmail or Facebook accounts. If not, you can assign your own picture of the contact, a photo that reminds you of the contact, or something wholly inappropriate.

To use the Android's camera to snap a contact picture, heed these directions:

1. Edit the contact's information.

2. Tap the contact's picture or the Picture Placeholder icon.

The placeholder may feature a Camera icon, like the one shown in the margin.

3. Choose Take Photo.

Some devices may skip this step, automatically displaying the Camera app (or a variation).

4. Use the device's camera to snap a picture.

Chapter 13 covers using the Camera app. Both the front and rear cameras can be used (though not at the same time). Tap the Shutter icon to take the picture.

5. Review the picture.

Nothing is set yet. If you want to try again, tap the Retry icon, similar to what's shown in the margin. Repeat Step 4. This icon might appear as a Minus (–) icon on the Camera app.

6. Tap the Done icon to confirm the new image and prepare for cropping.

Some devices skip this step, automatically setting the image you just took. If so, skip to Step 9.

7. **Crop the image.**

   Adjust the cropping box so that it surrounds only the portion of the image you want to keep. Refer to Chapter 14, which specifically covers how to use the cropping tool.

8. **Tap the DONE button to crop the image.**

9. **Tap the SAVE button to save and update the contact's information.**

The contact's image appears onscreen when the person calls, as well as when referenced in other apps, text messaging, Gmail, and so on.

If the contact isn't around, or nothing nearby is worthy of snapping a picture, you can assign one of the device's images to the contact. In Step 3, choose the action Select New Photo or Choose Photo. Browse the device's images to pluck out something suitable.

TIP

If you select the Choose Photo action, you might be prompted with a Complete Action Using card. My advice is to choose an app and tap JUST ONCE. See Chapter 20 for details on setting a default app.

» To remove an image from a contact, edit the contact and tap their image icon, as described in this section. Choose the action Remove Photo or tap the Minus (–) icon to reset the image.

» To replace an existing image, choose the action Select New Photo in Step 3. Or, on some devices, you're presented with the Camera app and can immediately shoot a new image.

» A generic image or icon appears for a contact without an assigned photo or image.

» Some stored images may not work for contact icons. For example, images synchronized with your online photo albums may be unavailable.

Playing favorites

A *favorite* contact is someone you stay in touch with most often. The person doesn't have to be someone you like — just someone you (perhaps unfortunately) contact often, such as your parole officer.

To make a contact a favorite, display the contact's information and tap the Favorite (star) icon by the contact's image, as shown in Figure 7-2. When the star is filled, the contact is one of your favorites and is stored in the Favorites group.

To remove a favorite, tap the contact's star again and it loses its highlight.

>> The Contacts app lists favorites first, atop the list. You may see a Star icon in the index, or the favorites might be shown on their own tab.

>> Favorite contacts are often displayed separately on an Android phone's Phone app. Refer to Chapter 5.

>> Removing a favorite doesn't delete the contact, but instead removes it from the Favorites group.

>> By the way, contacts have no idea whether they're among your favorites, so don't believe that you're hurting their feelings by not making them favorites.

Managing contacts

Older versions of the Contacts app allowed you to find duplicate contacts and glue them together. The process was called *joining, linking,* or *merging.* Likewise, you could separate contacts improperly joined. With the current iteration of the Contacts app, this process has become automated.

To review your Android's address book for potential duplicate contacts, follow these steps while using the Contacts app.

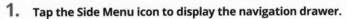

1. **Tap the Side Menu icon to display the navigation drawer.**

2. **Choose Suggestions.**

   A description card may appear. If so, tap the GOT IT button.

3. **Peruse the suggestions.**

On some Samsung devices, tap Action Overflow in the Contacts app. Choose the Manage Contacts action and then Merge Contacts.

The suggestions include merging potential duplicate contacts as well as updating contact information pulled in from other sources.

TIP

It's up to you whether you merge the contacts shown, and it's not something you must do. For example, different individuals at an organization might have the same main phone number, but different email addresses. In that case, don't merge the contacts.

Removing a contact

Every so often, consider reviewing your Android's address book. Purge the folks whom you no longer recognize or you've forgotten. It's simple:

1. Edit the forlorn contact.

For some versions of the Contacts app, this step isn't necessary. Instead, display the contact's info, and then move on with Step 2.

2. Tap Action Overflow and choose Delete.

If you don't see the Delete item, the contact is brought in from another source, such as Facebook. You need to use that app to disassociate the contact.

3. Tap DELETE button to confirm.

Poof! They're gone.

 On some devices, you may find a Delete icon (shown in the margin) directly on the contact's details card. Tap that icon to remove it, and then tap the OK button to remove the contact.

>> To mass-purge contacts, long-press the first one in the address book list. This step activates mass-selection mode: Continue tapping unwanted contacts. When you've built the list, tap the Delete icon to remove the batch.

WARNING

>> Because the Contacts list is synchronized with your Google account, the contact is also removed there — and on other Android devices.

>> Removing a contact doesn't kill the person in real life.

Chapter **8**

Text Me

Texting is the popular name for a cell phone's capability to send short, typed messages to another cell phone. The process echoes earlier technology, including telegraph and teletype. Curiously, the acronym *LOL* dates to a telegraph message sent in the 1880s:

```
Butch Cassidy robbed the 302 out of Belle Fourche.
It was carrying steer manure. LOL.
```

Despite its seemingly anachronistic nature, texting remains a popular form of communications. Indeed, some young people text more than they use the phone to place a call. It's a convenient and popular way to quickly communicate.

» Android tablets do not have the capability to send or receive text messages. Yes, even LTE tablets, though they may have a phone number assigned, cannot do text messaging.

» It's possible to configure Google Voice on an Android tablet to send and receive text messages, though it's not the easiest thing to do.

TECHNICAL STUFF

» The nerdy term for text messaging is *SMS,* which stands for Short Message Service.

Msg 4U

Text messaging allows you to send short quips of text from one cell phone to another. As long as the other phone is on and receiving a signal, the message is received instantly. That makes texting a quick and worthy form of communication.

WARNING

>> Don't text while you're driving.

>> Don't text in a movie theater.

>> Don't text in any situation where it's distracting.

>> Most cell phone plans include unlimited texting; however, some older plans may charge you per text. Check with your cellular provider to be sure.

>> If you're over 25, you might want to know that the translation of this section's title is "Message for You."

Opening the texting app

The stock Android text messaging app is called Messages. The previous version was called Messenger. And various phones from different manufacturers might call the app Messaging, Text Messaging, or some similar variation.

Regardless of the name, the text messaging app is found on the Home screen in the favorites tray, usually right next to the Phone app. Tap this launcher to open the text messaging app.

>> Many Android phones have multiple text messaging apps, such as Samsung's current Message+ app. These apps are in addition to the stock Android text messaging app. See the section "Choosing another texting app," later in this chapter.

>> The Facebook Messenger app is used for text chat within Facebook. It is not a text messaging app.

Texting a contact

You must desperately tell your friend Cody that kitty has been rescued from the tree. Here's how to convey your joy as a text message:

1. **Open the phone's address book app.**

   Refer to Chapter 7 for details on the address book app, usually named Contacts.

WHETHER TO SEND A TEXT MESSAGE OR AN EMAIL

Sending a text message is similar to sending an email message. Both involve the instant electronic delivery of a message to someone else. And both methods of communication have their pros and cons.

The primary limitation of a text message is that it can be sent only to another cell phone. Email, on the other hand, is available to people who have an email address, which might be in addition to their cell phone.

Text messages are pithy: short and to the point. They're informal, because the speed of reply is more important than trivia such as proper spelling and grammar. And just like with email, sending a text message doesn't guarantee a reply.

An email message can be longer than a text message. You can receive email on just about any Internet-connected device. Email message attachments (pictures, documents) are handled better and more consistently than text message (MMS) media.

When sending to multiple people, I strongly recommend using email instead, because it's easier to manage. A multi-person message, or "group text," is the bane of many smartphone users.

Finally, email is considered a bit more formal than a text message. Still, when you truly desire formal communications, make a phone call or send a letter.

2. **Select a contact.**

   For example, select Cody.

3. **Tap the Text Messaging icon next to the phone number.**

   The stock Android icon for text messaging is shown in the margin. The icon might also resemble an envelope.

   On a Samsung phone, swipe the contact's entry right-to-left.

   Upon success, you see a text message window. Any previous conversation you've had appears on the screen, similar to what's shown in Figure 8-1.

4. **Tap the text field, labeled *Type an SMS Message*.**

   The field might also read *Type a Message* or something similar.

5. **Type the message.**

The person you're texting

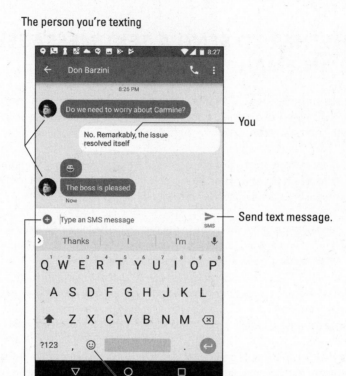

You

Send text message.

FIGURE 8-1:
FIGURE 8-1:
Sending a text
message.

Attachment   Access emoji keyboard.

6. **Tap the Send icon to send the message.**

The Send icon may look like the one shown in the margin, or it might be the word *SEND*.

The message is delivered (almost) instantly, though getting an instant reply isn't guaranteed.

WARNING

>> You can send text messages only to cell phones. Aunt Opal cannot receive text messages on her landline that she's had since the 1960s.

>> Do not text and drive. Do not text and drive. Do not text and drive.

Composing a new text message

When you know only a cell phone number and don't yet have a contact for that person in your address book, follow these steps to send a text:

1. **Open the phone's texting app.**

2. **If it opens a specific conversation, tap the Back navigation icon to view the main screen.**

3. **Tap the Add icon to start a new conversation.**

The Add icon may look similar to what's shown in the margin, or it could be a Pencil icon or something similar.

4. **Type the phone number.**

As you type, matching contacts appear. You could also type a contact name, if the person is already in the phone's address book.

5. **Tap the DONE button on the onscreen keyboard.**

6. **Type the message in the Type an SMS Message box.**

The box might instead say *Send Message* or *Type a Message*.

7. **Tap the Send icon or SEND button to send the message.**

Sending a text to multiple contacts

To send the message to multiple contacts, repeat the steps from the preceding section but in Step 4 continuing typing phone numbers or contact names. That's what makes the message a group text.

WARNING

When you receive a group text message (one that has several recipients), you can choose whether to reply to everyone. Look for the REPLY ALL button when composing your response. Please use caution when replying to everyone. Many people don't like group text messages, because they're persistently tedious and interminable.

Continuing a text message conversation

The text messaging app keeps track of old conversations, and you can pick up where you left off at any time: Open the texting app, peruse the list of existing conversations, and tap one to review what has been said or to begin something new.

Typing emojis

The current trend in text messaging communications dates to the Egyptians, though people don't call them "hieroglyphics." No, they're *emojis*, which is from the Japanese words for "picture letter/character." These teensy symbols frequently inhabit text messages.

To type an emoji, tap the happy face symbol, either near the text field where you type the message or on the onscreen keyboard, as illustrated in Figure 8-1. You can then pluck out an emoji from the many palettes displayed.

TIP

In the Samsung Message+ app, when you type a word strongly associated with an emoji, like *cake*, the word turns into a button. Tap the button to choose the associated emoji and insert it into your text message.

>> Computer scientists (I kid you not) have created hundreds of emoji symbols. These are common across all cell phones, though the pictures may not look the same.

>> Some emojis are rather simple, such as the happy face or sad face. Some can be complex and even have specific meanings as full words.

>> Don't be surprised to see a parade of emojis in a text message. They could express a complete thought.

Receiving a text message

New text messages are heralded by a notification atop the screen, similar to the one shown in the margin. If the phone is on, you may even see a card slide in with the message, as illustrated in Figure 8-2.

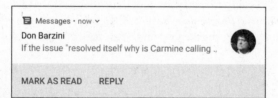

FIGURE 8-2:
A new message
has arrived.

If you see the message card, tap it to view the message to tap the REPLY button. Some phones may show more buttons, which offer more control. Otherwise, you can ignore the message card and it goes away. The message itself (and the notification icon) remains until you view the message in the text messaging app.

>> Choose the new text message notification to view any new text message.

>> The text messaging app may show a counter flag, similar to what's shown in the margin, indicating unread text messages.

Forwarding a text message

It's possible to forward a text message, but it's not the same as forwarding email: Your phone lets you forward only the information in a text messaging cartoon bubble, not the entire conversation. Here's how it works:

1. **If necessary, open a conversation in the phone's texting app.**

2. **Long-press the text entry (the cartoon bubble) you want to forward.**

3. **Choose Forward or Forward Message.**

   The forwarding command may appear as a text, or you may see an action bar atop the screen. If so, choose the Forward icon, shown in the margin, from the action bar.

From this point on, forwarding the message works like sending a new message from scratch: Choose a recipient or type a person's contact name or phone number. The text from the cartoon bubble you selected (refer to Step 2) is pasted into the Send Message text box. Tap the Send icon or SEND button to forward the message.

Other icons that may appear on the action bar (refer to Step 3) include Share, Copy, Info, and Delete (trash).

Multimedia Messages

The term *texting* sticks around, yet a text message can contain media — usually a photo — although short videos and audio can also be shared with a text message. Such a message ceases to be a mere text message and becomes a multimedia message.

TECHNICAL STUFF

» Multimedia messages are handled by the same app you use for text messaging.

» Not every cell phone can receive multimedia messages. Rather than receive the media item, the recipient may be directed to a web page where the item can be viewed on the Internet. Or the message may never show up.

» The official name for a multimedia text message is Multimedia Messaging Service, abbreviated MMS.

Creating a multimedia text message

As with other things on your Android phone, you need to think of sharing when it comes to attaching media to a text message. Obey these steps:

1. **Open the app that contains or shows the item you want to share.**

   For example, open the Photos app to view a picture or view a page in the web browser app.

2. **View the item and tap the Share icon.**

3. **Choose the phone's text messaging app from the list of apps.**

4. **Continue sending the text message as described earlier in this chapter.**

It's also possible to attach media to a message from within the text messaging app. To do so, tap the Add icon or Plus icon to the left of the text message box, similar to what's shown in the margin. Choose the media to attach. Optionally, type some text. Tap the Send icon.

In just a few, short, cellular moments, the receiving party will enjoy your multimedia text message.

Some text messaging apps may use the Attachment icon, shown in the margin, to add media to a text message. Tap that icon and then choose an app to pluck out the item to attach.

Receiving a multimedia message

A multimedia attachment comes into your phone just like any other text message. You may see a thumbnail preview of whichever media was sent, such as an image, a still from a video, or the Play icon to listen to audio. To preview the attachment, tap it.

TIP

To do more with the multimedia attachment, long-press it and then select an action from the list. For example, to save an image attachment, long-press the image thumbnail and choose Save Picture.

Text Message Management

You don't have to manage your messages. I certainly don't. But the potential exists: If you ever want to destroy evidence of a conversation, or even do something as mild as change the text messaging ringtone, it's possible.

Removing messages

Although I'm a stickler for deleting email after I read it, I don't bother deleting my text message threads. That's probably because I have no pending divorce litigation. Well, even then, I have nothing to hide in my text messaging conversations. If I did, I would follow these steps to delete a conversation:

1. Open the conversation you want to remove.

Choose the conversation from the main screen in your phone's text messaging app.

2. Tap the Action Overflow and choose Delete.

3. Tap the DELETE button to confirm.

The entire conversation is gone.

 If these steps don't work, an alternative is to open the main screen in the text messaging app and long-press the conversation you want to zap. Tap the DELETE button and then tap the DELETE or OK button to confirm.

Individual cartoon bubbles can be removed from a conversation: Long-press the bubble and then tap the Trash icon or the DELETE button.

Setting the text message ringtone

The sound you hear when a new text message floats in is the text message ringtone. It might be the same sound you hear for all notifications, though on some Android phones it can be changed to something unique.

Follow these steps in the Messages app to set a new text message ringtone:

1. Tap Action Overflow.

2. Choose Settings.

3. Choose Notifications.

4. Choose Sound.

5. Select a sound from the list and tap OK.

On Samsung phones running the Message+ app, follow these steps:

1. At the main screen, tap Action Overflow.

2. Choose Customize.

3. **Choose Tones.**

4. **Choose a sound from the list.**

5. **Tap the BACK navigation button to exit.**

You might also be able to change the notification ringtone from the Settings app. Refer to Chapter 21.

Choosing another texting app

Your phone might have more than one text messaging app. For example, it may have the manufacturer's app plus the stock Android app. You can use either one, but you must tell the phone which you prefer. Obey these directions:

1. **Open the Settings app.**

   The app is in the Apps drawer, though a handy shortcut can be found among the quick actions, as covered in Chapter 3.

2. **Choose Apps & Notifications.**

3. **If necessary, tap the chevron by the item titled Advanced.**

4. **Choose Default Apps.**

5. **Choose SMS App.**

6. **Select your preferred text messaging app from the list.**

On Samsung phones, attempt these steps:

1. **Open the Settings app.**

2. **Choose Apps.**

3. **Select the messaging app from the list of All Apps.**

4. **Choose Messaging App.**

5. **Choose the app.**

   The app is shown along with other messaging apps on the phone.

On some devices, the item you choose in Step 2 is titled Apps or App Manager.

Other default apps you can choose include the web browser, Home screen app, and even the Phone app. See Chapter 20 for more details on setting default apps.

Chapter **9**

You've Got Email

The first official telegraph message was, "What hath God wrought?" The first telephone call was supposedly, "Mr. Watson. Come here. I want you." The first email message, sent back in the early 1970s by programmer Ray Tomlinson, was probably something like "QWERTYUIOP." It's one for the history books.

Today, email has become far more functional and necessary, well beyond Mr. Tomlinson's early tests. Although you could impress your email buddies by sending them "QWERTYUIOP," you're likely to send and reply to more meaningful communications. Your Android is happily up to the task.

Android Email

Historically, Android devices used two apps for electronic mail: Gmail for Google's email service and Email for everyone else, including web-based email such as Yahoo! email or Outlook mail and so on.

Recently, the Gmail app has been updated to handle all email. This change hasn't occurred across all devices, however. Your phone or tablet might still have separate apps for Gmail and all other email. The good news is that both apps work in a similar manner, so your sanity should remain intact.

>> Both the Gmail and Email apps are in the Apps drawer. You may also find launchers on the Home screen. Look for Gmail in the Google folder if you don't find it elsewhere.

>> The Gmail app is updated frequently. To review any changes since this book went to press, visit my website at

> wambooli.com/help/android

TIP

>> You can use the web browser app to visit the Gmail website, but I recommend that you use the Gmail app instead to pick up your Gmail. Likewise, you can access a web page to read most other email, but instead use the Email app.

>> If you forget your Gmail password, visit this web address:

> google.com/accounts/ForgotPasswd

Setting up the first email account

The first email account on your Android is your Gmail account, which is required in order to use an Android mobile gizmo. After that, you add email accounts as described in the next section, "Adding more email accounts."

If your Android features an Email app, setting up the first email account works differently from when you're adding additional accounts. You must know the email account's *sign-in* (your email address) and password. When you have that information, follow these steps in the Email app to configure that first account:

1. **Start the Email app.**

Look for it in the Apps drawer. If it's not there, use the Gmail app instead, as described in the next section.

The first screen you see is Set Up Account or Set Up Email. If you've already run the Email app, you're taken to the Email inbox and you can skip these steps. See the next section for information on adding additional accounts.

2. **Type the email address you use for the account.**

For example, if you have a Comcast email account, use the onscreen keyboard to type your *me*@comcast.net email address in the Email Address box.

TIP

Look for a .com (dot-com) key on the onscreen keyboard, which you can use to more efficiently type your email address.

3. **Type the account's password.**

4. **Tap the NEXT button or, if you can't see that button, tap the Done button on the onscreen keyboard.**

   If you're lucky, everything is connected and you can move on to Step 5. Otherwise, you must specify the details as provided by your ISP. See the later section "Adding an account manually."

5. **Set account options.**

   You might want to reset the Inbox Checking Frequency option to something other than 15 minutes. I recommend keeping the other items selected until you become familiar with how your Android handles email.

6. **Tap the NEXT button.**

7. **Give the account a name and confirm your own name.**

   For example, I name my primary email account Main because it's my main account.

   The Your Name field shows your name as it's applied to outgoing messages. So, if your name is really Annabelle Leigh Meriwether and not amer82, you can make that change now.

8. **Tap the DONE button.**

   You're done.

After you configure the account, messages are immediately synchronized between the email service and your Android. Messages, new and already read, appear in the inbox. See the later section "You've Got Mail" for what to do next.

TIP

If you use Yahoo! Mail, get the Yahoo! Mail app, which handles your Yahoo! mail far better than the Email app (or the Gmail app). The Yahoo! Mail app gives you access to other Yahoo! features you may use and enjoy. Obtain the Yahoo! Mail app from Google Play. See Chapter 17.

Adding more email accounts

The Email app, as well as the newest version of Gmail, can be configured to pick up email from multiple sources. This feature allows you to collect all your Windows Live, Cox Cable, Yahoo!, and other messages to arrive in one app.

Both the Email and Gmail apps offer different ways to add a new email account. A more generic approach is to use the Settings app. Obey these directions:

1. **Open the Settings app.**

It's found in the Apps drawer.

2. **Choose Users & Accounts.**

On some devices, this item is titled Accounts.

3. **Tap the Add Account item.**

If you don't see this item, first choose Accounts.

In stock Android, the three options for adding email accounts are

- *Exchange or Microsoft Exchange ActiveSync:* For a corporate email account hosted by an Exchange Server (Outlook mail)

- *Personal (IMAP):* For web-based email accounts, such as Microsoft Live

- *Personal (POP3):* For traditional, ISP-email accounts, such as Comcast

See the later section "Adding a corporate email account" for information on the Exchange option. The other two options work pretty much the same. In fact, on some Androids you might see only a single option, Email.

4. **Choose the proper Personal email account type.**

5. **Type your email address and tap the NEXT button.**

6. **Type the email account password and tap the NEXT button.**

7. **Continue working through the email setup as prompted on the screen.**

Most of the preset settings are okay, though feel free to change the account name and confirm that your name is listed properly for outgoing email. Also see the nearby sidebar, "Deleting email from the server."

The new email account is synchronized immediately after it's added, and you see the inbox. See the later section "Checking the inbox."

» The big difference between creating the first email account and additional accounts is that you're asked whether the account you just added is the primary or default account. See the later section "Setting the primary email account" for details.

» Some Androids may add the new email account to the Email app, but others may add the account to Gmail. The only way to tell is to look inside each app for the account's email.

DELETING EMAIL FROM THE SERVER

One question you may see when configuring an email count is Delete Email from Server. The answer I recommend is Never. The other choice is When I Delete from Inbox.

The server is the online software that collects and distributes email. The messages stay on the server until they're picked up *and* deleted by the email client, such as the Gmail or Email apps on your Android or the Email program on a computer. If the mail isn't deleted, it can be picked up again as unread.

If you prefer to use your computer as your primary email location, set the Delete Email from Server option to Never. That way, you'll pick up messages on both your Android and the computer. If you plan to use your Android as your only email resource, set the option to When I Delete from Inbox.

Adding an account manually

TECHNICAL STUFF

If your email account isn't recognized, or some other boo-boo happens, you must manually add the account. The steps in the preceding sections remain the same, but you need to provide more specific and technical details. This information includes tidbits such as the server name, port address, domain name, and other incommodious details.

TIP

If you know trouble lies ahead, tap the MANUAL SETUP button when you choose to add a new account. Complete this step before you type your email address.

My advice is to contact your ISP or email provider: Look on their website for specific directions on connecting an Android device to their email account. Contact them directly if you cannot locate specific information.

The good news is that manual setup is very rare these days. Most ISPs and webmail accounts are added painlessly, as described in this chapter.

Adding a corporate email account

TIP

The easiest way to set up your evil corporation's email on your Android is to have the IT people do it for you. Or you may be fortunate and you'll find directions on the organization's intranet. I present this tip because configuring corporate email, also known as Exchange Service email, can be an arduous and terrifying ordeal.

It's possible to add the account on your own, but you still need detailed information. Specifically, you need to know the domain name, which may not be the same as the outfit's website domain. Other details may be required as well.

Above all, you must apply a secure screen lock to access Outlook email. This means you need to add a PIN or password to the device, which is covered in Chapter 22. You cannot access the Exchange Server without that added level of security.

And there's more!

You also need to grant Remote Security Administration privileges. This means your organization's IT gurus will have the power to remotely wipe all information from your phone or tablet. You're required to activate this feature, which is part of the setup process.

The bonus is that when you're done, you'll have full access to the Exchange Server info. That includes your email messages as well as the corporate address book and calendar. Refer to Chapter 7 for information on the address book app; the Calendar app is covered in Chapter 16.

You've Got Mail

New email arrives into your Android automatically, picked up according to the Gmail and Email apps' synchronization schedules. On newer devices, use the Gmail app to read all your email. Otherwise, use the Email app to read non-Gmail email.

Getting a new message

The arrival of a new email missive is heralded by a notification icon. Each email app generates its own version.

 For a new Gmail message, the New Gmail notification, similar to the one shown in the margin, appears at the top of the touchscreen.

 For a new email message, you see the New Email notification.

 For email you receive from an Exchange Server, or corporate email, you see the New Exchange Mail notification.

Conjure the notifications drawer to review the email notifications. Tap a notification to be whisked to an inbox for instant reading.

Checking the inbox

To peruse your Gmail, start the Gmail app. The Gmail inbox is shown in Figure 9-1.

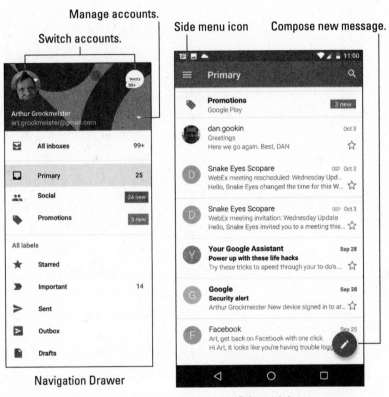

FIGURE 9-1:
The Gmail inbox.

To choose a non-Gmail account, tap the account icon from the navigation drawer (refer to Figure 9-1). You can view only one account's inbox at a time.

If your Android has an Email app, open it to view its inbox. You see a single account's inbox, or you can choose to view the universal inbox, shown as Combined view in Figure 9-2.

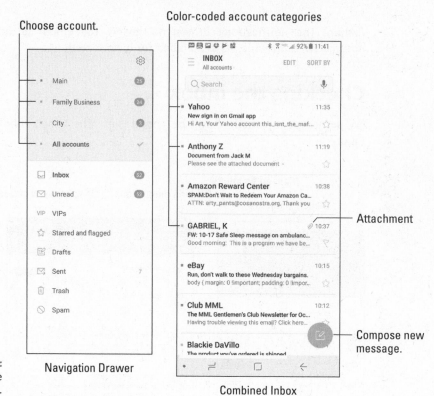

Choose account.

Color-coded account categories

Attachment

Compose new message.

FIGURE 9-2:
Messages in the Email app.

Navigation Drawer

Combined Inbox

REMEMBER

>> Gmail messages don't show up in the Email app. Use the Gmail app to read your Google mail.

>> To access the combined inbox in the Gmail app, tap the Side Menu icon and choose All Mail.

>> Multiple email accounts are color-coded. When messages are presented in the combined inbox, you see the color codes to the left of each message.

>> To view an individual account's inbox, choose that account from the navigation drawer, as illustrated in Figures 9-1 and 9-2.

Reading email

To view a specific email message, tap its entry in the inbox. You can also choose the message's notification to open and view its contents. Reading and working with a message operates much the same whether you're using the Gmail or Email app:

>> To read a message, use your finger to swipe it up or down.

>> Swipe a message left or right to browse between messages.

>> To return to the inbox, tap the left-pointing arrow or chevron at the top-left corner of the screen.

To work with the message, use the icons that appear above or below the message. These icons, which may not look exactly like those shown in the margin, cover common email actions:

Reply: Tap this icon to reply to a message. A new message window appears with the To and Subject fields reflecting the original sender(s) and subject.

Reply All: Tap this icon to respond to everyone who received the original message, including folks on the Cc line. Use this option only when everyone else must get a copy of your reply.

Forward: Tap this icon to send a copy of the message to someone else.

Delete: Tap this icon to delete a message.

If you don't see all these icons, look for them on the message's Action Overflow. You can also try turning the device to a horizontal orientation.

Compose a New Email Epistle

I frequently use my Android to check email, but I don't often use it to compose messages. That's because most email messages don't demand an immediate reply. When they do, you'll find that both the Gmail and Email apps are up to the task.

Writing a message

Creating a new email message dispatch works similarly in both the Gmail and Email apps. The key is to locate the Compose icon. This icon is illustrated in both Figures 9-1 and 9-2.

After you tap the Compose icon, you're presented with a new message card. Your job is to fill in the blanks, adding a recipient, subject, and message text. Figure 9-3 illustrates how a new message card might look. Its features should be familiar to you if you've ever written email on a computer.

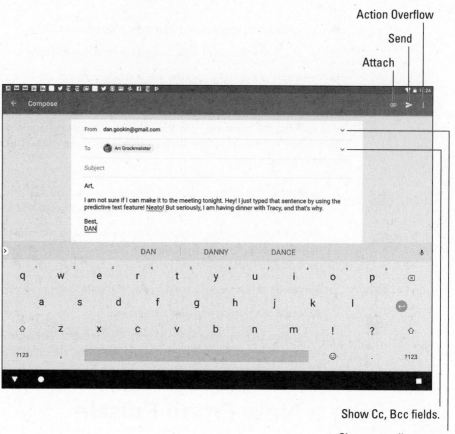

Action Overflow

Send

Attach

Show Cc, Bcc fields.

Choose email account.

FIGURE 9-3:
Composing a new email dispatch.

 To send the message, tap the Send icon, shown in the margin, or tap the SEND button.

>> To select a specific email account for sending, tap the chevron or down arrow next to your name atop the new message card, shown in Figure 9-3. This choice might also be presented in the From field. In the Email app, you set the default email account when you add it, or as described in the later section "Setting the primary email account."

>> You need only type a few letters of the recipient's name. Matching contacts are fetched instantly from the Android's address book, and they appear in a list. Tap a contact to automatically fill in the To field.

>> To view the CC and BCC fields, tap the chevron, shown in Figure 9-3. If that doesn't work, tap Action Overflow or the MORE button and choose Add Cc/Bcc.

» To cancel a message, tap Action Overflow or the MORE button to choose Discard. This action might also be found on the Compose screen. Tap the DISCARD button or OK button to confirm.

» To save a message, tap Action Overflow and choose the Save Draft action. Drafts are saved in the Drafts folder. You can open unfinished email in that folder for further editing or sending.

» Save a message by choosing the Save Draft action from Action Overflow. Drafts are saved in the Drafts folder (or *label*, as Gmail calls them). You can open them there for further editing or sending.

» Some versions of the Email app feature a formatting toolbar. Use the toolbar to change the way the text looks in your message.

Sending email to a contact

A quick and easy way to compose a new message is to find a contact and then create a message with the contact as a recipient. Heed these steps:

1. Open the Android's address book app.

Refer to Chapter 7 for details on the address book app.

2. Locate the contact to whom you want to send an electronic message.

3. Tap the contact's email address.

4. Choose Gmail to compose the message.

You can also choose the Email app or another specific app, such as Yahoo! Mail or a custom email app you've obtained from Google Play.

At this point, creating the message works as described in the preceding section.

Message Attachments

 The key to understanding email attachments on your Android is to look for the Paperclip icon. When you find that icon, you can either deal with an attachment for incoming email or add an attachment to outgoing email.

Receiving an attachment

Attachments are presented differently between the Gmail and Email apps, yet your goal is the same: to view or save the attachment. Sometimes you can do both!

Figure 9-4 shows both the Gmail app and Email app methods of presenting an email attachment. To deal with the attachment, tap it. In most cases, the attachment opens an appropriate app. For example, a PDF attachment might be opened by the Quickoffice app.

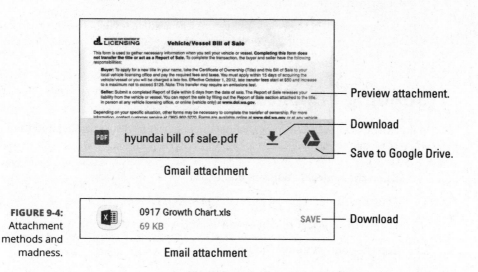

Gmail attachment

FIGURE 9-4: Attachment methods and madness.

Email attachment

Potential actions you can perform with an attachment include

Preview: Open the attachment for viewing.

Save to Google Drive: Send a copy of the attachment to your Google Drive (cloud) storage.

Save: Save the attachment to the device's storage.

Download Again: Fetch the attachment from the mail server.

As with email attachments received on a computer, you may discover that your Android lacks the app required to deal with the attachment. When an app can't be found, you must either suffer not viewing the attachment or request that the attachment be resent in a common file format.

>> Sometimes pictures included in an email message aren't displayed. Tap the SHOW PICTURES button to see the images.

>> Common image file formats include PNG and JPEG. Documents are shared by using the HTML (web page), DOCX (Microsoft Word), and PDF (Adobe Acrobat) file formats.

>> You may see a prompt displayed when several apps can deal with the attachment. Choose one and tap the JUST THIS ONCE button to view the attachment. Also see Chapter 20 for information on the default app prompt.

TECHNICAL STUFF

>> Attachments are saved in the Downloads folder. If your device features removable storage (the microSD card), the attachment is found in the Downloads folder on that storage media. See Chapter 19 for details on Android storage, including how to view downloaded files.

Sharing an attachment

To fully appreciate the Android operating system, you must accept that adding a message attachment in email doesn't start in the Gmail or Email app. No, you start in the app that created the item you want to attach. Heed these steps:

1. **Open the app that created the item you want to attach.**

   Popular apps for sharing include Photos, Gallery, the web browser app, Maps, Play Store, Drive or any other cloud storage app, and so on.

2. **View the item you want to share.**

3. **Tap the Share icon.**

   You see a list of apps.

4. **Choose the Gmail or Email app.**

5. **Complete the message as described earlier in this chapter.**

   The item you're sharing is automatically attached to the message or included as a link.

When you start a message and then discover that you need to attach something, fret not! Look for and tap the Attachment icon lurking somewhere on the Compose card, shown in Figure 9-3. This action might also appear as an ATTACH button. Choose the app or category and then select the item to share.

TIP

>> The variety of items you can attach depends on which apps are installed on the phone or tablet.

>> The Gmail and Email apps sometimes accept different types of attachments. So if you cannot attach something by using the Gmail app, try using the Email app instead.

Email Configuration

You can have oodles of fun and waste oceans of time confirming and customizing the email experience on your Android. The most interesting things you can do are to customize the account, modify or create an email signature, and assign a default email account.

Creating a signature

Don't be one of the uninformed mobile users whose email signature is the same as everyone else's. Why not set your own, unique signature? Here's mine:

```
DAN
This was sent from my Android.
Typos, no matter how hilarious, are unintentional.
```

To create a custom signature for your email accounts, follow these steps:

1. **Open the Settings app.**

The App is found on the Apps drawer.

2. **Choose Users & Accounts.**

On some Androids, this item is titled Accounts.

3. **Tap an email account item.**

It may be titled Personal (IMAP), or Email — it doesn't matter because you're not really done yet.

4. **Choose Account Settings.**

Now you see a list of email accounts, along with an item titled General Settings. This is the screen where you can modify general email behavior or change aspects of specific accounts.

5. **Choose a specific email account from the left side of the screen.**

6. **Choose Signature.**

   Any existing signature appears on the card, ready for you to edit or replace it.

7. **Type or dictate your signature.**

8. **Tap OK when you're done.**

You can repeat these steps (5 through 8) for each of your email accounts, applying to each one a unique signature. Or you can select the signature you create in Step 7 and copy and paste that text into the other accounts' signature cards.

If your device has the Email app, open it and follow these steps:

1. **Tap the Side Menu icon to view the navigation drawer.**

2. **Choose Settings or tap the Settings icon.**

3. **Choose an account.**

4. **Choose Signature.**

5. **Type a new signature. Or edit and replace the existing signature.**

The signature you set is appended automatically to all outgoing email you send.

Setting the primary email account

When you have more than one email account, the main account — the default — is the one used by the Email app to send messages. To change that primary mail account, follow these steps:

1. **Start the Email app.**

2. **Tap the Side Menu icon.**

3. **Tap the Settings icon in the navigation drawer or choose Settings.**

4. **Tap Action Overflow and choose Set Default Account.**

5. **Choose an email account from the list and tap the DONE button.**

The messages you compose and send in the Email app are sent from the account specified in Step 5.

REMEMBER

In the Gmail app, choose the sending account by tapping the chevron next to the From field, as illustrated in Figure 9-3.

» **Adding a bookmark**

» **Working with tabs**

» **Searching for text on a web page**

» **Sharing web pages**

» **Downloading images and files**

» **Configuring the web browser app**

Chapter **10**

Web Browsing

When Tim Berners-Lee developed the World Wide Web back in 1990, he had no idea that people would one day use it on a mobile device with a tiny screen. Nope, the web was designed to be viewed on a computer. Back then, cell phones had teensy LED screens. Browsing the web on a cell phone would have been like viewing the Great Wall of China through a keyhole.

The good news is that the web has adapted itself to mobile viewing. Whether you have a phone or a tablet, the web presents itself in a comfortable viewing size. You won't miss any information, especially after you've read the tips and suggestions in this chapter.

TIP

» If possible, activate the phone's or LTE tablet's Wi-Fi connection before you venture out on the web. Though you can use the mobile data connection, a Wi-Fi connection incurs no data usage charges.

» Many places you visit on the web can instead be accessed directly and more effectively by using specific apps. Facebook, Gmail, Twitter, YouTube, and other popular web destinations have apps that you may find are already installed on your device or otherwise available free from Google Play.

>> One thing you cannot do with your Android is view Flash animations, games, or videos on the web. The web browser app disables the Flash plug-in, also known as Shockwave. I know of no method to circumvent this limitation.

The Web Browser App

All Androids feature a web browsing app. The stock Android app is Google's own Chrome web browser. Your gizmo may use another web browser app, and it may be given a simple name such as Web, Browser, or Internet. Each of these apps works in a similar way and offers comparable features.

>> If your Android doesn't have the Chrome app, you can obtain it for free at Google Play. See Chapter 17.

>> A benefit of using Chrome is that your bookmarks, web history, and other features are shared between all your devices on which Chrome is installed. So if you use Chrome as your computer's web browser, it's logical to use Chrome on your Android as well.

>> The first time you fire up the web browser app on certain Samsung devices, you may see a registration page. Register your device to receive sundry Samsung bonus stuff — or not. Registration is optional.

Behold the Web

It's difficult these days to find someone who has no experience with the World Wide Web. More common is someone who has used the web on a computer but has yet to sample the Internet waters on a phone or tablet. If that's you, consider this section your quick mobile web orientation.

Surfing the web on a mobile device

When you first open the Chrome app, you see the last web page you viewed. In Figure 10-1, I was just on Wikipedia, so when I fired up Chrome, it returned to that page.

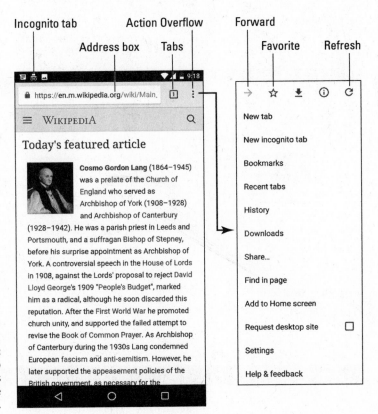

Incognito tab   Action Overflow   Forward

Address box   Tabs   Favorite   Refresh

FIGURE 10-1:
The Chrome app
beholds
Wikipedia's home
page.

Figure 10-1 shows the Chrome app on an Android phone. It looks different on a tablet, as shown in Figure 10-2.

TIP

Here are some handy Android web browsing tips:

>> Drag your finger across the touchscreen to pan and scroll the web page. You can pan up, down, left, or right when the page is larger than the device's screen.

>> Pinch the screen to zoom out, or spread two fingers to zoom in.

>> The page you see may be the mobile page, or a customized version of the web page designed for small-screen devices. To see the nonmobile version, tap the Action Overflow icon and choose Request Desktop Site (refer to the right side of Figure 10-1).

REMEMBER

>> You can orient the Android to read a web page in portrait or landscape orientation. One view may look better than the other. For example, portrait (vertical) orientation makes long lines of text shorter and easier to read.

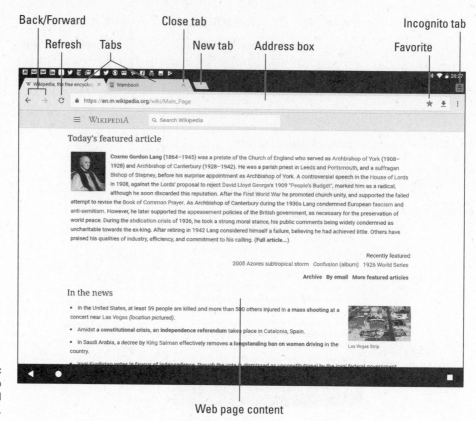

Back/Forward   Close tab   Incognito tab

Refresh   Tabs   New tab   Address box   Favorite

FIGURE 10-2:
The Chrome app
on an Android
tablet.

Web page content

Visiting a web page

To visit a web page, heed these directions in the web browser app:

1. Tap the address box.

Refer to Figures 10-1 and 10-2 for the address box's location. If you don't see the address box, swipe your finger from the top of the screen downward.

2. Use the onscreen keyboard to type the address.

You can also type a search word or phrase if you don't know the exact web page address.

3. Tap the Go button on the onscreen keyboard to visit the specific web page or search the web.

To "click" links on a page, tap them with your finger. If you have trouble stabbing the correct link, zoom in on the page and try again. You can also long-press the screen to see a magnification window to make tapping links easier.

>> The onscreen keyboard may change some keys to make it easier to type a web page address. Look for a www (World Wide Web) or .com (dot-com) key.

>> Long-press the .com key to see other top-level domains, such as .org, .net, and so on.

>> To reload a web page, tap the Refresh icon (refer to Figure 10-1). If you don't see that icon on the screen, tap the Action Overflow icon to find the Refresh or Reload action. Refreshing updates a website that changes often. Using the command can also reload a web page that may not have completely loaded the first time.

>> To stop a web page from loading, tap the Cancel (X) icon that appears by the Address box.

Browsing back and forth

To return to a previous web page, tap the Back navigation icon. On an Android tablet, the Back icon also appears next to the address bar.

Tap the Forward icon to go forward or to return to a page you were visiting before you tapped the Back icon. On an Android phone, this icon is found on the Action Overflow, as illustrated in Figure 10-1.

To review web pages you've visited in the long term, visit the web browser's history page. Follow these steps:

1. **Tap the Action Overflow.**

2. **Choose History.**

3. **Tap an entry in the list to revisit that site.**

You'll notice that the History list is adorned with Delete (trash) icons. See the later section "Clearing your web history" for information on purging items from the History list.

TIP

If you find yourself frequently clearing the web page history, consider using an incognito tab. See the later section "Going incognito."

Dropping a bookmark

You might call them bookmarks, but in the mobile world, your Android calls your bookmarks favorites. To mark a web page as a favorite, tap the Favorite (star) icon for that site. The icon appears on the Action Overflow on an Android phone, or on the address bar on an Android tablet. Refer to Figures 10-1 and 10-2, respectively.

To add more details or help organize your favorites, tap the Favorites star icon again. You see the Edit Bookmark card, which makes you wonder why it's not called Edit Favorite. See? Consistency is a thing that's lacking in the Android universe. Anyway, use the Edit Bookmark card to change the bookmark's name, organize it into a specific folder, or edit the address or URL.

TIP

As an example of editing a bookmark, you can change the official name of the page *Wikipedia, the free encyclopedia* and edit it to just *Wikipedia*. That makes the bookmark more relevant and easier to read.

>> Placing bookmarks into a specific folder is a bit of organization overload on a mobile device. Chrome prefers to shove it into the Mobile Bookmarks folder, which is fine.

>> Another reason to set bookmarks: Their websites appear rapidly as you type a web page address into the address bar. See the next section.

>> If you're compulsive about organization, consider adding your mobile bookmarks to the Bookmarks Bar folder. When you do so, the bookmark is also made available to Chrome on any computers you use.

>> To remove the bookmark, visit the same site and tap the Favorites icon again.

REMEMBER

>> Making a favorite web page isn't the same as saving the page. See the later section "Saving a web page."

>> A great way to find which sites to bookmark is to view the web page history: Tap the Action Overflow and choose History.

Visiting a favorite (bookmarked) web page

To view bookmarks in the Chrome app, tap the Action Overflow icon and choose Bookmarks. You see the Bookmarks card. It's organized by folder, similar to the Bookmarks bar on the computer version of Chrome.

Tap a folder to browse bookmarks stored in that folder.

Tap the Back icon on the screen (not the Back navigation icon) to go up a folder.

Tap a bookmark to visit that page.

TIP

To quickly visit a bookmarked website, just start typing the site's name in the Address box. Tap the bookmarked site from the matching list of results displayed below the Address box.

Managing web pages in multiple tabs

The Chrome app, as well as other Android web browsers, uses a tabbed interface to help you access more than one web page at a time. This feature is useful, but be aware that tabs in the Chrome app work differently between an Android phone and an Android tablet.

In Figure 10-1, you see the TABS button on the phone version of the Chrome app. The number in the button indicates how many tabs are open.

In Figure 10-2, you see the tabs appear atop the app window, marching left-to-right. This is how the tabs look in the computer version of Chrome.

> **Open a Blank Tab:** To open a blank tab, tap the Action Overflow and choose New Tab. On an Android tablet, you can tap the blank tab stub to the right of the last open tab, illustrated in Figure 10-2.

> **Open a Link in a New Tab:** To open a link in another tab, long-press the link and choose Open in New Tab.

> **Open a Bookmark in a New Tab:** To open a bookmark in a new tab, long-press the bookmark and choose Open in New Tab.

> **Switch Tabs:** On an Android tablet, tap the tab you want to view. On a phone, tap the Tabs icon. Choose a new tab from the list shown, as illustrated in Figure 10-3.

To close a tab on a phone, tap the TABS button and tap the close (X) icon by the tab thumbnail (refer to Figure 10-3). On a tablet, tap a tab's Close (X) icon.

TIP

You can also close a tab from the Overview: Tap the Recent navigation icon and then close or swipe the tab's thumbnail off the list.

After you close the last tab, you see a blank screen in the Chrome app. Tap the Add (plus) icon to summon a new tab.

TABS button (and open tab count)

Add new tab.   Close tab.

Incognito tab

FIGURE 10-3:
Switching tabs on
an Android
phone.

Tap a tab to view.

Going incognito

TIP

Shhh! For secure browsing, use an incognito tab: Tap the Action Overflow and choose New Incognito Tab. The incognito tab takes over the screen, changing the look of the Chrome app and offering a description page.

When you go incognito, the web browser doesn't track your history, leave cookies, or provide other evidence of which web pages you've visited. For example, if you go shopping in an incognito window, advertiser tracking cookies don't record your actions. That way, you aren't bombarded by targeted advertising later.

» When an incognito tab is open, the Incognito notification appears on the status bar, like the one shown in the margin.

» Choose the Incognito notification to close all open incognito tabs.

>> On an Android phone, to switch between incognito and regular tabs, tap the Tabs icon. Swipe the Tabs screen right-to-left to choose an open incognito tab. (Refer to the preceding section.)

>> On an Android tablet, tap the Incognito icon in the top-right corner of the Chrome app's screen to view any open incognito tabs. (Refer to Figure 10-2.)

>> The incognito tab is about privacy, not security. Going incognito doesn't prevent viruses or thwart sophisticated web-snooping software.

Searching the web

The best way to find things on the web is to use the Google widget, found floating on the Home screen. Type your search item into that box, or utter "OK, Google" and speak the search text.

While you're using the web browser app, type search text into the Address bar. Or you can visit any number of search engines, though Google would most enjoy your use of google.com.

Finding text on a web page

To locate text on a web page, tap the Action Overflow and choose Find in Page. Use the onscreen keyboard to type search text. As you type, matching text on the page is highlighted. Use the up and down chevrons to page through found matches.

Tap the Back navigation icon when you've finished searching.

Sharing a web page

There it is! That web page you just *have* to talk about to everyone you know. The gauche way to share the page is to copy and paste it. Because you're reading this book, however, you know better. Heed these steps:

1. **Visit the web page you desire to share.**

Actually, you're sharing a link to the page, but don't let my obsession with specificity deter you.

2. **Tap the Action Overflow icon and choose Share.**

   The command might be called Share Via or Share Page. Either way, you see an array of apps displayed. The variety and number of apps depends on what's installed on the device.

3. **Choose an app.**

   For example, select Gmail to send the web page's link by email, or Facebook to share the link with your friends.

4. **Do whatever happens next.**

   Whatever happens next depends on how you're sharing the link: Compose the email, write a comment in Facebook, or do whatever. Refer to various chapters in this book for specific directions.

You cannot share a page you're viewing on an incognito tab.

Another way to share a page is to print it. See Chapter 19 for details.

The Art of Downloading

The most important thing you need to know about downloading is that it's a transfer of information from another source to your gizmo. For your mobile device, the other source is the Internet. The information transferred is accessed on a web page. It can be a picture, a file, or something else that I can't think of right now.

>> The Downloading Complete notification appears after your Android has downloaded something. You can choose that notification to view the downloaded item.

>> New apps on your Android are downloaded, but not by using the web browser app. Instead, you use the Google Play Store app, which is a topic covered in Chapter 17.

>> Most people use the term *download* when they really mean transfer or copy. Those people must be shunned.

TECHNICAL
STUFF

>> The opposite of downloading is *uploading*. That's the process of sending information from your gizmo to another to another source, such as the Internet.

Grabbing an image from a web page

The simplest thing to download is an image from a web page:

1. **Long-press the image.**

You see an action card appear.

2. **Choose Download Image or Save Image.**

You may be prompted to allow Chrome to access the device's media. If so, tap the ALLOW button.

See the later section "Reviewing your downloads," for details on how to access the image.

Downloading a file

The web is full of links that don't open in a web browser window. For example, some links automatically download, such as links to Microsoft Word documents or other types of files that a web browser is too frightened to display.

To save other types of links that aren't automatically downloaded, long-press the link and choose the Save Link action. If this action doesn't appear, your Android is unable to save the link, because either the file is of an unrecognized type or it presents a security issue.

Saving a web page

To save the entire web page you're viewing, tap the Download icon, shown in the margin.

> >> On the phone version of Chrome, tap the Action Overflow to find the Download icon.
>
> >> On the tablet version of Chrome, the Download icon is located on the right end of the address bar.

One reason for downloading an entire page is to read it later, especially when the Internet isn't available. This tip is one of my Android travel suggestions. More travel tips are found in Chapter 23.

Reviewing your downloads

To access any image, file, or web page you've downloaded or saved on your Android, follow these steps in the Chrome web browser app:

1. **Tap the Action Overflow.**

2. **Choose Downloads.**

   A list of cards appears on the Downloads screen, each one representing something you've downloaded.

3. **Tap a card to open and view the item you downloaded.**

Photos can also be viewed in the Photos app, which is covered specifically in Chapter 14. In that app, tap the Side Menu icon and choose Devices Folders on the navigation drawer. You'll find all downloaded images saved in the Download folder or album.

REMEMBER

TECHNICAL STUFF

>> You can choose the Download notification to quickly review any single downloaded item.

>> If you're quick, you can tap the OPEN button that appears on the toast (pop-up message) immediately after an item is downloaded.

>> Some web pages load dynamic information. If you open a saved web page and find some of the artwork absent or other features disabled, it's that missing dynamic information that's making the page look odd.

Web Browser Controls and Settings

More options and settings and controls exist for web browser apps than for just about any other Android app I've used. Rather than bore you with every dang-doodle detail, I thought I'd present just a few of the options worthy of your attention.

Clearing your web history

When you don't want the entire Internet to know what you're looking at on the web, open an incognito tab, as described in the earlier section "Going incognito." When you forget to do that, follow these steps to purge one or more web pages from the browser history:

1. **Tap the Action Overflow icon and choose History.**

2. **Tap the X icon next to the web page entry you want to remove.**

   It's gone.

If you want to remove *all* your web browsing history, after Step 1 tap the button CLEAR BROWSING DATA. You see the Clear Browsing Data screen. The prechecked items are what you need, so tap the CLEAR DATA button to rid your Android of your sordid past.

You don't need to clean up your web browsing history when you use an incognito tab.

Changing the web's appearance

As I ranted at the start of this chapter, the web on a mobile device never looks as good as the web on a computer. You do have a few options for making it look better.

First and foremost, remember that you can orient the device horizontally and vertically, which rearranges the way a web page is displayed:

1. **Tap the Action Overflow icon.**

2. **Choose Settings.**

3. **Choose Accessibility.**

   This item might be titled Screen and Text in some web browser apps.

4. **Use the Text Scaling slider to adjust the text size.**

   The preview text below the slider helps you gauge which size works best.

You can spread your fingers to zoom in on any web page, but when you find your-self doing that too often, consider resetting the screen text size:

Setting privacy and security options

The Chrome web browser app presets optimum security settings. The only issue you should consider is how information is retained and automatically recalled. You may want to disable some of those features. Obey these steps:

1. **Tap the Action Overflow icon.**

2. **Choose Settings.**

3. **Choose Autofill and Payments.**

4. **Set the master control by Autofill Forms to the Off position.**

   This setting disables Chrome's capability of filling in forms with your personal information: name, address, account numbers, and so on.

5. **Tap the Back navigation icon to return to the main Settings screen.**

6. **Choose Save Passwords.**

7. **Set the master control by Save Passwords to the Off position.**

8. **Remove the check mark by the Auto Sign-in item.**

   Both settings on the Save Passwords screen prevent your device from filling in passwords and automatically logging in to various websites.

TIP

Incidentally, I strongly recommend that you make such settings with Chrome on your computer as well. When the web browser memorizes and automatically enters passwords and other sensitive information (such as credit card numbers), that makes it easier for the Bad Guys to do their Bad Guy Stuff.

With regard to general online security, my advice is always to be smart and think before doing anything questionable on the web. Use common sense. One of the most effective ways that the Bad Guys win is by using human engineering to try to trick you into doing something you normally wouldn't do, such as click a link to see a cute animation or a racy picture of a celebrity or politician. As long as you use your noggin, you should be safe.

Also see Chapter 22 for information on applying a secure screen lock, which I highly recommend.

Chapter **11**

Digital Social Life

Long ago, social networking eclipsed email as the number-one reason for using the Internet. It has nearly replaced email, has definitely replaced having a personalized website, and has become an obsession for millions across the globe. Your Android is ready to meet your social networking desires.

Share Your Life on Facebook

Of all the social networking sites, Facebook is the king. It's the online place to go to catch up with friends, send messages, express your thoughts, share pictures and video, play games, and waste more time than you ever thought you had.

>> The best way to access Facebook is to use the Facebook app. This app is preinstalled on some devices. If not, you can obtain the Facebook app for free at the Google Play Store. See Chapter 17.

>> You can use the Facebook app to sign up for a Facebook account, or you can use your existing account.

TIP

>> After signing in to Facebook the first time, you must perform configuration. I recommend choosing the option to synchronize Facebook with your Android's Contacts app.

>> The Facebook app is updated frequently. Visit my website to review any new information:

```
wambooli.com/help/android
```

Running Facebook on your Android

The main Facebook screen is illustrated in Figure 11-1. The News Feed tab is shown for both a phone and a tablet. Other tabs display different information. The Notifications icon alerts you to new friend requests, comments, and other updates.

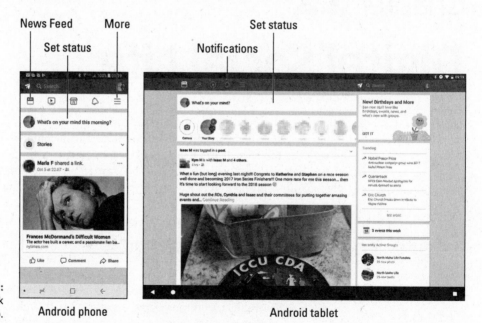

News Feed   More

Set status

Set status

Notifications

FIGURE 11-1:
The Facebook app.

Android phone   Android tablet

To set Facebook aside, tap the Home icon to return to the Home screen. The Facebook app continues to run until you either sign out of the app or turn off your device.

To sign out of the Facebook app, tap the More icon (refer to Figure 11-1) and choose the Log Out action (from the bottom of the list). Tap the LOG OUT button to confirm.

TIP

>> To update the News Feed, tug downward on the screen: Swipe from just below the status bar to the center of the touchscreen.

>> Use the Like, Comment, or Share icons below a News Feed item to like, comment, or share something, respectively. Existing comments appear only when you choose the Comment item.

>> The Facebook app generates notifications for news items, mentions, chat, and so on. This notification icon looks similar to the one shown in the margin.

Setting your status

The primary thing you live for on Facebook, besides having more friends than anyone else, is to update your status. It's the best way to share your thoughts with the universe, especially intimate moments like when you're waiting in the doctor's office to have your tonsilloliths removed.

To set your status, follow these steps in the Facebook app:

1. **Switch to the News Feed.**

   Tap the News Feed icon (refer to Figure 11-1).

2. **Tap the status update area.**

   This area is highlighted in Figure 11-1. It typically shows the text *What's on your mind?*

   Upon success, you see the Post to Facebook screen, where you can type your musings as well as perform other activities, as illustrated in Figure 11-2.

3. **Choose a sharing audience.**

   Tap the Sharing Audience button (refer to Figure 11-2). Chose Public so that everyone can see the message, or Friends so that only people you're friends with can see it.

4. **Type the post.**

   If necessary, tap the Back navigation icon so that you can see the *What's On Your Mind* text. Anything you type replaces that text.

5. **Tap the POST button to share your thoughts.**

Choose the sharing audience.

Share your status.

Status update text

Choose a background.

Share your location.

Set the mood.

Go live.

Add a photo.

FIGURE 11-2:
Updating your
Facebook status.

To cancel the post, tap the Back navigation icon. Tap the DISCARD POST button to confirm.

TIP

» If you've added the Facebook widget to the Home screen, you can use that widget to share a quick post.

» The color palette below your post text lets you set a background color for the post.

» Other options include adding a photo, setting a location, and so on. When you tap one of these icons (illustrated in Figure 11-2), you see a complete list of potential actions and activities.

Uploading a picture or video to Facebook

The Facebook app can access your Android's camera to snap a photo or shoot a video specifically for Facebook. You can also share any photo or video stored on the device, making the various intimate and private moments of your life visible to the ogling throngs of the Internet.

To share a picture or video in the Facebook app, follow these steps:

1. **Update your status.**

   Refer to the preceding section, though you don't need to type any text if you just want to post a photo or video.

2. **Tap the Add Photo icon.**

   Refer to Figure 11-2. After you tap the icon, you see a long slate of potential actions.

3. **Choose Photo/Video.**

4. **Select an image stored on your phone or tablet.**

   You can, optionally, tap additional images to share an album.

5. **Tap the DONE button.**

   The image(s) or video(s) are presented in the post.

6. **Tap the POST button to share.**

 You can also snap a picture or record a video on the spot: In Step 4, tap the Add Photo icon or Add Video icon, both of which are shown in the margin. Use the device's camera to shoot the image or record a video snippet. Specifics on using the Camera app are covered in Chapter 13.

» I find it easier to use the Camera app to take a bunch of images or record video and then choose that item later to upload it to Facebook.

» If you're unhappy with the photo you took, tap the RETRY button to take another image, or tap DONE / OK and get ready to post the image or video to Facebook. Tap Cancel (in the top-left corner of the screen) to abandon your efforts.

» Another popular photo-sharing option is 360 Photo, which lets you capture a wider panoramic shot or the entire area around you. Not every device shows this option in the Facebook app.

 » The Facebook app appears on the various Share menus available in other apps on the phone or tablet. Tap the Share icon to send to Facebook a YouTube video, an image, a web page, some music, and so on.

Going live

When you opt to share a video on Facebook, you have several options. You can

>> Share a video that's already recorded and saved.

>> Record a video and then share it.

>> Go live and share the video as you record it.

The first two options are covered in the preceding section. To go live, choose the Go Live option instead of Photo/Video. If presented with Permission cards, tap ALLOW to let the Facebook app access your Android's camera and microphone. Tap the Video icon to start broadcasting.

The video is presented live to anyone who's on Facebook at the time. It's recorded for playback later.

A Virtual Hangout

The great Googly way to hang out with your Google friends is to use an app called Hangouts. It offers text chat, voice chat, and video chat. It even has a feature that lets you make phone calls on an Android tablet.

Using Hangouts

The Hangouts app is located on the Home screen, found in the Google folder. If it isn't, you can open the app from the Apps drawer.

When you first open the Hangouts app, it may ask whether you want to make phone calls. Choose the option to install the Hangouts Dialer app, especially if that's your desire for an Android tablet. If you don't see this prompt, you can obtain the Hangouts Dialer app from the Google Play Store. See Chapter 17.

 You can do anything else on the phone while the Hangouts app stays active. You're alerted via notification of an impending Hangouts request. The Notification icon is shown in the margin.

Typing at your friends

Text chatting is one of the oldest forms of communication on the Internet. People type text back and forth at each other, which can be tedious, but it remains popular. To text-chat in the Hangouts app, obey these steps:

1. **Choose a contact or select a previous conversation from the main Hangouts screen.**

   To choose a new contact, tap the Add icon and choose New Conversation. Select a contact from the list presented.

2. **Type a message, as shown in Figure 11-3.**

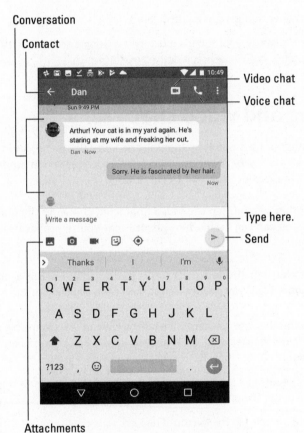

FIGURE 11-3: Text-chatting in Hangouts.

Conversation

Contact

Video chat

Voice chat

Type here.

Send

Attachments

3. **Tap the Send icon to send your text tidbit.**

   You type, your friend types, and so on, until you grow tired or the device's battery dies.

   >> To add more people to the hangout, tap Action Overflow and choose Create New Group. Choose more friends from those listed to invite them into the hangout.

>> Tap an attachment icon to add a photo, take a new picture, record a video, or add other interesting items, as illustrated in Figure 11-3.

>> Conversations are archived in the Hangouts app. To peruse a previous text chat, tap its entry on the main screen.

>> To remove a previous conversation, long-press it. Tap the Delete icon that appears atop the screen.

>> Group conversations cannot be deleted.

>> To use Hangouts, your friends must have a Google account. They can use a computer or mobile device; it doesn't matter which.

REMEMBER

Talking and video chat

Take the hangout up a notch by tapping the Voice Chat icon, shown in the margin and in Figure 11-3. When you do, your friend receives a pop-up invite. After that person taps the Accept icon, you begin talking.

To see the other person, tap the Video Chat icon, shown in the margin. As soon as they agree, you can see each other. Ensure that you're properly attired before you tap this icon.

To end the call, tap the red END CALL button, like ending a phone call on an Android phone. Well, say goodbye first, and then tap the button.

>> During the chat, the person you're talking with appears in the big window; you're in the smaller window. That's in case you don't remember what you look like.

>> If other people join the conversation, they appear in smaller windows at the bottom of the screen. Tap a window to enlarge it.

>> To mute the call, tap the Microphone icon.

>> Tap the Video icon to disable the camera and return to voice or text chat.

>> The onscreen controls may vanish after a second; tap the screen to see the controls again.

>> Video calls aren't archived, but you can review when the call took place, and with whom, by choosing a video-chat item.

Placing a Hangouts phone call

If you've obtained the Hangouts Dialer app, you can use Hangouts to place a live phone call — even on an Android tablet. It works like this:

1. **Tap the Phone Calls tab in the Hangouts app.**

    If you don't see the Phone Calls tab, you haven't yet installed the Hangouts Dialer app.

2. **Type a contact name or a phone number.**

3. **Tap the matching contact or tap the phone number (when it doesn't belong to a contact) to dial.**

    The call is placed.

 If you'd rather dial a number directly, tap the Dialpad icon, shown in the margin. Type the phone number and then tap the green Dial icon to place the call.

Tap the red End Call icon to end the call.

>> To the person you're calling, an incoming Hangouts call looks just like any other call, although the number may be displayed as Unavailable.

>> The good news: Hangouts calls are free!

>> The bad news: You can't use Hangouts to dial every phone number.

Let's All Tweet

Twitter is a social networking site that lets you share short bursts of text, or *tweets*. You can create your own or just choose to follow others, including news organizations, businesses, governments, celebrities, and creatures from alien planets.

If your Android didn't come with the Twitter app, obtain it from the Google Play Store, as described in Chapter 17. Install and run the app to sign in to Twitter using an existing account, or create a new account on the spot.

Figure 11-4 illustrates the Twitter app's main screen, which shows the current tweet feed. The Twitter app is updated frequently, so its exact appearance may change after this book has gone to press.

Twitter Home

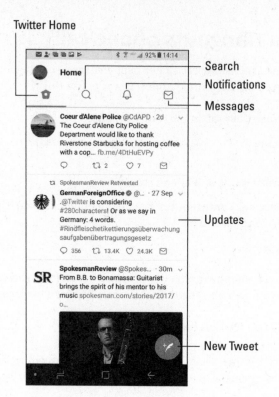

Search

Notifications

Messages

Updates

New Tweet

FIGURE 11-4:
The Twitter app.

To read tweets, choose the Home category, shown in Figure 11-4. Recent tweets are displayed in a list, with the most recent information at the top. Tug the list downward to update the tweets; swipe from just below the status bar to center screen.

To tweet, tap the New Tweet icon, shown in Figure 11-4. The "What's happening?" screen appears, where you can compose your tweet.

REMEMBER

A tweet has a limited number of characters. An indicator on the New Tweet screen informs you of how many characters remain.

Tap the Tweet button to share your thoughts with the twitterverse.

TIP

>> A message posted on Twitter is a *tweet*.

>> To access the Twitter app's navigation drawer, swipe in from the left side of the touchscreen.

>> The Twitter app comes with companion widgets that you can affix to the Home screen. Use the widgets to peruse recent tweets or compose a new tweet. Refer to Chapter 20 for information on affixing widgets to the Home screen.

>> To share material from other apps on Twitter, visit the other app and view the information. For example, open the Photos app to view a picture. Tap the Share icon and choose Twitter as the sharing destination.

Skype the World

Skype is one of the most popular Internet communications programs, allowing you to text-, voice-, or video-chat with other Skype users. But the big enchilada is Skype's capability to place honest-to-goodness phone calls, including international calls. This feature works on both Android phones and tablets.

Obtaining the Skype app and signing in

Odds are good that your device didn't come with the Skype app preinstalled. To get Skype, visit the Google Play Store and obtain the Skype app. See Chapter 17 for details on accessing the Google Play Store.

To use Skype, you need a Skype account. You can sign up when you first open the app. You must confirm your new account, and that confirmation must take place before you can start using the app. Otherwise, you can use an existing account to sign in.

To sign out of Skype, tap your account bubble at the top of the main Skype screen. On your account-info screen, tap the Settings icon. Swipe down the screen and choose the Sign Out action.

TIP

>> If you plan to use Skype a lot, get a good headset.

>> Text, voice, and video chat on Skype over the Internet are free. When you use a Wi-Fi connection, you can chat without consuming your cellular plan's data minutes.

>> You're free to do other things on your device while Skype runs. If any text message arrives, a Skype notification appears, similar to what's shown in the margin. Voice and video chats feature full-screen invitations.

>> After you initially sign in to Skype, the app continues to run. Only when you turn off your Android or deliberately sign out of Skype does the app stop.

Placing a Skype phone call

Skype's popular features include text chat as well as voice and video chat, though you can use these features only with fellow Skype users. The big enchilada in Skype is making phone calls.

TIP

Calls to real phones can be made only when you have Skype Credit on your account. To ensure that you have Skype Credit, tap your account icon atop the main Skype screen. Tap the Settings icon and swipe down the screen to view available credit. If you see $0.00, tap that item to either make a one-time Skype Credit purchase or get a subscription. You don't need a lot of Skype Credit to make calls — the rates are quite cheap.

After you've confirmed your Skype Credit, you can use an Android phone or tablet to make a "real" phone call, which is a call to any phone number on the planet (Planet Earth). Heed these steps:

1. **Tap the Phone icon on the Skype app's main screen.**

2. **Tap the Use Dialpad icon.**

   The Dialpad icon is shown in the margin. After you tap this icon, you see the Skype dial screen, illustrated in Figure 11-5.

FIGURE 11-5:
The Skype app
dialing screen.

3. **Use the keypad to punch in the phone number.**

Or you can tap the address book icon (near the top-right corner of the screen) to choose a Skype contact. When you do, you're calling their phone, not initiating a new voice chat.

The +1 prefix is required for dialing to the United States, even when the number is local. Don't erase it!

TIP

For international dialing, the number begins with a plus sign (+) followed by the country code and then the phone number. You can choose a country by tapping the screen, as shown in Figure 11-5.

4. **Tap the PHONE (DIAL) button at the bottom of the screen to place the call.**

5. **Talk.**

As you talk, the cost of the call is displayed on the screen. That way, you can keep tabs on the toll.

6. **To end the call, tap the END CALL button.**

Lamentably, you can't use Skype to receive a phone call on an Android tablet. The only way to make that happen is to pay for a Skype online number. In that case, you can use Skype to both send and receive regular phone calls.

>> In addition to the per-minute cost, you may be charged a connection fee for making the call.

>> You can check the Skype website at skype.com for a current list of call rates, for both domestic and international calls.

REMEMBER

>> You can use the Hangouts app to place free phone calls, though it doesn't support the same broad range of phone numbers as Skype. Hangouts is incapable of placing international calls (as this book goes to press). Refer to the earlier section "Placing a Hangouts phone call."

TIP

>> Unless you've paid Skype to let you use a specific number, the phone number shown on the recipient's Caller ID screen is something unexpected — often the text *Unknown.* Because of that, you might want to email the person ahead of time and inform him or her that you're placing a Skype call. That way, the call won't be skipped because the Caller ID isn't recognized.

Other Social Networking Opportunities

The Internet is nuts over social networking. Facebook may be the king, but you'll find lots of landed gentry out for that crown. It almost seems as though a new social networking site pops up every week. Beyond Facebook, Google Hangouts, Skype, and Twitter, other social networking sites include, but are not limited to:

>> Google+

>> LinkedIn

>> Meebo

>> Myspace

Apps for these services are obtained from the Google Play Store, which is covered in Chapter 17. Use the app itself to sign up for an account, or use an existing account. As with other online sites, use the app and not the web browser app to access the service.

TIP

>> If you find yourself overwhelmed with social networking sites and sources, consider obtaining the HootSuite app. Use that lone app to share your thoughts on a multitude of social networking platforms.

>> Use the Share icon to access your favorite social networking app. It's the quick way to post pictures, share web links, or forward YouTube videos: Tap the Share icon and then choose your favorite social networking app.

3

Amazing Android Feats

» Choosing a different map type

» Saving a map for later

» Finding your location

» Sharing your location

» Searching for places

» Getting directions and navigation

Chapter 12
There's a Map for That

The group were all stunned and disoriented. Dr. Cornelius explained it would happen. The room rocked, and gravity tugged left and right instead of down.

Eventually, Ira righted himself; his nausea abated. "They're never going to sell teleportation to the masses with this kind of aftereffect," he grunted.

Phyllis agreed. Holding a hand to her spinning forehead, she asked, "Where are we? And where is a good Hungarian restaurant?"

That's when Dan whipped out his Android. "I'll let you know in just a second," he said proudly. "And the reader will know as well, thanks to the marvelous information in this chapter."

Map 101

To find your location, as well as the location of things near and far, summon the Maps app. Good news: You run no risk of improperly folding the Maps app. Better news: The Maps app charts the entire country, including freeways, highways, roads, streets, avenues, drives, bike paths, addresses, businesses, and various points of interest.

Unfolding the Maps app

To start the Maps app, tap its launcher on the Home screen. You might find the launcher inside a Google folder. And, like all apps, it can be located on the Apps drawer.

If you're starting the app for the first time or it has been recently updated, you can read the What's New screen; tap the OK or GOT IT button to continue.

Your Android uses its own GPS radio to communicate with global positioning system (GPS) satellites to hone in on your current location. That location appears on the map, as illustrated in Figure 12-1, which shows the Maps app running on an Android phone.

Search for stuff.

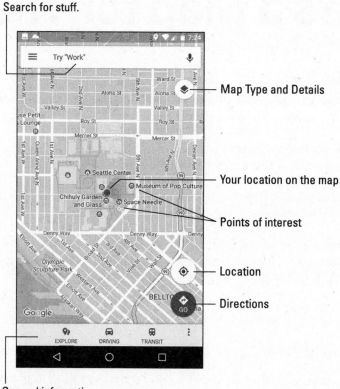

Map Type and Details

Your location on the map

Points of interest

Location

Directions

FIGURE 12-1: The Maps app on a phone.

General information

Android tablets are afforded a larger canvas, so the Maps app's gizmos are relocated, as illustrated in Figure 12-2. Despite this difference in presentation, both versions of the app offer the same features.

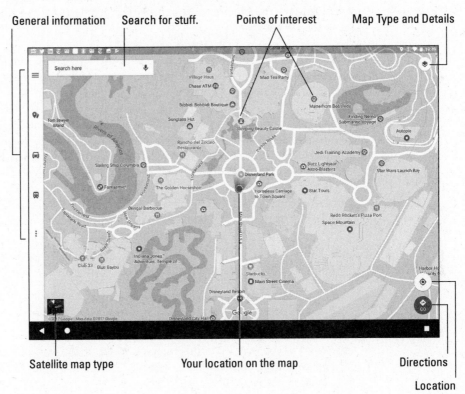

General information   Search for stuff.   Points of interest   Map Type and Details

Satellite map type   Your location on the map   Directions

Location

FIGURE 12-2:
The Maps app on a tablet.

Your position appears as a blue dot, illustrated in Figures 12-1 and 12-2. This location is accurate to within a given range, shown by a blue circle around your location. The Android's direction, if detected, is shown by the blue fuzzy triangle that pokes out from under the circle.

Here are some fun things you can do when viewing the map:

Zoom in: To make the map larger (to move it closer), double-tap the screen. You can also spread your fingers on the touchscreen to zoom in.

Zoom out: To make the map smaller (to see more), pinch your fingers on the touchscreen.

Pan and scroll: To see what's to the left or right or at the top or bottom of the map, swipe your finger on the touchscreen. The map scrolls in the direction you swipe.

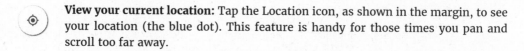

View your current location: Tap the Location icon, as shown in the margin, to see your location (the blue dot). This feature is handy for those times you pan and scroll too far away.

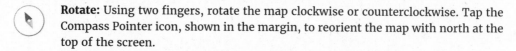

Rotate: Using two fingers, rotate the map clockwise or counterclockwise. Tap the Compass Pointer icon, shown in the margin, to reorient the map with north at the top of the screen.

Perspective: Touch the screen with two fingers and swipe up or down to view the map in perspective. You can also tap the Location icon to switch to Perspective view, though that trick works only for your current location. To return to flat-map view, tap the Compass Pointer icon.

The closer you zoom in on the map, the more detail you see, such as street names, address block numbers, businesses, and other sites — but no tiny people.

>> See the nearby sidebar "Activate location technology!" to confirm that the device's GPS radio presents your location accurately.

>> When the location icon is blue, you're viewing your current location on the map. Tap the icon to enter perspective view. Tap the Perspective icon, shown in the margin, to return to flat view.

>> When all you want is a virtual compass, similar to the one you lost as a kid, get a compass app from the Google Play Store. See Chapter 17 for more information about the Google Play Store.

ACTIVATE LOCATION TECHNOLOGY!

The Maps app works best when you activate all the device's location technologies, including both GPS and Wi-Fi radios. To ensure that these technologies are in use, open the Settings app. Choose the item Security & Location and then Location. On older Androids, the Location item appears on the main Settings app screen. For Samsung devices, choose the Connections category to find the location.

Ensure that the master control for Location is in the On position. Further, if a Mode or Locating Method item is available, choose it and select either the High Accuracy or the GPS and Wi-Fi option.

Changing the map type

The standard map type is the street map. Two other types are available: Satellite and Terrain. To change the view, follow these steps:

1. **Tap the Map Type and Details icon.**

   You see the Map Type and Details card.

2. **Choose another map type.**

   The Satellite map type is shown in Figure 12-3.

FIGURE 12-3: The Satellite map type.

The map type can also be combined with details, such as mass transit, traffic, and bicycle paths. Tap the Map Type and Details icon to choose one of those layers to apply over the map type.

TIP

>> The standard street map is called the *Default* map. Choose it from the Map Type and Details icon to return to that view.

>> To remove a layer, choose it again from the Map Type and Details card.

>> You can quickly switch between Satellite and Default (street) map types on an Android tablet: Tap the Preview icon located in the lower left corner of the screen, illustrated earlier, in Figure 12-2.

Saving an offline map

For times when an Internet connection isn't available (which is frequent for a Wi-Fi–only tablet), you can still use the Maps app, though only in a limited capacity. The secret is to save the portion of the map you need to reference. Obey these steps:

1. View the map chunk you desire to save.

Zoom. Pan. Square in the area to save on the screen. It can be as large or as small as you need. Obviously, smaller maps occupy less storage.

2. Tap the Side Menu icon.

3. Choose Offline Maps from the navigation drawer.

Any maps you've previously saved appear in the list.

4. Tap the button SELECT YOUR OWN MAP.

Because you've already selected the map in Step 1, you can move on with Step 5:

5. Tap the DOWNLOAD button.

The map's details are downloaded. Eventually, it appears in the list of offline maps.

To use an offline map, display the navigation drawer and choose Offline Areas. Tap the offline map to view, and it shows up on the screen, even when an Internet connection is unavailable. You can browse the map, but you cannot search or use navigation features while the device is offline.

>> Offline maps remain valid for 30 days. After that time, you must update the map to keep it current. A notification reminds you to update.

>> To update an offline map, choose it from the Offline Maps screen and tap the UPDATE button.

>> To name a map something better than MAP1, tap Action Overflow by the map's entry and choose Rename. Be descriptive.

>> To remove an offline map, choose it and tap the DELETE button. Tap YES to confirm.

>> If you're out traveling and the Android's Wi-Fi is on, the offline map may display your location. Don't count on this feature to work properly for navigation.

TIP

It Knows Where You Are

Many war movies have this cliché scene: Some soldiers are looking at a map. They wonder where they are, when one of them says, "We're not even on the map!" Such things never happen with the Maps app. That's because it always knows where you are.

Well, unless you're on the planet Venus. I've heard that the Maps app won't work there.

Finding a location

The Maps app shows your location as a blue dot on the screen. But where is that? I mean, if you need to contact a tow truck, you can't just say, "I'm the blue dot on the gray slab by the green thing."

Well, you can say that, but it probably won't do any good.

If you desire more information about your location, or any spot on the map, long-press the screen in the Maps app. Up pops a card, like the one shown in Figure 12-4. The card gives your approximate address.

On an Android phone, tap the card to see a screen with more details and additional information, as shown on the right in Figure 12-4. Android tablets show the card on the left side of the screen — no need to tap.

>> Use the DIRECTIONS button to get directions to the location. See the later section "Android the Navigator."

>> When you have way too much time on your hands, play with the Street View command. Choosing this option displays the location from a 360-degree perspective. In Street view, you can browse a locale, pan and tilt, or zoom in on details to familiarize yourself with an area, for example — whether you're familiarizing yourself with a location or planning a burglary.

TIP

Long-press a location to see the address.

Dropped Pin

near 1-9 Oak St
Nantucket, MA 02554

SAVE · LABEL · SHARE · DOWNLOAD

Measure distance

SHOW MAP · DIRECTIONS

Dropped Pin

near 1-9 Oak St, Nantucket, MA 02554

MORE INFO · DIRECTIONS

FIGURE 12-4:
Finding an
address.

Information card   Route   Street view

Helping others find your location

TIP

It's possible to use the Maps app to send your current location to a friend. If your pal has a mobile device with smarts like your Android phone or tablet, he can use the coordinates to get directions to your location. Maybe he'll even bring some tacos!

To send your current location, obey these steps:

REMEMBER

1. **Long-press your current location on the map.**

   To see your current location, first tap the Location icon in the lower right corner of the Maps app screen.

   After long-pressing your location (or any location), you see a card displayed, showing the approximate address, like the card shown on the right in Figure 12-4.

2. **Tap the card's Share icon.**

3. **Choose the app to share the location.**

For example, choose Messages or the phone's text messaging app; Gmail to send the location data in an email message; Hangouts to instantly chat with someone; and so on.

4. **Continue using the selected app to complete the process of sending your location to someone else.**

When the recipient receives the message, he can tap the link to open your location in the Maps app — provided he has an Android device. When the location appears, he can buy this book and follow my advice in the later section "Android the Navigator" for getting to your location. And don't loan anyone this book, either; have them purchase their own copy. Thanks.

Find Things

The Maps app can help you find places in the real world, just like the Google Search app helps you find places on the Internet. Both operations work the same: Open the Maps app and type something to find in the Search box. What can you type? Keep reading this section.

Looking for a specific address

To locate an address, type it in the Search box. For example:

```
1313 N. Harbor Blvd., Anaheim, CA 92803
```

You may not need to type the entire address: As you tap the keys, suggestions appear onscreen. Tap a matching suggestion to view that location. Otherwise, tap the onscreen keyboard's Search key, and that location is shown on the map.

After you find a specific address, the next step is to get directions. See the later section "Android the Navigator."

>> You don't need to type the entire address. Oftentimes, all you need is the street number and street name and then either the city name or zip code.

>> If you omit the city name or zip code, the Maps app looks for the closest matching address near your current location.

>> Tap the X button in the Search box to clear the previous search.

Finding a business, restaurant, or point of interest

You may not know an address, but you know when you crave sushi or perhaps the exotic flavors of Manitoba. Maybe you need a hotel or a gas station, or a combination hotel-and-gas-station. To find a business entity or a point of interest, type its name in the Search box. For example:

```
Movie theater
```

This search text locates movie theaters on the current Maps screen. Or, to find locations near you, first tap the Location icon (shown in the margin) and then type the search text.

To look for points of interest at a specific location, add the city name, district, or zip code to the search text. For example:

```
Asian market San Diego
```

After typing this command and tapping the onscreen keyboard's Search key, you see the assortment of Asian markets located in the San Diego metropolitan area, similar to the results shown on the left in Figure 12-5.

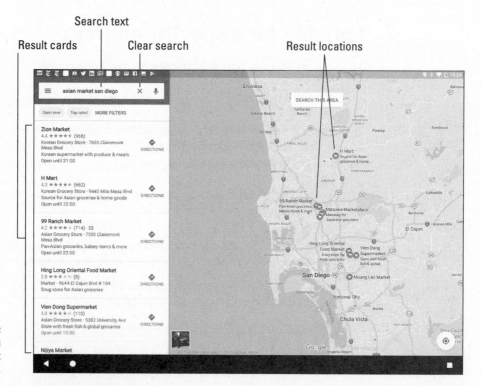

FIGURE 12-5: Finding a Japanese market near San Diego.

Tap a card from the list to view more details, including the exact address, hours of operation, phone number, website, and so on.

>> Figure 12-5 shows the results on an Android tablet. On a phone, the DIRECTIONS button is replaced by a Call icon. Tap the icon to phone the business.

>> Every letter or dot on the search-results screen represents a matching location. For each dot, a card is available, as shown in Figure 12-5.

>> Spread your fingers on the touchscreen to zoom in on the map.

Marking a favorite place

For locations you visit frequently, consider adding them to your favorite places list. To do so, follow these steps:

1. **Tap the SAVE button on a location's card.**

   A card appears, showing location lists available to you. The three preset lists are Favorites, Want to Go, and Starred Places.

2. **Choose a list, such as Favorites.**

   The location is saved.

No difference exists between Favorite, Want to Go, and Starred locations. All are saved, just in different lists. See the next section.

Searching for favorite or recent places

Places that you've marked as favorites, as well as all locations you've visited recently, are memorized by the Maps app. To review these locations, heed these steps:

1. **Tap the Side Menu icon.**

2. **On the navigation drawer, choose Your Places.**

The Your Places screen features multiple tabs across the top of the screen. The SAVED tab lists places you've marked as favorites, categorized by lists.

The VISITED tab records locations you've wandered through.

Other tabs list relevant information related to the tab title. For example, the LABELED tab shows your home and work locations, if you've set those (as covered in the next section).

To access any location on the Your Places list, tap its card.

Setting your Home and Work locations

Two places that you frequent most in the real world are where you live and where you work. The Maps app lets you create shortcuts for these locations. They're called, logically enough, Home and Work.

To set the Home and Work locations, follow these steps in the Maps app:

1. **Tap the Side Menu icon to display the navigation drawer.**

2. **Choose Your Places.**

3. **On the LABELED tab, choose Home.**

   If a home location isn't set, you see the text *Set Home Address* appear below the Home label.

4. **Type your home address.**

5. **Repeat Steps 3 and 4 for your work address.**

You can use the Home and Work shortcuts when searching for a location or getting directions. For example, type **Home** into the Search box to instantly see where you live, or whichever place you call home. To get directions from your current location to work, type **Work** as the destination. Keep reading in the next section.

>> If you choose Home or Work from the Your Places menu, you see that location displayed on the map.

>> To reset your home or work locations, display the Your Places screen (refer to Steps 1 and 2), but tap the Action Overflow icon and choose Edit Home or Edit Work, respectively.

Android the Navigator

The real point of having a map and finding a location is to get somewhere else. In the old days, you'd use your eyeballs to plot your route or rely upon directions from an acquaintance or friendly local, or you'd struggle with a folding map you bought at a gas station.

Things are better now. With your Android mobile gizmo, you tap the DIRECTIONS button and you're on your way. In case you need specifics, here are the steps involved:

1. Tap the DIRECTIONS button on a location's card.

You see a screen similar to the one shown in Figure 12-6. A card lists your starting and ending points. Methods of travel are listed with estimated arrival times. The route is plotted in blue on the screen, with alternative routes shown in gray.

Mode of transportation

Starting point

Destination

Starting location

Navigation

FIGURE 12-6: Planning a journey.

Route card

Destination

2. Set a starting point.

The starting point is listed as Your Location, which is the Android's current location. You can type in another location or use the Home or Work shortcuts, as described in the preceding section.

TIP

If the starting point and destination are reversed, tap the Action Overflow and choose Reverse.

3. **Choose a mode of transportation.**

The available options vary, depending on your location. In Figure 12-6, the items are (from left to right) Car, Public Transportation, On Foot, Ride Services, and Bicycle. Ride-services options, including Uber and Lyft, appear only where available.

4. **If necessary, tap the alternative route.**

Alternative routes appear in gray (refer to Figure 12-6). You might choose that route because it's faster, avoids slow traffic, skirts toll roads, and so on. You can also drag the route lines on the map to set your own directions.

Tap the ROUTE INFO button to view turn-by-turn directions and potentially see Street View previews as you go.

Tap the START button to begin voice navigation, where the Android narrates directions as you proceed to your destination.

WARNING

>> The map shows your route, highlighted as a blue line on the screen. Detailed directions also appear. Traffic jams show up as red, with slow traffic as yellow.

>> While the Android is navigating, the Navigation notification appears on the status bar, as shown in the margin. This icon is important to note because:

>> Turn-by-turn navigation consumes a lot of battery power, especially when the device's screen is on and the voice is narrating.

>> I recommend plugging the Android into the car's 12-volt power receptacle while navigating. Car adapters are available at any electronics or phone store.

>> If you tire of hearing the voice, tap the Speaker icon on the screen and set the Mute option.

>> The Speaker Mute icon is shown in the margin.

>> Navigation works best on Android phones and LTE tablets. Wi-Fi-only tablets can't use navigation without Internet access. Even with a saved or offline map, navigation isn't possible.

>> To exit from Navigation mode, tap the Close icon on the screen.

>> The START button appears as PREVIEW whenever you get directions not involving your current location.

REMEMBER

>> The Android stays in Navigation mode until you exit. A navigation notification can be seen atop the touchscreen while you're in Navigation mode.

Chapter **13**

Everyone Say "Cheese!"

I have no idea why people say "Cheese" when they get their pictures taken. Supposedly, it's to make them smile. Even in other countries, where the native word for *cheese* can't possibly influence the face's smile muscles, they still say their word for *cheese* whenever a picture is taken. Apparently, it's a tradition that's present everywhere.

Alexander Graham Bell never thought anyone would utter "cheese" around his invention. That's because the notion of integrating the phone with a camera didn't occur until just before his death. Folks had to wait decades for a phone to take a picture. You don't have to wait any time at all.

The Android's Camera

A camera snob gladly tells you, "No true camera has a ringtone." You know what? He's correct: Phones and tablets don't make the best cameras. Regardless, the mobile device has completely replaced cameras for all but professionals and serious amateur photographers.

Getting to know your device's camera

Cameras have improved over the years, getting better with each new generation of Android mobile devices. Some phones and tablets take pretty good pictures. That's great. The problem, however, is that not every Android has the same type of camera. Worse: Each manufacturer has its own Camera app.

The Camera app is the app you use to control the Android's cameras. Details are offered throughout this chapter. In the big picture, taking still shots or recording video works pretty much the same. All Camera apps offer similar, basic controls. You can get the job done — take that photo or capture that movie — with a minimum of stress.

>> All Androids feature front and rear cameras, though some low-end models may lack one or the other.

>> Both cameras can take still shots and record video.

>> The front camera isn't as powerful as the rear camera. Therefore, the rear camera is considered the primary camera.

>> If your pictures or videos appear blurry, ensure that the camera lens on the back of the device isn't dirty. Or you may have neglected to remove the plastic cover from the rear camera when you first set up your Android.

>> Only the rear camera features an LED flash, which can be used for both still shots and video. Some tablets may lack the LED flash.

>> The Camera app sets the camera's resolution as well as the zoom and whether the flash activates. It's also used to switch between front and rear cameras.

>> You can take as many pictures or record as much video as you like, as long as the device doesn't run out of space.

Using basic camera controls

Here are some pointers that apply to all Android Camera apps:

>> Use your phone or tablet in either landscape or portrait orientation while taking a still shot. Don't worry either way: The image is always saved with the proper side up.

>> I strongly recommend that you record video in horizontal orientation only. This presentation appears more natural.

>> The device's touchscreen serves as the viewfinder; what you see on the screen is exactly what appears in the final photo or video.

>> Tap the screen to focus on a specific object. You'll see a focus ring or square that confirms how the camera lens is focusing. Not every device's camera hardware can focus; the front-facing camera features a fixed focus.

>> Spread your fingers on the screen to zoom in.

>> Pinch your fingers on the screen to zoom out.

>> Some Androids let you use the volume key to zoom in or out, though, more commonly, pressing the volume key snaps a still shot — even while recording video.

REMEMBER

>> Hold the Android steady! I recommend using two hands for taking a still shot *and* shooting video.

TECHNICAL
STUFF

>> All Androids store pictures and videos in the DCIM/Camera folder. Still images are saved in the JPEG or PNG file format; video is stored in the MPEG-4 format. If your Android offers removable storage, the Camera app automatically saves images and videos to that media, though you might be able to control this feature. See the later section "Choosing the storage device."

The Google Camera App

It would be impossible to cover every Android Camera app variation, so in this book I focus on the Google Camera app, which is included in stock Android. Your device's Camera app may be identical or subtly different.

>> The big difference between Camera apps is how the controls are presented on the screen.

>> The Camera app's basic shooting modes are Still Shot and Video. Additional modes include Panorama, Photo Sphere, and others. Some manufacturers include a host of different shooting modes.

>> Like many apps, the Camera app takes over the entire touchscreen. To summon the navigation icons (Back, Home, Recent), tap the screen or swipe top-to-bottom.

>> Other apps beyond the Camera app can access the device's cameras. Sometimes these apps use their own camera apps, but mostly they use the device's default Camera app to capture stills and videos.

>> The Google Camera app is available for any Android gizmo from the Google Play Store. See Chapter 17 for details on Google Play.

Capturing a still shot

Taking a still image requires only two steps. First, ensure that the Camera app is in Single-Shot mode. Second, tap the Shutter icon to snap the photo.

 In Still Shot mode, you see the Shutter icon appear, as shown in Figure 13-1. If you don't, tap the Still Shot icon, similar to what's shown in the margin. If that icon doesn't appear on an Android tablet, swipe the screen left-to-right.

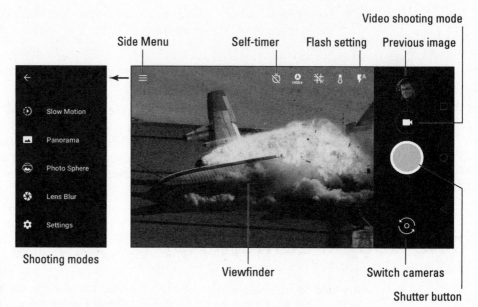

FIGURE 13-1: Still Shot shooting mode.

Frame the image. Pinch or spread your fingers on the touchscreen to zoom out or in, respectively.

Tap the shutter icon to snap the photo, as illustrated in Figure 13-1. You may hear a shutter noise. The picture is saved and appears as a thumbnail preview in the Camera app, also illustrated in Figure 13-1.

REMEMBER

>> Set the resolution before you shoot. See the later section "Setting resolution and quality."

>> To review the image, tap the Thumbnail icon. You can swipe through the various shots you've taken. Tap the Back navigation icon to return to the Camera app.

>> If you don't like a photo you just took, tap the Thumbnail icon to view the image. Tap the Delete (trash) icon to remove it.

Recording video

To record video, switch the Camera app to Video mode. For the Google Camera app, tap the Video shooting mode icon, illustrated in Figure 13-1. On the Android tablet version of the app, swipe the screen right-to-left. Other Camera apps may show a Video icon, similar to what appears in the margin. Some Samsung devices may show both the Shutter button and Video Record icon at the same time, so switching modes isn't necessary.

To start recording the video, tap the Record icon, shown in the margin. The elapsed time, and maybe even storage consumed, appears on the touchscreen as video is being recorded. The Record icon changes to a Stop icon, as illustrated in Figure 13-2.

Video time   Snap still shot.

Stop recording.

FIGURE 13-2:
Recording video.

Viewfinder   Pause recording.

To snap a still shot while recording, tap the icon, illustrated in Figure 13-2. You might also try pressing the device's volume key.

The Pause icon is used to halt recording but not end the video. After you tap this icon again (which changes to look like the Record icon), recording resumes.

Tap the Stop icon to end the recording.

REMEMBER

>> Video quality is set before you shoot. See the later section "Setting resolution and quality."

>> On some Samsung devices, the Record icon appears on the Camera app's main screen. Tap the icon to start recording.

>> Hold the Android horizontally when you record video. Keep your hands steady. Do not zoom in and out!

Exploring other shooting modes

Beyond still shots and video, all Camera apps offer additional shooting modes. The variety depends on the app, though common modes include Panorama and Photo Sphere.

In the Google Camera app, tap the Side Menu icon to view the various shooting modes, as illustrated in Figure 13-1. Choose one to set that mode for the Camera app. You may see directions on the screen, offering details on how to operate the specific mode.

>> See Chapter 25 for specifics on shooting a panorama.

>> The Google Camera app automatically exits a special shooting mode, returning to Still Shot or Video mode. Other Camera apps, however, may require that you reselect Still Shot or Video mode.

>> Beyond shooting modes, some Camera apps may feature special-effects modes or other enhancements to basic image-taking duties.

Camera Settings and Options

The variety of Camera app controls can be overwhelming, especially when a manufacturer gussies up the app with multiple shooting modes. Among the many choices, a few settings and options are common and necessary to properly use the Android's camera.

Switching cameras

You can do more with the device's front-facing camera than take those infamous selfie shots. Exactly what more you can do, I can't think of right now, but the point is how to switch between front and rear cameras while using the Camera app.

The Switch Cameras icon is usually found right on the main Camera app screen, as illustrated in Figure 13-1. Variations on these icons appear in Figure 13-3. If you don't see such an icon on your gizmo's Camera app screen, tap the Action Overflow or Settings icon to look for the Switch Cameras icon or action.

FIGURE 13-3:
Switch Camera
icons.

Another technique is popular on some Samsung Camera apps: Swipe the screen from top to bottom. This action flips the display as you switch between front and rear cameras.

Tap the same icon again to switch back to the rear camera. The icon may change its appearance, but you should find it in the same location on the Camera app's screen.

Setting the flash

Camera apps feature three flash settings, illustrated in Table 13-1. The current setting appears on the screen (refer to Figure 13-1), or you may have to access the flash setting control to view the current setting.

TABLE 13-1   Flash Settings

Setting	Icon	When the Flash Activates
Auto		During low-light situations but not when it's bright out
On		Always
Off		Never, even in low-light situations

To change or check the flash setting in the Google Camera app, tap the current flash icon shown on the app's main screen. Tap that icon to cycle through and set the camera's flash setting. In other Camera apps, tap a Settings icon to access the Flash setting.

TIP

>> Not all Android tablets feature a flash on the rear camera.

>> No Android — phone or tablet — features a flash for the front camera, which is a good thing.

>> A good time to turn on the flash is when taking pictures of people or objects in front of something bright, such as Aunt Ellen showing off her prized peach cobbler in front of a burning munitions factory.

>> A "flash" setting is also available for shooting video in low-light situations. In that case, the flash LED is on the entire time. This setting is made similarly to setting the flash, though the options are only On and Off. It must be set before you shoot video, and yes, it devours a lot of battery power.

Using the self-timer

One common feature found on just about every Camera app is the self-timer. Though it's normally disabled, you can enable this feature to delay taking a still image for a given number of seconds after you tap the Single-Shot shutter icon. Supposedly, that gives you enough time to run in front of the device so that you, too, can be in the photo.

To activate the self-timer feature, tap its icon. In the Google Camera app, tap the Self-Timer icon to choose no delay, a 3-second delay, or a 10-second delay. The icon you tap is one of those shown in Table 13-2.

TABLE 13-2   **Self-Timer Icon Round-Up**

Icon	Setting
⏱	The self-timer function is disabled; photos snap instantly.
3s	The photo snaps 3 seconds after you tap the icon.
10s	The photo snaps 10 seconds after you tap the icon.

After you set the timer, tap the Still Shot shutter icon. Then dash out in front of the Android so that it can take your photo.

Oh: You probably want to prop up the phone or tablet on something stable, or even get a mobile device tripod mount. The self-timer is pretty useless without one.

REMEMBER

Turn off the self-timer when you want to return to standard Still Shot mode or when you're exhausted from running around.

Setting resolution and quality

You don't always have to set the highest resolution or top quality for images and videos. Especially when you're shooting for the web or uploading pictures to Facebook, top quality is a waste of storage space and upload time because the image is shown on a relatively low-resolution computer monitor or mobile device screen.

As you may suspect, setting the image resolution or video quality is done differently by the various Camera apps. No matter what, you must set the new still-shot resolution or video quality *before* you shoot.

In the Google Camera app, follow these steps to access still-shot resolution and video quality settings:

1. **Tap the Side Menu icon to display the Camera app's shooting modes.**

   Refer to Figure 13-1.

2. **Tap the Settings icon.**

   You see categories for Photo and Video. Each has an item for the front and rear cameras.

3. **Choose a mode and a camera.**

   For example, tap Back Camera Photo Resolution to set the still-image resolution for the rear camera. Or tap Front Camera Video Resolution to set the video quality for the device's front-facing camera.

4. **Choose a resolution or video-quality setting from the list.**

   Options are presented in aspect ratio and megapixels for still images; video-quality settings are rated in HD, UHD, and vertical pixel resolution.

   Options are presented in aspect ratio and in megapixels.

For other Camera apps, tap the Action Overflow or Settings icon to view resolution and video quality options. The item may be titled Resolution, Picture Size, or Photo Size. You may also have to switch cameras (back or front) before setting the resolution.

>> The *aspect ratio* expresses the relationship between an image's horizontal and vertical dimensions. The 4:3 aspect ratio is 4 units wide by 3 units tall. The typical widescreen computer monitor has an aspect ratio of 16:9.

>> A picture's *resolution* describes how many pixels, or dots, are in the image. The more dots, the better the image looks when enlarged.

>> The video quality settings HD and SD refer to High Definition and Standard Definition, respectively. Qualities shown with a "p" value indicate vertical resolution, with higher values for higher quality.

>> The resolution and video quality choices are more limited on the front-facing camera because it's not as sophisticated as the rear camera.

TIP

>> If I were taking a photo for uploading to Facebook, I'd choose a medium resolution. For recording vacation photos or family events, higher resolution is best because you can print the images and get better quality.

>> Choose lower video quality for recordings you want to share on social media or send as an email or text message attachment.

TECHNICAL
STUFF

>> *Megapixel* is a measurement of the amount of information stored in an image. One megapixel is approximately 1 million pixels, or individual dots that comprise an image. It's often abbreviated MP.

Checking the location tag feature

The Camera app not only takes pictures but also keeps track of where you're located when you take the picture — if you've activated that option. The feature is called *location tag*, *geotag*, or *GPS-tag*.

To confirm the location tag setting in the Google Camera app, follow these steps:

1. **Tap the Side Menu icon and choose Settings.**

2. **Enable or disable the Save Location feature.**

   The master control by the Save Location item is either on or off, reflecting the location tag setting.

For some Samsung Camera apps, obey these steps to check the location tag feature:

1. **Tap the Settings icon on the main Camera app screen.**

2. **Set the master control by the Location Tags item on or off.**

Other Camera apps may require you to jump through various hoops, such as wade through an Action Overflow or Settings icon menu, to locate the Location Tag item.

» Deactivating the location tag feature doesn't remove that information from photos you've already taken.

» The location tab information is stored in the picture itself. This means that other devices, apps, and computer programs can read the GPS information to determine where the image was taken.

» See Chapter 14 for information on reviewing a photograph's location.

Choosing the storage device

When you place a microSD card in your Android's removable storage slot, the Camera app automatically chooses that location to save new photos and videos. To confirm or change this setting, follow these steps in the device's Camera app:

1. **Tap the Action Overflow or Settings icon.**

2. **Choose Storage Location.**

   The option may have a name that's different from, but similar to, Storage Location.

3. **Set the location.**

   The options are Device or Internal for internal storage; or microSD, Memory Card, or External Storage for the removable media card.

REMEMBER

Not every phone or tablet features removable storage.

- » **Adding a new album**

- » **Finding an image's location**

- » **Checking out your pictures online**

- » **Editing images**

- » **Cropping and rotating pictures**

- » **Publishing a video on YouTube**

- » **Sharing images and videos**

Chapter **14**

Your Digital Photo Album

Those photos you snap on your Android must go somewhere. The nerds know about folders and files, so they're happy. But how can mere mortal users access their wealth of images and videos? The answer is to open the digital photo album app. It lets you review, manage, edit, and share your visual treasures.

The Photos App

The stock Android app for viewing pictures and videos is called Photos. It's the natural companion to the Camera app, covered in Chapter 13. To start the app, tap its launcher, which may be lurking on the Home screen in the Google folder or, like all apps, found on the Apps drawer.

> » Not only does the Photos app let you look at pictures and watch videos, but you can also manage that media, edit, and share your visual creations online.

TECHNICAL STUFF

>> The traditional Android photo-management/album app is Gallery. You may still find the Gallery app on your device, though this chapter is specific to the Photos app.

Viewing pics and vids

The Photos app organizes your photos and videos in multiple and confusing ways. The Photos screen, shown in the center in Figure 14-1, lists items by date. Tap the Photos icon at the bottom of the screen to ensure that this view is active.

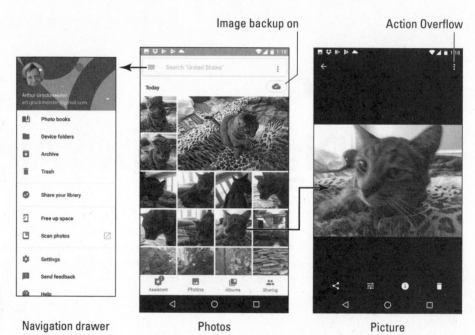

Image backup on   Action Overflow

FIGURE 14-1: Image organization in the Photos app.

Navigation drawer   Photos   Picture

To see any photo albums, tap the Albums icon at the bottom of the screen. Albums are closely associated with your online photos accessed from your Google account, covered elsewhere in this chapter, so these could be albums created on another device that uses your same Google account.

To view an image, tap its thumbnail. You see the image appear full-screen, as shown on the right in Figure 14-1. Swipe the screen left or right to browse your images.

Videos thumbnails feature a Play icon, shown in the margin. Tap that icon to view the video. As the video is playing, tap the screen again to view onscreen controls.

>> While you're viewing an image or a video full-screen, the navigation icons may disappear. Tap the screen to view them.

>> Tap the Back navigation icon to return to an album after viewing an image or a video.

Creating an album

If you prefer to organize your images by album instead of by date, follow these steps in the Photos app:

1. **View an image that you want to add to an album.**

   Ensure that the image is shown full-screen, as shown on the far right in Figure 14-1.

2. **Tap Action Overflow.**

3. **Choose Add to Album.**

4. **Tap Album on the Create New card.**

   The image is added to a new, empty album.

5. **Type a name for the album.**

6. **Tap the Done icon to create the album and add the first image.**

To add more images to the album, repeat these steps, but choose the specific album in Step 4.

TIP

To add a swath of images to an album, long-press the first one. Continue tapping images to build up a group. Tap the Add (plus) icon, and choose the album from the list.

REMEMBER

To switch between Album and Photos mode, tap the proper icon at the bottom of the Photos app's main screen, as shown in Figure 14-1.

Starting a slideshow

The Photos app can display a slideshow of your images, but without the darkened room and sheet hanging over the mantle. To view a slideshow, follow these steps:

1. **View an image full-screen.**

2. **Tap the Action Overflow icon.**

3. **Choose Slideshow.**

   Images from that particular album or date appear one after the other on the screen.

Tap the Back navigation icon to exit the slideshow.

 Slideshows don't have to remain in your Android. If a nearby HDMI TV or monitor features a Chromecast dongle, tap the Chromecast icon, as shown in the margin. Choose a specific Chromecast gizmo from the list to view the slideshow on a larger screen. See Chapter 19 for more details on using Chromecast to stream media.

Finding a picture's location

In addition to snapping a picture, your Android's camera records the specific spot on Planet Earth where the picture was taken. This feature, often called a *location tag*, is covered in Chapter 13. To exploit its efforts and view the map information, heed these steps:

1. **View the image in the Photos app.**

 2. **Tap the Info icon.**

   The icon is found below the image, as shown in the margin. On some Androids, you may have to tap Action Overflow and choose Details.

The Info card that's displayed shows details about when, how, and where the image was taken. Map information, if available, appears on the card.

Refer to Chapter 13 for directions on disabling the location tag feature.

Visiting Google Photos online

The Photos app is linked to your Android account, and your device's photos have a home on the Internet called Google Photos. To visit that site on a computer, go to photos.google.com and sign in to your Google account.

Your Android automatically synchronizes your photos and videos with Google Photos, so don't be surprised when you see them online. The process is called *image backup,* and you can disable it, if you prefer. Follow these steps:

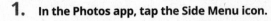

1. **In the Photos app, tap the Side Menu icon.**

2. **On the navigation drawer, choose Settings.**

3. **Choose Back Up & Sync.**

4. **Slide the master control by Back Up & Sync to the Off position.**

Changing this setting doesn't affect any images already backed up to Google Photos, though any new images you snap or videos you record are no longer shared online. Likewise, you won't be able to access those images from other Android devices.

Edit and Manage Images

The best tool for image editing is a computer amply equipped with photo editing software, such as Photoshop or a similar program that's also referred to as "Photoshop" because the term is pretty much generic. Regardless, you can use the Photos app to perform some minor image surgery.

Editing an image

To enter image editing mode in the Photos app, view the image you want to modify and tap the Controls icon, shown in the margin. (This icon is actually the old Settings icon from the 1954 version of the Android operating system, Apple Pie.) The icon might also appear as a pencil. If you don't see the editing icon, tap the screen and it shows up.

Editing tools are presented in three categories, shown at the bottom of the screen and illustrated in Figure 14-2: preset effects, image settings, and crop/rotate.

>> The Preset Effects item presents a scrolling palette (swipe left-to-right) of options, each of which adjusts the image's tonal qualities.

>> The Image Settings control lets you adjust specific aspects of an image: light, color, and pop. A chevron by the Light and Color items provides more detailed image control.

>> The crop and rotate functions are covered in the later sections "Cropping an image" and "Rotating a picture."

Cancel edits.   Save changes.   Action Overflow

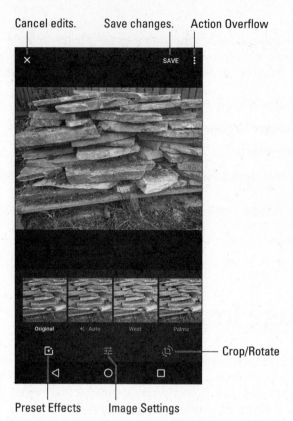

FIGURE 14-2:
Image editing in
the Photos app.

Crop/Rotate

Preset Effects   Image Settings

Tap the SAVE button when you're done editing. This action replaces the image with your edited copy.

Tap the CANCEL button to discard your edits. Tap the DISCARD button to confirm.

Un-editing an image

TIP

The changes you make are directly applied to the image; an original copy isn't retained. To remove any previously applied edits, crops, or rotation effects, view the image in the Photos app and follow these steps:

1. **Tap the Edit icon to edit the image.**

2. **Tap the Action Overflow.**

3. **Choose Undo Edits.**

4. **Tap the SAVE button.**

The original image is restored.

Cropping an image

To *crop* an image is to snip away parts you don't want or need, similar to taking a pair of scissors to a photograph of you and your old girlfriend, though the process is far less cathartic. To crop an image, obey these steps:

1. **View the image in the Photos app.**

2. **Tap the Edit icon.**

3. **Tap the Crop / Rotate icon.**

   The icon is shown in the margin. The screen changes as illustrated in Figure 14-3. The tools that are presented crop and rotate the image.

4. **Drag any of the four corners to crop the image.**

   As you drag, portions of the image are removed.

   You can also drag the image within the cropping rectangle to modify the crop action.

   TIP

Cropping corners   Cropping rectangle

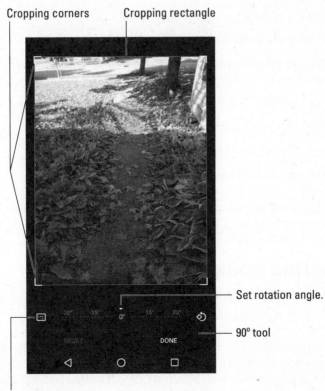

Set rotation angle.

90° tool

FIGURE 14-3:
Rotating and
cropping an
image.

Set aspect ratio.

5. **Tap the DONE button.**

   The image is cropped. You can continue to edit, or tap the SAVE button to make the changes permanent.

If you're unhappy with the changes after tapping the DONE button, tap the Action Overflow and choose Undo Edits.

Use the Aspect Ratio icon (refer to Figure 14-3) to adjust the cropping box for the image to a new presentation, such as square, or widescreen.

Rotating a picture

Showing someone else an image on a mobile device can be frustrating, especially when the image is a vertical picture that refuses to fill the screen when the Android is in vertical orientation. To fix this issue, rotate the image in the Photos app. Follow these steps:

1. **Display the cockeyed image.**

2. **Tap the Edit icon.**

3. **Choose the Crop / Rotate tool.**

4. **Tap the 90° icon to rotate the image in 90-degree increments, or drag the sliders to set a specific angle.**

   Refer to Figure 14-3 for the location of these controls on the editing screen.

5. **Tap the DONE button to save the changes.**

   You can continue editing.

6. **Tap the SAVE button to make the changes permanent.**

Rotating an image to a specific angle also crops the image. This step is necessary to maintain the image's aspect ratio.

Deleting images and videos

It's entirely possible, and often desirable, to remove unwanted, embarrassing, or questionably legal images and videos from the Photos app.

To banish something to the bit dumpster, tap the Delete (trash) icon on the screen when viewing an image or a video. It's not really gone; no, it's moved to the Trash album. You might even see a MOVE TO TRASH button after you tap the Delete icon.

>> If you don't see the Delete icon, the item cannot be deleted. It's most likely a copy pulled in from a web photo-sharing service or a social networking site.

>> To view the Trash album, tap the Side Menu icon and choose Trash from the navigation drawer.

>> Items held in the Trash album are automatically deleted after 60 days. To hasten the departure, long-press items in the Trash album and then tap the Delete icon atop the screen.

Set Your Pictures and Videos Free

Keeping your precious moments and memories in your phone or tablet is an elegant solution to the problem of lugging around photo albums. But when you want to show your pictures to the widest possible audience, you need a bigger stage. That stage is the Internet, and you have many ways to send and save your pictures.

Posting a video to YouTube

The best way to share a video is to upload it to YouTube. As a Google account holder, you also have a YouTube channel. It's like Channel 6 on the TV when you grew up, but far fewer people watch it. That's because you've not yet populated your channel with videos. Start now:

1. **Ensure that the Wi-Fi connection is activated.**

The best way to upload a video is to turn on the Wi-Fi connection, which (unlike the mobile cellular network) doesn't incur data surcharges. In fact, if you opt to use the 4G LTE network for uploading a YouTube video, you see an onscreen reminder about data surcharges.

2. **Open the Photos app.**

3. **View the video you want to upload.**

You do not need to play the video; just have it on the screen.

4. **Tap the Share icon.**

If you don't see the Share icon, tap the screen and it shows up.

5. **Choose YouTube from the list of sharing apps.**

The Add Details card appears. You may first see a tutorial on trimming the video, which is the next step.

6. **Trim the video, if necessary, resetting the starting and ending points.**

   If you opt to trim, drag the starting and ending points for the video left or right. As you drag, the video is scrubbed, allowing you to preview the start and end points.

7. **Type the video's title.**

8. **Set other options.**

   Type a description, set the privacy level, add descriptive tags, and so on.

9. **Tap the Send icon.**

   You return to the Photos app, and the video is uploaded. It continues to upload even if the screen locks itself out of boredom or you do other things on the Android.

When the upload has completed, a YouTube notification appears. When the video has finished processing on the Internet and is available for viewing, you receive a Gmail message, announcing your video's publication.

To view your video, open the YouTube app. See Chapter 16 for details.

Sharing images with other apps

Just about every app wants to get in on the sharing bit, especially when it comes to pictures and videos. The key is to view an item full-screen in the Photos app and then tap the Share icon, as shown in the margin. Choose an app to share the image or video, and that item is instantly sent to that app.

What happens next?

That depends on the app. For Facebook, Twitter, and other social networking apps, the item is attached to a new post. For Gmail, the item becomes an attachment. Other apps treat images and videos in a similar manner, somehow incorporating the item(s) into whatever wonderful thing that app does. The key is to look for that Share icon.

Chapter **15**

Music, Music, Music

Your Android's amazing arsenal of features includes the capability to play music. I'm not referring to the sounds made by the touchtone dialing on an Android phone, either. Playing music is why your phone or tablet is an all-in-one device. It's the reason why you don't need to lug around that Edison wax cylinder phonograph everywhere you go.

The Hits Just Keep On Comin'

Your Android mobile gizmo is ready to entertain you with music whenever you want to hear it. Plug in some headphones, summon the music-playing app, and choose tunes to match your mood.

The stock Android music-playing app is called Play Music. It might be in addition to other musical apps on your phone or tablet, including streaming music apps covered later in this chapter. For now, the topic is Play Music.

>> As with other Google services, music on your Android that's available through the Play Music app is also available online at play.google.com/music.

>> See the later section "Music from the Stream" for details on streaming music apps.

TIP

» When you first open the Play Music app, it bombards you with options to subscribe to Google's music service. The service offers instant music for a monthly fee, though subscribing to the service is optional. Merrily skip the prompts, if you desire.

Browsing your music library

The music stored on your Android, or available through your Google account on the cloud, is referred to as your *music library*. To view its collection of tunes, heed these directions:

1. **Open the Play Music app.**

2. **Tap the Side Menu icon to display the navigation drawer.**

The Side Menu icon is found in the upper left corner of the screen, similar to what's shown in the margin. If you see a left-pointing arrow instead, tap that arrow until the Side Menu icon appears.

3. **Choose Music Library.**

Figure 15-1 shows the Play Music app with the Music Library screen selected. Your music is organized by categories, shown as tabs on the screen. Tap a tab to switch categories, or swipe the screen left or right to browse your music library.

The categories make your music easier to find, because you don't always remember song, artist, or album names. The Genres category is for those times when you're in the mood for a certain type of music but don't know, or don't mind, who recorded it.

» Is your music library empty or pathetically small? Get some music! See the later section "Add Some Music to Your Life."

» Songs and albums feature the Action Overflow icon, shown in the margin. Use that icon to view actions associated with the album or artist.

» Two types of album artwork are used by the Play Music app. For purchased music, or music recognized by the app, original album artwork appears. Otherwise, the app shows a generic album cover.

» When the Play Music app doesn't recognize an artist, it uses the title Unknown Artist. This happens with music you copy manually to your device, but it can also apply to audio recordings you make.

Play Music notification

Chromecast

Categories

Action Overflow

Current song

Navigation drawer

FIGURE 15-1:
The Play Music
app, Albums
category.

Playing a tune

When you've found the proper tune to enhance your mood, play it! Tap on a song to play that song. Tap on an album to view songs in the album, or tap the album's large Play button, shown in the margin, to listen to the entire album.

While a song plays, controls appear at the bottom of the screen, as shown at the bottom of Figure 15-1. Tap that strip to view the song full-screen, as shown in Figure 15-2.

After the song is over, the next song in the list plays. The order depends on how you start the song. For example, if you start a song from Album view, all songs in that album play in the order listed.

The next song doesn't play when you have the SHUFFLE button activated (refer to Figure 15-2). In that case, the Play Music app randomly chooses another song from the same list. Who knows which one is next?

The next song also might not play when you have the Repeat option on: The three repeat settings, along with the shuffle settings, are illustrated in Table 15-1. To change settings, tap the SHUFFLE button or Repeat icon.

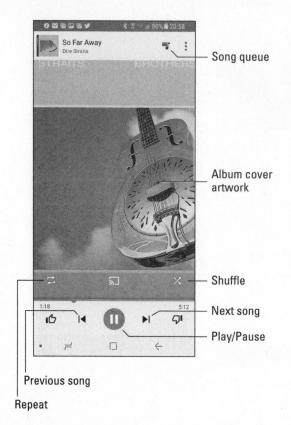

Song queue

Album cover artwork

Shuffle

Next song

Play/Pause

Previous song

FIGURE 15-2:
A song is playing.

Repeat

TABLE 15-1 **Shuffle and Repeat Icons**

Icon	Setting	What Happens When You Touch the Icon
	Shuffle Is Off	Songs play one after the other.
	Shuffle Is On	Songs are played in random order.
	Repeat Is Off	Songs don't repeat.
	Repeat Current Song	The same song plays over and over.
	Repeat All Songs	All songs in the list play over and over.

While the song plays, you're free to do anything else on your Android. In fact, the song continues to play even when the device is locked. Choose the Play Music notification, shown in the margin, to return to the Play Music app, or you can use the controls on the notification drawer or on the lock screen to pause the song or skip to the next or previous tune.

To stop the song from playing, tap the Pause icon, labeled in Figure 15-2.

>> On an Android phone, an incoming call stops the music. You hear the ringtone and can answer the call. After the call ends, you must restart the song: Visit the Play Music app and tap the Play icon.

>> Use the device's volume key to set the volume.

>> Music on your Android is streamed from the cloud. That means music won't play when an Internet connection is unavailable.

>> You can download music to play it without an Internet connection. Directions are offered in Chapter 17.

>> Use the Play Music app's Search command to locate tunes in your music library. Tap the Search icon, illustrated in the margin. Type a song name, artist, or album, and then tap the Search icon on the onscreen keyboard. Choose the song you want to hear from the list that's displayed.

>> When a song is playing or paused, its album artwork might appear as the lock screen wallpaper. Don't let the change alarm you.

Queuing up the next song

It's fun to randomly listen to your music library, plucking out tunes like a mad DJ. Oftentimes, however, you don't have the patience to wait for the current song to finish before choosing the next tune. The solution is to add songs to the queue. Follow these steps:

1. **Browse your music library for the next song (or album) you want to play.**

2. **Tap the song's Action Overflow.**

3. **Choose Add to Queue.**

   The Play Music app adds the song to the list of tunes to play next.

Songs are added to the queue in the order you tap them. That is, unless you choose instead the Play Next command in Step 3, in which case the tune is inserted at the top of the queue.

To review the queue, tap the Song Queue icon, shown in the margin as well as in Figure 14-2. Songs in the queue play in order, from the top down. To change the order, drag a song card up or down. To remove a song from the queue, swipe its card left or right.

TIP

If you like your queue, consider making a playlist of those same songs. See the section "Saving the song queue as a playlist," later in this chapter.

Being the life of the party

You need to do four things to make your Android the soul of your next shindig or soirée:

» Connect it to external speakers.

» Use the Shuffle setting.

» Set the Repeat option.

» Provide plenty of drinks and snacks.

To connect external speakers, you need an audio cable with a mini-headphone connector for the Android's headphone jack and an audio jack that matches the output device. Look for any store where the employees wear name tags. But why use wires?

The Play Music app lets you cast music to a Chromecast device. Tap the Chromecast icon, shown in the margin as well as in Figure 15-1, to send your tunes to an HDTV or another Chromecast-connected output gizmo. See Chapter 19 for specific directions.

Enjoy your party, and please drink responsibly.

Add Some Music to Your Life

Consider yourself fortunate if your Android came with music preinstalled. Otherwise, your music library may be a little light. To pack it full of those songs you adore, you have two options:

» Buy lots of music from the Google Play Store, which is what Google wants you to do.

» Borrow music from your computer, which Google also wants you to do, just not as enthusiastically as the first option.

For information on buying music at Google Play, see Chapter 17. You can also sub-scribe to its streaming service, which will annoy you again if you haven't yet accepted the monthly subscription offer.

The options for borrowing music from your computer are covered in the next two sections.

Getting music into the Google cloud

Realizing that you probably don't want to buy yet another copy of the Beatles' White Album, you can take songs from your computer and transfer them to your Google Play Music library on the Internet. Here's how that procedure works:

1. **On your computer, locate the music you want to upload to your Play Music library.**

    You can open a music jukebox program, such as Windows Media Player or whatever they're using on Windows 10. I don't know. I don't keep up. Or just have a folder window open that lists the songs you want to copy.

2. **Open the computer's web browser and visit** `music.google.com`

3. **If necessary, sign in to your Google/Gmail account.**

    You see a copy of your Play Music library, including your playlists and any recent songs. You can even listen to your music right there on the computer, but no: You have music to upload.

    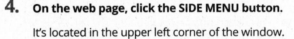

4. **On the web page, click the SIDE MENU button.**

    It's located in the upper left corner of the window.

5. **From the list of commands, choose Upload Music.**

6. **Drag music into the web browser window.**

Google may prompt you to configure your PC, so work through those gyrations described on the web page. Follow the steps presented on the web page to con-tinue uploading music.

>> You can repeat these steps to upload tens of thousands of songs. The limit was once 25,000, but I believe Google increased that number recently.

>> The songs you upload are available to your Android, just like any other songs in your music library.

Synchronizing music directly

Some Androids may let you copy music directly from the computer. The trick is to convince the computer's music jukebox program into believing that the Android is a portable MP3 player — which it is, of course. Then you transfer or "sync" the music, adding a copy of the computer's music to the Android.

The process works like this:

1. **Connect the Android to your PC.**

   See Chapter 19 for details on making the connection.

2. **On the PC, choose Windows Media Player from the AutoPlay notification or dialog box.**

   If the AutoPlay dialog box doesn't appear, start the Windows Media Player program: Press the Windows key on the PC's keyboard and type **windows media player**. Choose that program from the list of search results.

3. **Choose your Android in the Sync List, as illustrated in Figure 15-3.**

   Click the Next Device link until you see your gizmo, such as the Samsung phone shown in Figure 15-3.

4. **Drag music to the Sync area.**

   Drag an individual song or an entire album.

5. **Click the Start Sync button to transfer the music from the PC to your phone or tablet.**

   The Start Sync button may be located atop the list, as shown in Figure 15-3, or it might be found at the bottom.

6. **Close Windows Media Player and disconnect the Android.**

This technique may not work for all devices. In some cases, the manufacturer may configure the device to ignore Windows Media Player music files. Therefore, I recommend trying to sync a few tunes to start, and then confirm that they appear in the Play Music app.

WARNING

>> You cannot use iTunes to synchronize music with Android devices. Duh.

>> Your Android can store only so much music! Don't be overzealous when copying your tunes. In Windows Media Player (refer to Figure 15-3), a capacity-thermometer thing shows you how much storage space is used and how much is available on your Android. Pay heed to the indicator!

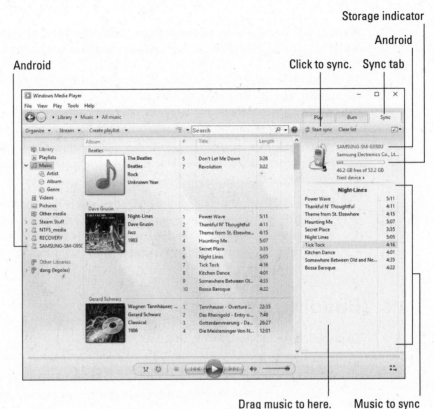

Storage indicator

Android

Click to sync. Sync tab

Android

Drag music to here.   Music to sync

FIGURE 15-3:
Windows Media
Player meets
Android phone.

Organize Your Music

The Play Music app categorizes your music by album, artist, song, and so forth, but unless you have only one album and enjoy all the songs on it, this organization probably won't do. To better manage your music, you can create playlists. That way, you can hear the music you want to hear, in the order you want, for whatever mood hits you.

Reviewing your playlists

To view available playlists, heed these directions:

1. **Tap the Side Menu icon in the Play Music app.**

2. **Choose Music Library.**

3. **Tap the Playlists tab on the Music Library screen.**

Playlists are displayed in two categories: Auto Playlists, generated by the Play Music app, and All Playlists, which contains playlists you created.

To see which songs are in a playlist, tap the playlist's card. To play the songs in the playlist, tap the first song in the list.

TIP

>> The Auto playlists include: Thumbs Up, which lists songs you've liked by tapping the Thumbs Up icon; Last Added, which includes songs recently purchased or added; and Free and Purchased, which includes just about everything.

>> Use the playlist feature to organize music that isn't otherwise organized in the Play Music app. For example, if you're like me, you probably have a lot of songs labeled *Unknown*. A quick way to remedy this situation is to name a playlist after the artist and then add those "unknown" songs to the playlist.

Building a playlist

To create a new playlist, follow these steps:

1. **Locate some music you want to add to a playlist.**

   Ensure that you're viewing a song or an album; otherwise, the Action Overflow icon and Add to Playlist action don't show up.

2. **Tap the Action Overflow icon by the album or song.**

3. **Choose Add to Playlist.**

4. **Tap NEW PLAYLIST.**

5. **Type a name for the playlist.**

   You got down this naming thing: Make it short and descriptive. *Elvis*. That's a playlist.

6. **Tap the CREATE PLAYLIST button.**

The song or album is added to the new playlist.

To add songs to an existing playlist, choose the playlist in Step 4.

>> Alas, you cannot long-press a song and start collecting a group of them to add to a playlist all at once. This feature might be included with a future release of the Play Music app, but for now you must add songs individually to each playlist.

» You can have tons of playlists and stick as many songs into them as you like. Adding songs to a playlist doesn't noticeably affect the device's storage capacity.

» To remove a song from a playlist, open the playlist and tap the Action Overflow by the song and choose Remove from Playlist.

» Removing a song from a playlist doesn't delete the song from the music library; see the later section "Removing unwanted music."

» Songs in a playlist can be rearranged: While viewing the playlist, use the tab on the far left end of a song's card to drag that song up or down in the list.

» To delete a playlist, tap the Action Overflow icon in the Playlist icon's lower right corner. Choose Delete and tap OK to confirm.

Saving the song queue as a playlist

If you've created a song queue, and it's a memorable one, consider saving that queue as a playlist that you can listen to over and over. Obey these directions:

1. **Tap the Song Queue icon to view the song queue.**

   Refer to the earlier section "Queuing up the next song" for details on the song queue.

2. **Tap the Action Overflow icon next to the Song Queue icon.**

3. **Choose Save Queue.**

4. **Tap the NEW PLAYLIST button.**

   Or you can add the songs to an existing playlist: Select the playlist from the Add to Playlist card.

5. **Fill in the New Playlist card with a name and description.**

6. **Tap the CREATE PLAYLIST button.**

The songs in the current queue now dwell in their own playlist, or have been added to an existing playlist. The queue's songs are now available from that playlist.

Removing unwanted music

To remove a song or an album, tap its Action Overflow icon. Choose the Delete action. Tap the OK button to remove the song. Bye-bye, music.

TIP

I don't recommend removing music. The music on your Android is actually stored in the cloud, on Google's Play Music service. Therefore, removing the music doesn't affect the device's storage. So, unless you totally despise the song or artist, removing the music has no effect.

>> Music can be stored locally by downloading it to the phone or tablet, as described in the earlier section "Synchronizing music directly." Again, if you remove such music, it's gone for good.

>> You can also download music to the device for listening when an Internet connection isn't available. See Chapter 17.

Music from the Stream

Though they're not broadcast radio stations, some sources on the Internet — *Internet radio* sites — play music. These Internet radio apps are available from Google Play. Some free services that I can recommend are

>> Pandora Radio

>> Spotify

>> TuneIn Radio

These apps, as well as other, similar apps, are available for free. Paid versions might also be found on Google Play. The paid versions generally provide unlimited music with no advertising.

>> Google offers an unlimited music listening service. You can tap the item SUBSCRIBE NOW on the navigation drawer to sign up. The service is free for 30 days, and then a nominal fee, currently $9.99, is charged monthly.

>> It's best to listen to Internet radio when your phone or tablet is connected to the Internet via a Wi-Fi connection.

WARNING

>> Be wary of music subscription services offered through your Android's manufacturer or cellular provider. Their services aren't as long-lasting and well-supported as the others mentioned in this section.

TECHNICAL STUFF

>> Music provided over the Internet is referred to as *streaming*. That's because the music arrives on your Android as a continuous download from the source. Unlike music you download and save, streaming music is played as it comes in and isn't stored long-term.

Chapter **16**

Various and Sundry Apps

E ven given the variety of things your Android can do, you will find some limi-
tations. For example, you cannot use an Android phone as a yoga block. An
Android tablet makes a poor kitchen cutting board. And despite efforts by
European physicists, an Android mobile device simply cannot compete with the
Large Hadron Collider. Still, for more everyday purposes, I believe you'll find your
device more than up to the task.

Clock

The Clock app is your Android's chronometric app, featuring a timer, a stopwatch,
an alarm, and world clock functions. Of these activities, setting an alarm is quite
useful: In that mode, your gizmo becomes a nightstand companion — and, potentially, your early morning nemesis.

To set an alarm in the Clock app, follow these steps:

1. **Tap the Alarm icon or tab atop the Clock app's screen.**

   The four tabs in the stock Android Clock app are Alarms, World Clock, Timer, and Stopwatch.

2. **Tap the Add icon.**

   A card appears, which you use to set the alarm time, days, name, and so on.

3. **Fill in details about the alarm.**

   Set the alarm's time. Determine whether it repeats daily or only on certain days. Choose a ringtone. Ponder over any other settings, as shown on the card. The alarm name appears when the alarm triggers.

4. **Set the alarm.**

   Slide the alarm card's master control to the On position to ensure that the alarm signals at the appropriate time and schedule.

You can confirm that an alarm is set when you see the Alarm Set status icon atop the touchscreen, as shown in the margin.

When the alarm triggers, slide the Dismiss icon or press the volume key. Some alarms may feature a Snooze icon. Tap it to be annoyed again after a few minutes.

REMEMBER

>> Alarms must be set to activate.

>> Of all the apps that come with an Android phone or tablet, the Clock app is the one that manufacturers customize the most. Your device's Clock app, which might be called Alarm, has standard features, but may do things differently from what's described in this section.

>> Your Android keeps its clock accurate by accessing an Internet time server. You never have to set the time.

>> Information about a set alarm appears on the Clock app's screen and on the lock screen.

>> Unsetting an alarm doesn't delete the alarm. To remove an alarm, tap the alarm to select it and then tap the Delete (trash) icon.

>> To make the alarm sound on specific days of the week, use the Repeat option or check box. Choose the days of the week when you want the alarm to sound. Otherwise, the alarm sounds only when you set it.

>> The alarm doesn't work when you turn off the Android. The alarm may not sound when Do Not Disturb mode is active. The alarm does trigger when the touchscreen is locked.

>> For a larger time display, you can add the Clock widget to the Home screen. Refer to Chapter 20 for more information about widgets on the Home screen.

>> So tell me: Do alarms go off, or do they go on?

Calculator

The Calculator is perhaps the oldest of all traditional cell phone apps. It's probably also the least confusing and frustrating app to use.

The stock Android calculator app appears in Figure 16-1. The version you see on your device may look different, although the basic operation remains the same.

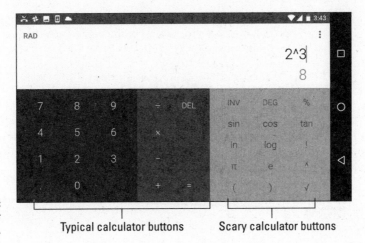

FIGURE 16-1: The Calculator app.

Typical calculator buttons   Scary calculator buttons

Tap various buttons on the Calculator app screen to input your equations. Parentheses buttons can help you determine which part of a long equation gets calculated first.

>> Also, consider changing the device's orientation to see more or fewer buttons; the image in Figure 16-1 uses horizontal orientation, which shows the calculator's more terrifying buttons.

TIP

>> Long-press the calculator's text (or results) to copy the results. This trick may not work in every Calculator app.

>> When a CLEAR ALL button isn't available, long press the DEL, CLR, or C button.

Calendar

Once upon a time, people toted around a bulky notebook thing called a *datebook*. It assisted primitive humans with keeping a schedule, reviewing appointments, and knowing where they needed to be and when. Such archaic technology is no longer necessary because your Android mobile gizmo comes with a Calendar app.

>> The Calendar app works with your Google account to keep track of your schedule and appointments. You can visit Google Calendar on the web at

```
calendar.google.com
```

TIP

>> Before you throw away your datebook, copy into the Calendar app some future appointments and info, such as birthdays and anniversaries.

Browsing your schedule

To check your schedule and browse events, open the Calendar app. You'll see upcoming dates shown in one of several views; Figure 16-2 shows the Calendar app's Month, Week, and Day views. Not shown are the 3 Day view or the Schedule view, which simply lists upcoming events.

To change views, tap the Side Menu icon and choose a view type from the navigation drawer.

Swipe the screen left or right to browse events. If you need to return to today's date, tap the Go to Today icon, illustrated in Figure 16-2. It may appear as a TODAY button in some calendar apps.

>> Schedule view might be called Agenda or Tasks in some versions of the Calendar app.

>> The 3 Day view is unavailable for Android tablets.

>> Some Calendar apps feature 4 Day view as well.

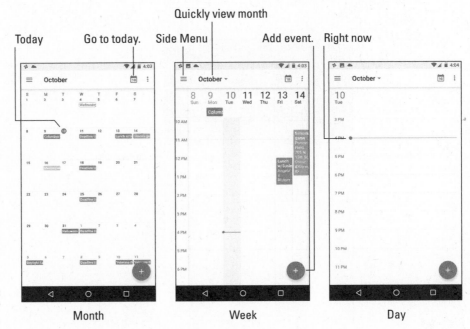

Quickly view month

Today   Go to today.   Side Menu   Add event.   Right now

Month   Week   Day

FIGURE 16-2:
The Calendar
app.

TIP

>> Use Month view to see an overview of what's going on, and use Week view or Day view to see your appointments.

>> I check Week view at the start of the week to remind me of what's coming up.

>> Swipe the screen left or right to change the view from month to month, week to week, or day to day.

>> Different colors flag your events, as shown in Figure 16-2. The colors can be assigned directly to events, or they represent a calendar category to which events are assigned. See the later section "Creating an event" for information on calendar categories.

Reviewing appointments

To see more detail about an event, tap it. When you're using Month view, tap the date to see a card displaying events for that day. Tap a specific event to see its details card, as shown in Figure 16-3.

The details you see depend on how much information was recorded when the event was created. Some events have only a minimum of information; others may have details, such as a location for the event, the time, and with whom you're meeting.

Close

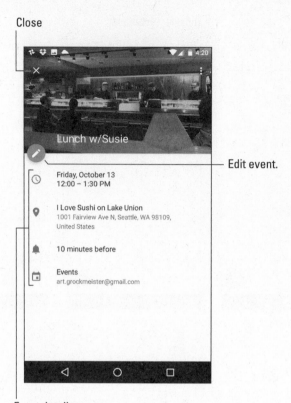

Edit event.

FIGURE 16-3:
Event details.

Event details

 Tap the Close icon to dismiss the event's details, or tap the Back navigation icon.

>> Birthdays and a few other events on the calendar may be pulled in from the Android's address book or from social networking apps. That probably explains why some events are listed twice — they're pulled in from two sources.

>> When the event's location is listed, you can tap that item to open the Maps app. See where the event is being held and get directions, as covered in Chapter 12.

TIP

>> The best way to review upcoming appointments is to choose Schedule view from the navigation drawer.

>> The Calendar widget also provides a useful way to see upcoming events directly on the Home screen. See Chapter 20 for information on applying widgets to the Home screen.

>> The Google app lists any immediate appointments or events. See the later section "Your Pal, Google."

Creating an event

The key to making the calendar work is to add events: appointments, things to do, meetings, or full-day events such as birthdays or root canal work. To create an event, follow these steps in the Calendar app:

1. **Go to the event's day, and tap the approximate time when the event starts.**

   It's easier to work in Week view when you want to tap a specific time on a specific day.

2. **Tap the square that appears on the calendar.**

   When you tap a specific time, a square appears with a teensy plus sign (+) in the center. That's secretly a NEW EVENT button.

   If you tap instead the Add icon at the bottom-right of the Calendar app screen (refer to Figure 16-2), choose Event to create a new event.

3. **Add information about the event.**

   The more information you supply, the more detailed the event, and the more you can do with it on your Android and on Google Calendar on the Internet. Here are some of the many items you can set when creating an event:

   - *Title:* The name of the event, person you're meeting, or a destination.

   - *Calendar Category:* Choose a specific calendar to help organize and color-code your events. The Calendar app, by default, chooses the Events calendar.

   - *Time/Duration:* If you followed Step 1 in this section, you don't have to set a starting time. Otherwise, specify the time the event starts and stops, or choose to set an all-day event such as a birthday or your mother-in-law's visit that was supposed to last for an hour.

   - *Location:* Type the location just as though you're searching for a location in the Maps app.

   - *Repeat:* Tap the MORE OPTIONS button if you don't see this item. Use the Repeat setting to configure events on a recurring schedule.

   - *Notification/Reminder:* Set an email, text message, or Calendar notification to signal an upcoming event.

4. **Tap the SAVE button to create the new event.**

The new event appears on the calendar, reminding you that you need to do something on such-and-such a day with what's-his-face.

When an event's date-and-time arrives, an event reminder notification appears, as shown in the margin. You might also receive a Gmail notification or text message, depending on how you chose to be reminded when the event was created. If your Android is handy, the event reminder appears on the lock screen.

>> Tap an existing event to modify it. Tap the Edit icon (refer to Figure 16-3) to make any changes.

TIP

>> For events that repeat twice a week or twice a month, create two repeating events. For example, when you have meetings on the first and third Mondays, you create two separate events: one for the first Monday and another for the third. Then have each event repeat monthly.

>> To remove an event, tap the event to bring up its card. Look for a DELETE button or icon. If you don't find it, tap the Action Overflow icon on the card and choose Delete. Tap OK to confirm. For a repeating event, choose whether to delete only the current event or all future events.

>> Setting an event's time zone is necessary only when the event takes place in another time zone or spans time zones, such as an airline flight. In that case, the Calendar app automatically adjusts the starting and stopping times for events depending on where you are.

WARNING

>> If you forget to set the time zone and you end up hopping around the world, your events are set according to the time zone in which they were created, not the local time.

>> Avoid using the Phone and Device categories for your events. Events in those categories appear on your Android, but aren't shared with your Google account.

TECHNICAL STUFF

>> Calendar categories are handy because they let you organize and color-code your events. They can be confusing because Google calls them *calendars.* I think of them more as *categories:* I have different calendars (categories) for my personal and work schedules, government duties, clubs, and so on.

>> New calendar categories are created on the web at `calendar.google.com`. You cannot create them from within the Calendar app.

eBook Reader

To sate your electronic-book-reading desires, your Android comes with Google's eBook reader app, Play Books. It offers you access to your eBook library, plus the multitudinous tomes available from the Google Play Store.

Open the Play Books app. You might find it in the Google folder on the Home screen or it might be in its own Play folder. The app is also located on the Apps drawer.

The first screen you see might instead be Google Play, trying to sell you books. If so, tap the Library button, shown in the margin (look at the bottom of the screen), to view your digital bookshelf.

Swipe the screen to browse and scroll through the library.

Tap a book's cover to open it. If you've opened the book previously, you're returned to the page you last read. Otherwise, you see the book's first page.

Figure 16-4 illustrates the basic book-reading operation in the Play Books app. You swipe the screen right-to-left to turn pages. You can also tap either the far left or right side of the screen to turn pages.

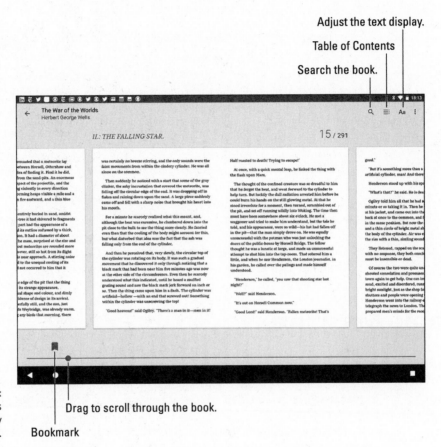

Adjust the text display.

Table of Contents

Search the book.

FIGURE 16-4:
eBook controls
in the Play
Books app.

Drag to scroll through the book.

Bookmark

TIP

The Play Books app works in both vertical and horizontal orientations. To lock the screen orientation, choose Settings from the navigation drawer and choose the Auto-Rotate Screen item. Select how you want the screen to present itself while you use the Play Books app.

>> If you don't see a book in the library, tap the Action Overflow icon and choose Refresh.

>> Books in your Play Books library are stored on the Internet and available to read only when an Internet connection is active. It's possible to keep a book

on your Android by downloading it to the device. Refer to Chapter 17 for details on downloading books.

» To remove a book from the library, tap the Action Overflow icon on the book's cover and then choose the Delete from Library command. Tap the DELETE button to confirm.

» If the onscreen controls (refer to Figure 16-4) disappear to make the text easier to read, tap the screen to see the controls again.

» Tap the *Aa* icon to display a menu of options for adjusting the text on the screen and the brightness.

» eBooks lack indexes. That's because the text layout on digital pages changes based on the book's presentation. Therefore, use the Search command (refer to Figure 16-4) to look for items in the text.

» A copy of your eBook library is available on the Play Books website:

```
play.google.com/books
```

» Refer to Chapter 17 for information on obtaining books from Google Play.

» If you have a Kindle device, you can obtain the Amazon Kindle app for your Android. Use the app to access books you've purchased for the Kindle, or as a supplement to Google Play Books.

Game Machine

For all its seriousness and technology, one of the best uses of an Android mobile device is to play games. I'm not talking about silly arcade games (though I admit that they're fun). No, I'm talking about some serious portable gaming.

To whet your appetite, your Android may have come with a small taste of what the device can do regarding gaming; look for preinstalled game apps on the Apps drawer. If you don't find any, choose from among the hordes available from Google Play, covered in Chapter 17.

» Game apps use the device's features, such as the touchscreen or the accelerometer, to control the action. It takes some getting used to, especially if you regularly play using a game console or PC, but it can be fun — and addicting.

» Look for the "lite" versions of games, which are free. If you like the game, you can fork over the pocket change that the full version costs.

TIP

Your Pal, Google

Your Android isn't out to control your life, but it's willing to help. Don't freak out! The device harbors no insidious intelligence, and the Robot Uprising is still years away. What I'm referring to is Google Assistant. It's an upgrade to the old Google Now app, which offers 2-way conversation and helpful information as you go about your daily routine.

The Google Assistant app is titled *Google.* You might also see a Google widget affixed to the Home screen. Tap that widget, open the Google app, or utter "Okay, Google" to access your Google Assistant. You may need to work through some setup, but eventually the assistant is ready to assist you.

Figure 16-5 illustrates a typical Google Assistant screen. The search box accepts onscreen keyboard input as well as voice input. You can also configure the app (it asks you) to use "Okay, Google" as the voice activation feature. Then you just speak your comments. See the nearby sidebar, "Barking orders to your Google Assistant," for suggestions.

Search for something.   Ask a question.

FIGURE 16-5:
Google Now is
ready for
business. Or play.

Cards

TIP

» Use your Google Assistant to search the Internet, just as you would use Google's main web page. In fact, don't even bother going to the web page on your Android; just say, "Okay, Google!"

» On some devices, the Google Assistant app dwells on the far left Home screen page.

» An update to the Google Assistant allows you to change the activation words to "Hey, Google."

» Samsung also offers its own personal assistant app, Bixby. On Samsung devices, Bixby occupies the far left Home screen page.

BARKING ORDERS TO YOUR GOOGLE ASSISTANT

You can speak simple search terms to your Google Assistant, such as "Find pictures of Megan Fox." Or you can give more complex orders, among them:

- Will it rain tomorrow?

- What time is it in Oslo?

- Set an alarm for 90 minutes from now.

- How many euros equal $25?

- Take a picture.

- What are the directions to Epcot?

- Where is the nearest Canadian restaurant?

- What's the score of the Lakers–Celtics game?

- What is the answer to life, the universe, and everything?

When asked such questions, your Google Assistant responds with a card and a verbal reply. When a verbal reply isn't available, you see Google search results.

Video Entertainment

Someday, it may be possible to watch "real" TV on your Android mobile device, but why bother? You'll find plenty of video apps available to sate your video watching desires. Two of the most common are YouTube and Play Movies. And when you tire of these apps, you can use the Camera app with the front-facing camera to pretend that you're the star of your own reality TV show.

>> Other video entertainment apps include the popular Netflix, Hulu, and HBO Now, and the list is pretty long. Many broadcast channels feature their own apps.

>> Also see Chapter 19 for information on screencasting video entertainment from your Android's diminutive screen to your humongous HDTV or monitor.

Watching YouTube

YouTube is the Internet phenomenon that proves that real life is indeed too boring and random for television. Or is it the other way around? Regardless, you can view the latest videos on YouTube — or contribute your own — by using the YouTube app.

 Tap the Search icon to find the video you want. Type the video's name, a topic, or any search terms to locate videos. Zillions of videos are available.

The YouTube app displays suggestions for any channels you're subscribed to, which allows you to follow favorite topics or YouTube content providers.

To view a video, touch its name or icon in the list.

>> Orient the device horizontally to view the video in a larger size.

>> Because you have a Google account, you also have a YouTube account. I recommend that you sign in to your YouTube account when using YouTube on your Android: Tap the Action Overflow icon and choose Sign In.

>> Refer to Chapter 14 for information on uploading a video you've recorded on your Android to your account on YouTube.

 >> To view the video in a larger size, rotate the phone or tablet to its horizontal orientation. You can also tap the Expand icon, shown in the margin, to view a video full-screen.

» Use the YouTube app to view YouTube videos, rather than use the web browser app to visit the YouTube website.

» Not all YouTube videos are available for viewing on mobile devices.

Buying and renting movies

You can use the Play Movies & TV app to watch videos you've rented or purchased from Google Play. Open the app and choose the video from the main screen. Items you've purchased show up in the app's library.

The actual renting or purchasing is done in the Google Play Store app. Check that app often for freebies and discounts. More details for renting and purchasing movies and shows are found in Chapter 17.

» Movies and shows rented from Google Play are available for viewing for up to 30 days after you pay the rental fee. After you start the movie, you can pause and watch it again and again during a 48-hour period.

» Not every film or TV show is available for purchase. Some are rentals only.

» Any videos you've purchased from Google Play are available on the Internet for anytime viewing. Visit:

```
play.google.com/movies
```

Chapter **17**

Google Play Shopping

The place to find more apps, books, music, and video for your Android mobile gizmo is a digital marketplace called Google Play. The good news is that most of the stuff available is free. Better news is that the non-free stuff is cheap. For little or no cost, you can add new apps and media to expand your Android's capabilities. Alas, I've still not located a Mow the Lawn or Do the Dishes app.

Welcome to the Store

It reads like the name of a kid's clothing store, but Google Play is where you obtain new apps, books, movies, music, and other goodies for your beloved Android gizmo. Google Play is the name of the store. And to keep you confused, the app is named Play Store.

TIP

» You obtain goodies from Google Play over an Internet connection. Therefore:

» I recommend that you connect your device to a Wi-Fi network when you shop at Google Play. Wi-Fi not only gives you speed but also helps avoid data surcharges. See Chapter 18 for details.

» The Play Store app is frequently updated, so its look may change from what you see in this chapter. Refer to my website for updated info and tips:

wambooli.com/help/android

» Google Play was once known as the Android Market, and you may still see it referred to as *the Market*. You may also see the term *Play Store* used, though that's the app's name and not the store's name.

Browsing Google Play

To access Google Play, open the Play Store app. You may find a Launcher icon on the Home screen; otherwise, it's located on the Apps screen.

After opening the Play Store app, you see the main screen, similar to what's shown in Figure 17-1. The store has two parts, one for Apps & Games and the other for entertainment: Movies, Music, Books.

If you don't see the main screen, similar to what's shown in Figure 17-1, tap the Side Menu icon (shown in the margin) to display the navigation drawer. Choose Apps & Games to view the apps portion of the store, or choose Movies, Music, Books to view entertainment and media items.

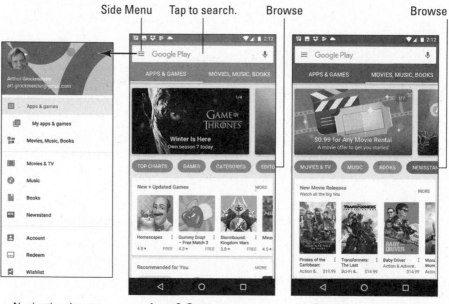

FIGURE 17-1:
Google Play.

Navigation drawer   Apps & Games screen   Entertainment screen

To browse, choose a top-level category. For Apps & Games, you can choose Top Charts, Games, and so on, as illustrated in Figure 17-1. For Entertainment, choose Movies & TV, Music, Books, and so on.

After you browse to a specific item, further categories help you browse. These categories include top sellers, new items, free items, and so on. Eventually, you see a list of suggestions, as shown on the left in Figure 17-2. Swipe the suggestions up and down to peruse the lot.

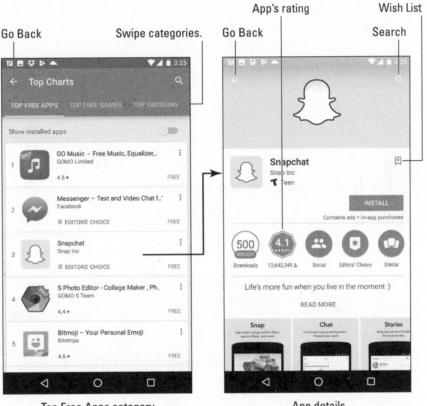

FIGURE 17-2:
App details.

Top Free Apps category   App details

To see more information about an item, tap its card. You see a more detailed description, screen shots, or perhaps a video preview, as shown on the right in Figure 17-2.

>> The first time you enter the Play Store app, or after the app is updated, you must accept the terms of service. To do so, tap the ACCEPT button. This process repeats whenever the app is updated.

>> You can be assured that all apps available on Google Play are compatible with your phone or tablet. You cannot download or buy an incompatible app.

 When you have an idea of what you want, tap the Search icon at the top of the Play Store screen. Type all or part of the item's title, such as an app name, an album name, a book author, or perhaps a description.

>> Pay attention to an app's ratings. Ratings are added by people who use the apps — people like you and me. A rating with more stars is better.

>> Another good indicator of an app's success is how many times it's been downloaded. Some apps have been downloaded more than 100 million times. That's a good sign.

 >> In Figure 17-2, the app's description (on the right) shows the INSTALL button. Other buttons that may appear on an app's description screen include OPEN, UPDATE, REFUND, and UNINSTALL. The OPEN button opens an already installed app. REFUND is available briefly after you purchase something. See Chapter 20 for information on using the UPDATE and UNINSTALL buttons.

TECHNICAL STUFF

Obtaining an item

After you locate an app, some music, or a book on Google Play, the next step is to download it. Apps are installed immediately, expanding what your Android can do. Entertainment items are made available at once, building your media library.

Good news: Most apps are free. Classic books are available at no cost. And, occasionally, Google offers movies and music *gratis.* Even the items you pay for don't cost that much. In fact, it seems odd to sit and stew over whether paying 99 cents for a game is "worth it."

 I recommend that you download a free app or book first, to familiarize yourself with the process. Then try downloading a paid item.

TIP

Free or not, the process of obtaining something from Google Play works pretty much the same. Follow these steps:

1. **If possible, activate the Wi-Fi connection to avoid incurring data overages.**

See Chapter 18 for information on connecting your Android device to a Wi-Fi network.

2. **Open the Play Store app.**

3. **Find the item you want and open its description.**

   All items in the Play Store app feature a description screen. It looks similar to the app description screen shown on the right in Figure 17-2.

4. **Tap the button to obtain the item.**

   A free app features an INSTALL button. A free book features an ADD TO LIBRARY button. For a free movie or TV show or music, look for a FREE button. You might also see a FREE TRIAL button for some items. In that case, tap the button to view or listen to a free sample of the media.

   Paid items feature a button that shows the price. For movies and TV shows, you may see a RENT or PURCHASE button. See the later section "Renting or purchasing videos."

5. **Tap the Accept button.**

   The Accept button appears on an access card. It describes which device features the app uses. The list isn't a warning, just a summary. Even so, you're prompted later as the app runs and it requests permission to access various items. See the later section "Granting permissions" as well as the nearby sidebar, "Avoiding Android viruses."

6. **For a paid item, tap the BUY button.**

   See the next section for further details on purchasing items at Google Play.

7. **Wait for the item to download or to become available.**

   Media items are available instantly. Apps are downloaded and installed, which may take some time. The Downloading notification appears as the app is transferred. Feel free to do something else while the app downloads. Installation takes place automatically.

8. **Tap the OPEN, PLAY, LISTEN, READ, or similar button to run the app, watch a video, listen to music, or read a book, respectively.**

Media arrives quickly to your Android because it's not actually copied to the device. Instead, the item is *streamed*, or made available only when you request it. This process works as long as an Internet connection is available. See the later section "Keeping stuff on the device" for information on accessing media when an Internet connection isn't available.

>> The Play Store app prompts you for payment information if you haven't yet supplied it. This prompt appears even for free items, in which case you can skip the prompt: Tap the SKIP button. You can always supply payment information the first time you actually buy something.

If you chose to do something else while an app downloads, refer to the status bar to check for the Successfully Installed notification, shown in the margin. Choose that notification to open the recently obtained app.

>> Apps you download are added to the Apps drawer, made available like any other app on your phone or tablet. Additionally, you may find the app on the Home screen. See Chapter 20 for information on removing the app's launcher from the Home screen, if that is your desire.

>> Media you've obtained from Google Play is accessed from a specific app: Play Music for music, Play Books for books, and Play Movies & TV for video. Other chapters in this part of the book offer details.

>> After obtaining an item from Google Play, you receive a Gmail message confirming your purchase, paid or free.

>> Be quick on that refund: For a purchased app, you have only two hours to get your money back. You know when the time limit is up because the REFUND button on the app's description screen changes to UNINSTALL.

>> See Chapter 20 for information on uninstalling apps.

>> Google Play doesn't currently offer refunds on purchased media, which includes music, books, and movies.

TIP

>> Keep an eye out for special offers from Google Play. These offer a great way to pick up some free songs, movies, and books.

Making a purchase at Google Play

To purchase an app or media on Google Play, you tap the BUY button. A card appears, listing your preferred payment method, such as the example shown in Figure 17-3.

In the figure, the album *Invisible Touch* is listed for $9.53. The chosen payment method is a Visa card ending in 6797. To use that payment method, follow these steps:

1. **Tap the BUY button.**

   For security, you're prompted to type your Google password.

2. **Type your Google password.**

WARNING

   I strongly recommend that you *do not* choose the option Never Ask Me Again. You want to be prompted every time for your password.

3. **Tap the CONFIRM button.**

AVOIDING ANDROID VIRUSES

How can you tell which apps are legitimate and which might be viruses or evil apps that do odd things to your Android? Well, you can't. In fact, most people can't, because your typical evil app doesn't advertise itself as such.

The key to knowing whether an app is malicious is to look at its access card: Open the app's description in the Play Store app and see which permissions it's requesting. For example, if a simple grocery list app wants to access the address book, it's suspect.

In the history of the Android operating system, only a handful of malicious apps have been distributed, and most of them were found only on devices used in Asia. Google routinely removes malicious apps from its inventory. It can also remotely uninstall malicious apps, so you're safe.

Avoid "hacker" apps, porn apps, and apps that use social engineering to make you do things that you wouldn't otherwise do, such as visit an unknown website to see racy pictures of politicians or celebrities.

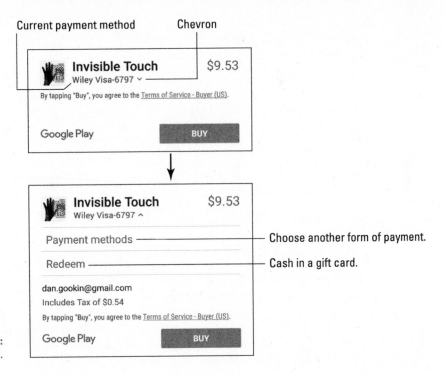

FIGURE 17-3:
The Buy card.

4. **Type the credit card's security code.**

   This is the CVC code, found on the back of the card.

5. **Tap the VERIFY button.**

   The app is downloaded or the media made available to your phone or tablet.

To select another payment method, tap the chevron by the current payment method, shown in Figure 17-3. The Buy card expands, as illustrated at the bottom of the figure. Choose Payment Methods, and select another credit or debit card or use your Google Play balance. After another payment method is selected, continue with Step 1 in this section.

If you've not yet set up a payment method, the chevron appears by the item's price, not below the item purchased (refer to Figure 17-3). Tap the chevron and then choose a payment method. You can add a credit or debit card, bill via your cellular provider, use PayPal, or redeem a Google Play gift card.

>> After you purchase the item, it's made available to your phone or tablet. Apps are downloaded and installed; music, eBooks, movies, and videos are available but not necessarily downloaded. See the later section "Keeping stuff on the device."

>> Information about any potential refund is provided in the Gmail message you receive after the purchase. Review the message for refund details.

>> Be quick on that refund: For a purchased app, you have only two hours to get your money back. You know when the time limit is up, because the REFUND button on the app's description screen changes to UNINSTALL.

>> The credit or debit cards listed in Google Play are those you've used before. Don't worry: Your information is safe.

>> All music sales are final. Don't blame me; I'm just writing down Google's current policy for music purchases.

Renting or purchasing videos

When it comes to movies and TV shows available at the Google Play Store, you have two options: Rent or purchase.

When you desire to rent a video, the rental is available to view for the next 30 days. Once you start watching, however, you have 48 hours to finish — you can also watch the video over and over again during that time span.

NEVER BUY ANYTHING TWICE

Any apps or media you obtain from Google Play are available to all your Android devices as well as from your Google account on the Internet. These items include apps, books, music, videos, and anything else.

For example, if you have an Android phone and a tablet, those apps you've paid for on the phone are available on the tablet: Open the Play Store and install the paid apps. You don't have to buy it twice. The same goes for purchased music, books, and videos. These media are available in the Play Music, Play Books, and Play Movies & TV apps on all your Android devices.

To review your purchased apps, display the Play Store app's navigation drawer (refer to the left side of Figure 17-1). Choose My Apps & Games. (If you don't see this item, first choose Apps & Games.) Tap the LIBRARY button to review apps, both paid and free, that you've previously obtained on your current device as well as other Android gizmos. You can install any item on the list without paying for it a second time.

Purchasing a video is more expensive than renting it, but you can view the movie or TV show at any time, on any Android device. You can also download the movie so that you can watch it even when an Internet connection isn't available, as described in the later section "Keeping stuff on the device."

One choice you must make when buying a movie is whether to purchase the SD or HD version. The SD version is cheaper and occupies less storage space (if you choose to download the movie). The HD version is more expensive, but it plays at high definition only on certain output devices. Obviously, when watching on an Android phone, the SD option is preferred.

>> See Chapter 16 for information on the Play Movies app.

>> Also see Chapter 19 for information on casting videos from your Android to a large-screen device, such as an HDTV.

Google Play Tricks

Like most people, you probably don't want to become a Google Play expert. You just want to get the app you want or music you desire and get on with your life. Yet more exists to the Play Store app than just obtaining new stuff.

Granting permissions

The Play Store is the guardian of all apps. One of its jobs is to remind you when an app requests to access some part of your phone or tablet. These requests are listed on the Accept card when you purchase the device, but you also see reminders as you use your gizmo, such as the card illustrated in Figure 17-4.

This *permissions card* describes which feature of your Android the app wants to access. It could be a hardware device, such as the microphone or camera, or it could be something else, such as the address book (shown in Figure 17-4), Google account, or another item.

Specific request

FIGURE 17-4:
A permissions
card.

If the request fits in with the app's purpose, such as Facebook wanting to peruse your contacts in Figure 17-4, tap the ALLOW button. Otherwise, tap DENY.

If you tap DENY, the app might quit, though sometimes the app continues to work but won't perform specific actions.

The purpose of the permissions card is to assure you that an app can't run amok or do anything else unless you say it's okay or "allowed." Seeing these cards is a normal part of using an app on the Android device. Further, once you tap ALLOW, you won't see the same permissions card again.

Using the wish list

While you dither over getting a paid app, music, book, or any other purchase at Google Play, consider adding it to your wish list: Tap the Wish List icon, shown in the margin (and refer to Figure 17-2).

To review your wish list, tap the Side Menu icon in the Play Store app (refer to Figure 17-1). Choose the Wish List item from the navigation drawer. You see all the items you've flagged. When you're ready to buy, choose one and buy it!

Sharing a Google Play item

Sometimes you love your Google Play purchase so much that you just can't contain your glee. When that happens, consider sharing the item. Obey these steps:

1. **Open the Play Store app.**

2. **Browse or search for the app, music, book, or other item you want to share.**

3. **When you find the item, tap it to view its description screen.**

4. **Tap the Share icon.**

   You may have to swipe down the screen to locate the Share icon, shown in the margin. After tapping the Share icon, you see a menu listing various apps.

5. **Choose an app.**

   For example, choose Gmail to send a Google Play link in an email message.

6. **Use the chosen app to share the link.**

   What happens next depends on which sharing method you've chosen.

The result of following these steps is that your friend receives a link. That person can tap the link on his Android device and be whisked instantly to the Google Play Store, where the item can be obtained.

Keeping stuff on the device

Books, music, movies, and TV shows you obtain from Google Play aren't copied to your Android. Instead, they're stored on the Internet. When you access the media, it's streamed into your device as needed. This setup works well, and it keeps your phone or tablet from running out of storage space, but the media is accessible only when an Internet connection is available.

When you plan on being away from an Internet connection, such as when you are flying across the country and are too cheap to pay for inflight Wi-Fi, you can download Play Store music, eBook, and movie purchases and save them on your device.

To see which media is on your Android and which isn't, open the Play Books, Play Music, or Play Movies & TV app. Follow these steps, which work identically in each app:

1. **Tap the Side Menu icon.**

2. **In the navigation drawer, set the master control by the Downloaded Only item to the On position.**

3. **Choose the Library item from the navigation drawer.**

   You see only those items stored on your Android. The rest of the library is held on the Internet.

To see the entire library again, repeat these steps but in Step 2 slide the master control to the Off position.

 Items downloaded to your Android's storage feature the On Device icon, similar to the one shown in the margin. The icon's color differs between Play Music, Play Books, and Play Movies & TV apps.

 To keep an item on the device's storage, look for the Download icon, shown in the margin. Tap that icon, and the item is fetched from the Internet and stored on your Android.

 Keeping media — specifically, movies — on your Android consumes a lot of storage space. That's okay for short trips and such, but for the long term, consider purging some of your downloaded media: Tap the On Device icon. Tap the REMOVE button to confirm.

WARNING

Removing a downloaded item from your Android doesn't delete it or prevent you from accessing it once an Internet connection is available. And you can download the movie, music, or book again and again without penalty or wrath.

Buying something remotely

Google Play is available as a website, accessible from a computer or laptop. The address is `play.google.com/store`.

This Google Play website features the same apps, videos, music, and books that are found in the Play Store app on your mobile device. Further, the website offers Android hardware for sale, including more phones and tablets, one for each limb.

A nifty trick you can pull on the Google Play website is to remotely install apps on your Android device: Visit the website and click the SIGN IN button if you haven't yet signed in. Use your Google account, the same one you use on your Android.

To remotely install an app from the Google Play website, click the INSTALL button. Then choose a device from the card presented. Only compatible gizmos appear in the list, so you can't remote-install the wrong app. Eventually, the app is transferred to the device, made available the next time you use your phone or tablet.

Don't worry! No one else can use the remote-install feature. Only when you use your Google (or Gmail) account to sign in is this service available.

4 Nuts and Bolts

Chapter **18**

It's a Wireless Life

Portable implies that something can be moved, but not how far or how easily. My first TV was a "portable" because it had a handle — never mind that it weighed about 25 pounds. *Cordless* implies a degree of freedom beyond portable, but still with limitations. *Wireless* is at the top of the mobility heap. It implies freedom from wires but is also lightweight and tiny.

Your phone or tablet is truly wireless, especially if it doesn't require a wire for charging. Even when you need that wire to charge the battery, after the process is complete, you can tote your Android anywhere and use it wire-free. You can access the mobile network, a Wi-Fi network, and wireless peripherals. Truly, it's a wireless life.

Android Wireless Networking

Your phone or tablet demands an Internet connection. To sate that desire, the device communicates with the information superhighway in a wireless way. Given how wireless networking has proliferated around the globe, finding an available connection is no longer a big deal. No, the issue is how to coax the Android into making this connection happen.

Using the mobile-data network

All Android phones and LTE tablets use the mobile-data network to connect to the Internet. For this service, you pay a handsome fee every month. (Phone users pay a second fee for the telephone service.) The fee grants your Android wireless Internet access anywhere the signal is available.

Several types of mobile-data network service are available:

> **4G LTE:** The fourth generation of wide-area data networks is the fastest and most popular network. Some providers may refer to this type of network as HSPA.

> **3G:** The third-generation mobile-data network is available in locations that don't offer 4G LTE service or where the signal is unavailable.

> **1X:** The original mobile-data network had no name, but is now called 1X. This service might be available when the two faster services have been obliterated by some moron with a backhoe.

Your phone or LTE tablet always uses the best network available. So, when the 4G LTE network is within reach, it's used for Internet communications. Otherwise, the 3G network is chosen, and then 1X networking in an act of last-ditch desperation.

> >> Your phone or LTE tablet shows a special icon that indicates the currently connected mobile-data network type.

> >> The H+ status icon represents the HSPA mobile-data network, which is equivalent to 4G LTE.

> >> The Signal Strength icon represents the mobile-data network connection, though on some phones it refers only to the telephone service.

> >> You can still place calls on an Android phone when the mobile-data network is unavailable.

TIP

> >> When both a mobile-data network and Wi-Fi are available, your Android uses Wi-Fi for all Internet access. To avoid data surcharges, I recommend connecting to and using a Wi-Fi network wherever possible.

> >> Non-LTE Android tablets use only the Wi-Fi connection for Internet access.

>> Your mobile-data network subscription has its limits — usually, a certain quantity of data you can use monthly for a flat fee. When you exceed that quantity, the costs can become prohibitive.

>> See Chapter 23 for information on how to avoid cellular data surcharges.

Understanding Wi-Fi

The mobile-data connection is nice, and it's available pretty much all over, but it costs you money every month. A better option for an Internet connection is Wi-Fi, the same wireless networking standard that computers use.

To make the Wi-Fi connection work requires two steps. First, you must activate the device's Wi-Fi radio. Second, connect to a specific wireless network. The next two sections cover these steps in detail.

Wi-Fi stands for *wireless fidelity*. It's brought to you by the numbers 802.11 and various letter suffixes too many to mention.

Activating Wi-Fi

Follow these steps to activate your Android's Wi-Fi radio under stock Android version 8.0, or *Oreo*:

1. **Open the Settings app.**
2. **Choose Network & Internet.**
3. **Ensure that the Wi-Fi master control is set to the On position.**

   To further access Wi-Fi settings, tap the Wi-Fi item.

On earlier versions of Android, choose Wi-Fi in Step 2.

For current Samsung devices, follow these steps:

1. **Open the Settings app.**
2. **Choose Connections.**
3. **Choose Wi-Fi.**

   The Wi-Fi master control is on the Wi-Fi screen.

To deactivate the Wi-Fi radio, which also disconnects the device from the Wi-Fi network, set the master control to the Off position.

» Use the Wi-Fi quick setting to instantly activate or deactivate the Wi-Fi connection. See Chapter 3 for information on accessing the quick settings.

» Once the Wi-Fi is activated, the phone or tablet automatically connects to any memorized Wi-Fi networks. See the later section "Managing connections."

» It's okay to keep the Wi-Fi radio on all the time. It is not a major drain on the battery.

» Using Wi-Fi to connect to the Internet doesn't incur data usage charges — unless you're accessing a metered network. See the later section "Configuring a metered Wi-Fi connection."

Connecting to a Wi-Fi network

After you've activated the Wi-Fi radio, your phone or tablet automatically connects to any known Wi-Fi network, one that you've accessed before where the password is still valid. If not, you can hunt down an available network. Follow these steps:

1. Visit the Wi-Fi screen in the Settings app.

Refer to the preceding section for details.

2. Select a wireless network from the list.

Available Wi-Fi networks appear on the screen, similar to what's shown in Figure 18-1. When no wireless networks are listed, you're out of luck regarding wireless access from your current location.

3. If prompted, type the network password.

Tap the Show Password check box so that you can see what you're typing; some of those network passwords can be long.

4. Tap the CONNECT button.

The network is connected immediately. If not, try the password again.

5. If prompted to remember the network, do so.

Some Androids may ask whether you want to automatically reconnect to the same Wi-Fi network in the future. I recommend choosing that option.

While your Android is connected to a wireless network, the Wi-Fi Connected status icon appears atop the touchscreen, looking like the one shown in the margin. This icon indicates that the Wi-Fi radio is on and the device is connected and communicating with a Wi-Fi network.

Available Wi-Fi networks

Wi-Fi master control

Wi-Fi

On

Imperial Wambooli
Connected

HP-Print-BE-Officejet Pro 8610

ByGraceAlone

513 Military

703Empire

ByGraceAlone-5G

CDA COTTAGE

Pinkertons - 2.4

Tritten Wi-Fi
Not in range

Underground Wambooli

703Empire

Password

☐ Show password

Advanced options

CANCEL   CONNECT

Wi-Fi network connection card

FIGURE 18-1:
Hunting down a
wireless network.

Signal strength

Password-protected
network

WARNING

>> Some public networks require that you sign in to their web pages after connecting. The sign-in page may appear automatically. If not, open the web browser app and visit any page to be redirected to the sign-in page. Heed the directions there to gain network access.

>> See the later section "Managing connections" for more information on dealing with an automatic connection where the password has changed.

>> A wireless network without a password is considered unsecure. The absence of security makes it easier for the Bad Guys to do bad-guy things on the network. My advice is to use the connection but avoid sending sensitive information over a nonsecured public network.

>> The Wi-Fi connection works best when you plan on being in a specific location for an extended time. That's because the Wi-Fi signal goes only so far. If you wander too far away, the signal — and your connection — are lost.

>> The Wi-Fi connection stays active until you wander out of range. To deliberately disconnect from a Wi-Fi network, turn off the device's Wi-Fi radio, as covered in the preceding section.

Connecting to a hidden Wi-Fi network

Some wireless networks don't broadcast their names, which adds security but also makes it more difficult to connect. In these cases, follow these steps to make the Wi-Fi network connection:

1. **Visit the Wi-Fi screen.**

Refer to the earlier section "Activating Wi-Fi."

2. **Tap the ADD NETWORK button.**

The button is found at the bottom of the list of available networks.

3. **Type the network name.**

The Network Name text box might be labeled SSID.

4. **Choose the security setting.**

How do you know which item to choose? Ask the person who gave you the network name. Otherwise, WPA/WPA2 PSK is the most common option.

If an option is available to reconnect automatically (Auto Reconnect), choose that setting.

5. **Tap the SAVE button or CONNECT button.**

6. **If prompted, type the network password.**

As with other Wi-Fi networks, after the connection is made, your Android memorizes the connection. You must toil through these steps only once.

SSID stands for Service Set Identifier. Any further information on this acronym would needlessly lower your blood pressure, so I'll leave it at that.

TECHNICAL
STUFF

Connecting to a WPS router

Many Wi-Fi routers feature WPS, which stands for Wi-Fi Protected Setup. It's a network authorization system that's simple and secure. If the wireless router features WPS, follow these steps to quickly connect your phone or tablet to the network:

TIP

1. **Visit the Wi-Fi screen in the Settings app.**

   Directions are found in the earlier section "Activating Wi-Fi."

2. **Tap the WPS connection button on the router.**

   The button either is labeled WPS or uses the WPS icon, shown in the margin.

3. **On your Android, choose Wi-Fi Preferences.**

   This item is found at the bottom of the list of available networks on the Wi-Fi screen. If not, tap Action Overflow and choose Advanced.

4. **Choose WPS Push Button or WPS Pin Entry, depending on how the router does its WPS thing.**

   If you don't see these items, expand the Advanced category.

   For a WPS push-button router, push the WPS button on the router.

   For a WPS PIN router, look on the device's touchscreen for a PIN. Type that number on the Wi-Fi router.

Connection with the router may take a few moments, so be patient. The good news is that, as on all Wi-Fi networks, once the initial connection is established, the connection is made again automatically in the future.

Configuring a metered Wi-Fi connection

Not every Wi-Fi network provides free, unlimited access. For example, a metered connection implies that the provider charges you per minute or per megabyte for Internet access. To help avoid surcharges, you can configure the connection as metered. Follow these steps:

1. **Connect to the network as you normally would.**

   Directions are found earlier in this chapter.

2. **Visit the Wi-Fi screen in the Settings app.**

   Refer to the earlier section "Activating Wi-Fi" for directions.

3. **Choose Data Usage.**

4. **Choose Network Restrictions.**

   This action might be titled Restrict Networks.

5. **Locate the current connection in the list and set its master control to the On position.**

When a Wi-Fi connection is set as metered, your phone or tablet monitors and restricts data access. You are warned when a large download or upload is attempted.

Managing connections

It's not necessary to review the list of memorized Wi-Fi networks — unless you need to change a network's password. In that case, you must direct the phone or tablet to forget the network so that you can reestablish the connection and set the new password.

To review the list of memorized networks, visit the Wi-Fi screen in the Settings app and choose Saved Networks. On Samsung devices, follow these steps:

1. **Open the Settings app.**

2. **Choose Connections.**

3. **Choose Wi-Fi.**

4. **Tap Action Overflow and choose Advanced.**

5. **Choose Manage Networks.**

   You see the list of saved Wi-Fi networks.

To forget a network, tap its entry. On the network's card, tap the FORGET button. The network is removed from the list. To input the new password, access the network again, as described earlier in this chapter. Set the new password, and you're good.

REMEMBER

Forgetting a network doesn't prevent you from connecting to that same network again. It means only that the connection isn't established automatically.

Share the Connection

Your Android phone or LTE tablet need not jealously guard its mobile-data connection. It's possible to share that Internet access in one of two ways. The first is to create a mobile *hotspot*, which allows any Wi-Fi–enabled gizmo to access the Internet via your device. The second is a direct connection between your Android and another device, which is a process called *tethering*.

Creating a mobile hotspot

To share your gizmo's mobile data connection with other Wi–Fi devices in the vicinity, heed these steps:

1. **Open the Settings app.**

2. **Choose Network & Internet.**

   If this category isn't available, skip to Step 3.

3. **Turn off the Wi-Fi radio.**

   Why create a Wi-Fi hotspot when one is already available?

4. **Connect your Android to a power source.**

   The mobile hotspot feature draws a lot of power.

5. **Choose Hotspot & Tethering.**

   This item might be located by tapping the More category in the Wireless & Networks section of the Settings app.

6. **Choose Set Up Wi-Fi Hotspot.**

7. **Fill in the card with the network and password, and then tap the SAVE button.**

   You can keep the default settings, which are unique to your phone or LTE tablet. Tap the Show Password box to view the preset password, or replace it with something less onerous to type.

8. **Set the Portable Wi-Fi Hotspot master control to the On position.**

   Your device may check with the cellular provider's mothership to affirm that your mobile-data subscription plan features the mobile hotspot feature. If so, the Wi-Fi net is up and running right away.

On a Samsung phone or tablet, follow these steps:

1. **Open the Settings app.**

2. **Choose Mobile Hotspot and Tethering.**

3. **Set the master control by Mobile Hotspot to the On position.**

   Your cellular subscription is checked. If you have access to this feature, Wi-Fi is automatically disabled.

4. **Once it's active, tap the Mobile Hotspot item again to set the password and other options.**

Once it's active, the Wi-Fi hotspot is accessed like any other network and by any device with a Wi-Fi radio.

To disable the mobile hotspot, repeat Steps 1 through 5, and then set the master control by Portable Wi-Fi Hotspot to the Off position.

TIP

>> Some devices feature a Mobile Hotspot app. If so, use it instead of following the steps in this section.

>> If your phone or LTE tablet is unable to create a mobile hotspot, check with your cellular provider about upgrading your plan to offer that feature. Or, instead, use the tethering feature covered in the next section.

>> While the mobile hotspot is active, a Hotspot Active status icon appears, similar to the one shown in the margin.

>> The range for the mobile hotspot is about 30 feet. Items such as walls and cement trucks can interfere with the signal, rendering it much shorter.

>> When you use the mobile hotspot, data usage fees apply. When a crowd of people are using the hotspot, a lot of data is consumed rather quickly.

REMEMBER

>> Don't forget to turn off the mobile hotspot when you're done using it.

Tethering the Internet connection

A more intimate way to share an Android's mobile data connection is to connect the device directly to a computer and activate the tethering feature. Follow these steps:

1. **Use the USB cable to connect the phone or LTE tablet to a computer or laptop.**

   I've had the best success with this operation when the computer is a PC running Windows.

2. **Open the Settings app.**

3. **Choose Network & Internet.**

4. **Choose Hotspot & Tethering.**

5. **Set the master control by the USB Tethering option to the On position.**

On a Samsung galactic gizmo, obey these steps to tether the cellular connection:

1. **Open the Settings app.**

2. **Choose Mobile Hotspot and Tethering.**

3. **Slide the master control by the USB Tethering option to the On position.**

The computer or laptop should instantly recognize the Android as a "modem" with Internet access. Further configuration may be required, which depends on the computer using the tethered connection. For example, you may have to accept the installation of new software in Windows.

To end the connection, repeat Steps 2 and 3 in this section, but disable tethering in Step 3. Then you can disconnect the USB cable.

>> While tethering is active, a Tethering status icon may appear, similar to what's shown in the margin.

REMEMBER

>> Sharing the mobile data connection incurs data usage charges against your cellular data plan. Mind your data usage when you're sharing a connection.

TECHNICAL STUFF

>> It's possible to use tethering on a Mac, but the driver required to recognize the Android as a modem is missing in OS X. You can obtain a free driver from the following site: joshuawise.com/horndis

The Bluetooth Connection

Bluetooth has nothing to do with the color blue or dental hygiene. No, it's a protocol for wirelessly connecting peripherals. Your Android happens to have a Bluetooth wireless radio in its belly, so it can pal around with Bluetooth devices, such as keyboards, headphones, and even your car.

Understanding Bluetooth

To make Bluetooth work, you need a Bluetooth peripheral, such as a wireless earpiece or keyboard. The goal is to pair that peripheral with your phone or tablet. The operation works like this:

1. **Turn on the Android's Bluetooth wireless radio.**

   The radio must be on for both your Android and the Bluetooth gizmo.

2. **Make the peripheral discoverable.**

   The peripheral must announce that it's available and willing to date other electronics in the vicinity.

3. **On your phone or tablet, choose the peripheral from the list of Bluetooth devices.**

4. **If required, confirm the connection.**

   For example, you may be asked to input or confirm a code. You might need to press a button on peripherals that have buttons.

5. **Use the Bluetooth peripheral.**

You can use the Bluetooth peripheral as much as you like. Turn off the Android. Turn off the peripheral. When you turn both on again, they're automatically reconnected.

 Bluetooth devices are branded with the Bluetooth logo, shown in the margin. It's your assurance that the gizmo works with other Bluetooth devices.

Activating Bluetooth

You must turn on the Android's Bluetooth radio before you can enjoy using any Bluetoothy peripherals. Heed these steps:

1. **Open the Settings app.**

2. **Choose Connected Devices.**

   On a Samsung device, this category is titled Connections. If you see neither the Connected Devices nor Connections categories, skip to Step 3.

3. **Choose Bluetooth.**

4. **Ensure that the Bluetooth master control is set to the On position.**

 When Bluetooth is on, the Bluetooth status icon appears. It uses the Bluetooth logo, shown in the margin.

To turn off Bluetooth, repeat the steps in this section but slide the master control to the Off position in Step 4.

 You'll also find a Bluetooth activation button in the quick settings, as foretold in Chapter 3.

TIP

Pairing with a Bluetooth peripheral

To make the Bluetooth connection between your Android and another gizmo, such as a Bluetooth keyboard, follow these steps:

1. Ensure that the Bluetooth radio is on.

Refer to the preceding section.

2. Make the Bluetooth peripheral discoverable.

Turn on the gizmo and ensure that its Bluetooth radio is on. Keep in mind that some Bluetooth peripherals have separate power and Bluetooth switches. If so, press the Bluetooth button or take whatever action is necessary to make the peripheral discoverable.

3. On the Android, open the Settings app to access the Bluetooth screen.

Refer to Steps 1 through 3 in the preceding section.

The Bluetooth screen shows already paired and available peripherals, similar to what's shown in Figure 18-2. If not, tap the SCAN button or tap Action Overflow and choose Refresh. If the Refresh icon is available, shown in the margin, tap it.

FIGURE 18-2: Finding Bluetooth gizmos.

4. **Choose the Bluetooth peripheral from the list.**

5. **If necessary, type the device's passcode or otherwise acknowledge the connection.**

   For example, with a Bluetooth keyboard, you may see on the touchscreen a prompt showing a series of numbers. Type those numbers on the keyboard, and then press the Enter or Return key. That action completes the pairing.

After the device is paired, you can begin using it.

Connected devices appear in the Bluetooth Settings window, under the heading Paired Devices, as shown in Figure 18-2.

>> Bluetooth peripherals stay paired whether you turn off the Android, turn off the device, or disable the Bluetooth radio. The connection is reestablished automatically when you turn things on again.

>> Yes, your car can be a Bluetooth peripheral, if it has a Bluetooth radio installed. That way, you can use an Android phone hands-free while driving. Pairing the phone with your car works differently for each vehicle, though the general steps proceed as outlined in this chapter. Do be aware that the car will not pair while it is in gear; stop the car to being the pairing process.

>> To stop using a device long-term, you unpair it. To do so, visit the Bluetooth screen (refer to Figure 18-2) and tap the Settings icon by the peripheral's entry. Tap the FORGET button or the Unpair action. The device is unpaired.

>> Unpair only the devices that you plan never to use again. Otherwise, turn off the Bluetooth device when you're done using it.

REMEMBER

>> The Bluetooth radio consumes a modicum of power. It's not a lot of juice for the Android, but could be for the peripheral. If you don't plan to use the peripheral for a while, turn it off.

Android, Beam It to Me

A handful of Android devices feature an NFC radio, where NFC stands for Near Field Communications and radio is a type of vegetable. NFC allows your Android to communicate wirelessly with other NFC devices. That connection is used for the quick transfer of information. The technology is called Android Beam.

To play with the Android Beam feature, ensure that the NFC radio has been activated. Follow these steps:

1. **Open the Settings app.**

2. **Choose Connected Devices.**

   On Samsung devices, choose Connections.

3. **Ensure that the NFC item is activated; set its master control to On.**

   This item might be titled NFC and Payment.

To make the Android Beam feature work, touch your Android to another NFC device, usually back-to-back. As long as both devices have an NFC radio and the Android Beam feature is active, they can share information.

On the sending device, tap the text *Tap to Beam.*

On the receiving device, choose the option to accept the item.

You can beam items such as a contact, map location, web page, YouTube video, or just about anything else you're viewing on the touchscreen.

>> Generally speaking, if an app features the Share icon, you can use Android Beam to share an item between two NFC gizmos.

>> NFC is not the same as the Nearby Devices feature found on some Samsung galactic gizmos. The Nearby Devices feature is used for sharing media over a network.

TECHNICAL STUFF

Chapter **19**

Connect, Share, and Store

No Android is an island. True, your gizmo is wireless, but it does need to communicate with other devices. You can use those avenues of communication to share photos, transfer files, print items, or beam movies and music to another technology gizmo. That way, your Android might think it's an island, but it's not a lonely one.

The USB Connection

The most direct way to connect an Android phone or tablet to a computer is to use a wire — specifically, the wire nestled at the core of a USB cable. Conveniently, such a cable came with the device. It has purposes beyond giving the battery a charge.

Configuring the USB connection

The USB connection is configured automatically whenever you connect your Android to a computer. Everything should work peachy. When it doesn't, you can try manually configuring the USB connection. Follow these steps:

1. **Swipe down the notifications drawer.**

2. **Choose the USB notification.**

The USB notification might appear at the bottom of the list, down where Android shows system activities. Figure 19-1 illustrates how the notification might appear. Some devices may show two notifications: one for charging the device and another for transferring files.

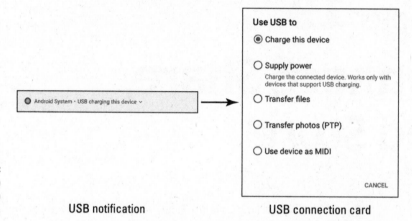

FIGURE 19-1:
USB connection configuration details.

USB notification   USB connection card

You might have to tap the USB connection notification twice before you see the connection card, shown on the right in Figure 19-1.

3. **Select a connection option.**

The USB connection card lists several options for configuring the USB connection:

Charge This Device: The USB connection charges the phone or tablet. This is the default action and no matter which option you select, the device charges while it's connected to the computer.

Transfer Files: This connection is ideal for transferring files. The computer views the Android as a thumb drive or similar storage device. Other titles for this setting are File Transfer, Transferring Media Files, MTP, and CTP.

Transfer Photos (PTP): In this mode, which might also be labeled Transferring Image, the computer sees the Android as a digital camera, which is ideal for importing photos and videos.

Use Device as MIDI: Choose this mode to use the Android as a keyboard or similar device for musical input.

At some point in the process, you may see a permissions card, asking for access to the device's storage. If so, tap the ALLOW button.

After configuring the connection, you may see a notification on the computer, prompting you to do something with the Android. Your choices are based on which option you choose in Step 4.

TIP

>> The titles of the items on the USB connection card differ from device to device. The functions, however, are the same.

>> If the computer fails to recognize the Android, select another USB connection option.

>> Often the connection fails because of the Android's security level. If so, unlock the device and then try the connection again.

>> If you're using a Macintosh, see the later section "Connecting to a Mac."

>> Some devices insist that you use their own file transfer software, which is annoying, but you must deal with it. For example, older Samsung gizmos require you to use the Samsung Kies utility to transfer files.

>> Your Android may not charge its battery when you connect the USB cable to a computer. To ensure that it charges, connect the device to a USB port on the computer's console as opposed to connecting to an external USB hub.

>> If your Android has a microSD card, its storage is also mounted to the computer, in addition to internal storage.

>> Androids with a USB 3.0 jack come with a USB 3.0 cable. You can still use the old-style, USB 2.0 micro-USB cables on such devices: Connect the micro-USB plug to the larger side of the USB 3.0 jack on the device's edge.

>> For data transfer to take place at top speeds over the USB 3.0 cable, you must connect the Android's USB 3.0 cable into the USB 3.0 port on a computer. These ports are color-coded blue.

>> Android mobile devices lack the capability to use the USB connection to add peripherals to the device, such as a mouse or thumb drive. Some devices may come with a multimedia dock that offers this connectivity, but it can't happen with a direct USB connection.

TECHNICAL STUFF

>> MTP stands for Media Transfer Protocol. This setting persuades the computer to believe that the Android is a portable media player or thumb drive. The PTP, or Picture Transfer Protocol, setting misleads the computer into thinking that the phone or tablet is a digital camera, which it is.

Connecting to a PC

Upon making the USB connection between an Android and a PC, a number of things happen. Don't let the flurry of activity frighten you.

You may see drivers install. That's normal Windows behavior when a new USB gizmo is connected.

You may also see a notification, such as the Windows 10 notification, shown in Figure 19-2. Click or tap that notification to see how to deal with the new connection.

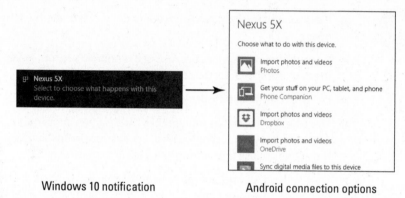

Windows 10 notification   Android connection options

FIGURE 19-2: Windows 10 connection choice.

For example, choose Open Devices to View Files (not shown in Figure 19-2, but it's on the scrolling list of options). This choice opens a File Explorer window listing files and folders on the Android. Or you can choose Import Photos and Videos to quickly copy over pictures and videos.

>> The choice you make from the list of items is retained by Windows 10. The next time you connect your Android, that option is chosen automatically.

>> Other versions of Windows also display a list of actions, though they appear in an AutoPlay dialog box. As with Windows 10, if you select a specific item, that choice is always selected for you when the Android is connected.

Connecting to a Mac

You need special software to deal with the Android-to-Macintosh connection. That's because the Mac doesn't natively recognize Android devices. Weird, huh? It's like Apple wants you to buy some other type of mobile gizmo. I just don't get it.

To help deal with the USB connection on a Mac, obtain the Android File Transfer program. On your Mac, download that program from this website:

```
android.com/filetransfer
```

Install the software. Run it. From that point on, whenever you connect your Android to the Mac, you see a special window appear, similar to the one shown in Figure 19-3. It lists the device's folders and files. Use that window for file management, as covered later in this chapter.

Internal storage

microSD card storage

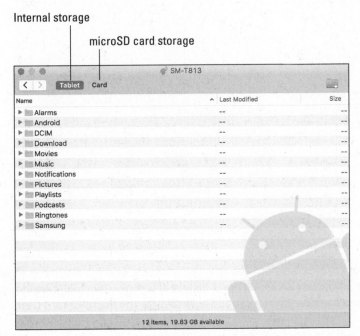

FIGURE 19-3:
The Android File
Transfer
program.

If the phone or tablet has a microSD card inserted, you see two buttons on the Android File Transfer program window: Tablet (or Phone) and Card, as shown earlier, in Figure 19-3. Click one or the other to see files and folders in that storage location.

Using the USB cable to transfer files

After you make the USB connection between your Android and a computer, you can transfer files back and forth. This is the traditional method of file exchange, though further, and mostly wireless, methods are offered in the later section "Files Back and Forth."

To best move files between the two devices, ensure that folder windows for both the Android and the computer are open. Figure 19-4 illustrates such an arrangement.

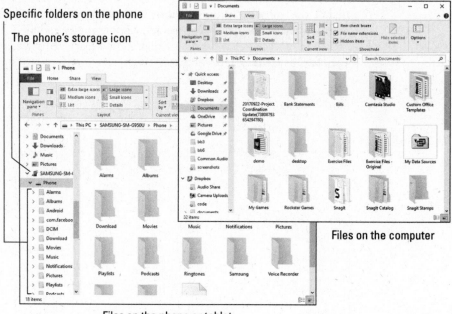

Specific folders on the phone

The phone's storage icon

Files on the computer

FIGURE 19-4:
Copying files
to an Android
phone or tablet.

Files on the phone or tablet

Drag file icons between the two windows to copy. And keep in mind that if your Android has a microSD card installed, it shows two folder windows on the desktop: one for internal storage and a second for the microSD card (removable) storage.

Here are some suggestions for transferring files:

TIP

>> Unless you know specifically where a file must go on the Android, copy the file to the Download folder.

>> Pictures and videos on the Android are stored in the DCIM/Camera folder.

>> Use the MTP configuration to import photos and videos over a USB cable. That way, photos and videos are copied from the Android into the proper folder or program on the PC.

>> If you're transferring music, use the Windows Media Player program, as described in Chapter 15.

When you're done copying files, close both windows and detach the phone or tablet, as described in the next section.

REMEMBER

Getting a file into your Android is no guarantee that you can do productive things with it. Specifically, don't expect to be able to read an eBook file you've copied from elsewhere.

TECHNICAL STUFF

A good understanding of basic file operations is necessary for successful file transfers between a computer and your gizmo. Knowing basic procedures such as copy, move, rename, and delete is an important part of the process. Understand how a folder works. The good news is that you don't need to manually calculate a 64-bit cyclical redundancy check on the data, nor do you need to know what a parity bit is.

Disconnecting from a computer

The process is cinchy: When you're done transferring files, music, or other media between a computer and your Android, close all programs and folders you have opened on the computer — specifically, those you've used to work with the device's storage. Then you can disconnect the USB cable. That's it.

WARNING

>> It's a Bad Idea to unplug the Android while you're transferring information or while a folder window is open on your computer. Doing so can damage the device's storage, rendering unreadable some of the information that's kept there. To be safe, close those programs and folder windows you've opened before disconnecting.

>> Unlike other external storage on the Macintosh, you don't need to eject the Android's storage when you're done accessing it. Quit the Android File Transfer program on the Mac, and then unplug the phone or tablet — or vice versa. The Mac doesn't get angry, either way.

Files Back and Forth

The USB connection provides only one way to transfer files between your Android and another device. Files can also flee to and fro on cloud storage, via the microSD card, to a printer, and to a screencasting gizmo. Set your files free!

Sharing files on the cloud

The wireless way to swap files between your Android and just about any other device is to use cloud storage. That's just fancy talk for storing files on the Internet.

Google's cloud storage is called Google Drive. Like other services, it's tied to your Google account. You have access to the storage on your Android or any other device that has Internet access. You sign in to your Google account — *boom!* — you see your files. (The boom is an exclamation; nothing actually explodes.)

On your Android, use the Drive app to browse and manage your Google Drive files. On the Internet, you access your Google Drive at `drive.google.com`. From that site, you can also obtain the Google Drive program for your computer, which I recommend installing.

To move an item from your Android to your computer via Google Drive, follow these steps:

1. **Locate the item you want to save or copy to your Google Drive storage.**

   It can be a picture, movie, web page, YouTube video, or just about anything.

2. **Tap the Share icon.**

   If you don't see the Share icon, the item you're viewing cannot be copied to Google Drive.

3. **Choose Save to Drive.**

   You may instead see the Google Drive icon, shown in the margin. Tap it.

   If you've not yet used Google Drive, you'll see a permissions card. Tap the ALLOW button.

4. **Fill in the Save to Drive card.**

   The card already lists the item's filename or title, but you can change it to something shorter or more descriptive. Also, because I'm organized, I tap the Folder action bar to choose a specific Google Drive folder on which to save the item. If you're unsure which folder is best, just use the main My Drive folder for now.

5. **Tap the SAVE button.**

The item is saved or copied to your Google Drive storage. In mere Internet moments, it's available to your computer or any other device where you can access your Google Drive storage.

>> To move a file from a computer to your Android, use Google Drive on your Computer: Copy the file to the Google Drive folder. When you next access the Drive app, open the proper folder and find the file.

>> Other cloud storage apps include the popular Dropbox, Microsoft's OneDrive, the Amazon Cloud, and more. Each of these works similarly to Google Drive; just choose the proper app in Step 3.

>> Cloud storage apps are free. You're provided with a modest amount of online storage at no charge. For a monthly subscription, you can obtain more storage.

Using the media card to transfer files

Welcome to the 1980s! Back before computers had networking capabilities, and long before Wi-Fi, files moved from one computer to another on removable storage media. The vehicle of choice was the floppy drive. The power came from your feet. The method was called "sneaker net." Everyone hated it.

If your Android features removable storage, you can use it to transfer files — just like those proto-geeks from the last century: Remove the microSD card from the phone or tablet and insert it into a computer. From that point, the computer can read the files just as they can be read from any media card.

>> Don't worry about getting the files on the microSD card. If your Android has one installed, it's the default location for photos and other media.

>> You can also use a file management app to move files to a microSD card while you use your Android. See the later section "Managing files."

>> Directions for removing the microSD card are found in the later section "Unmounting the microSD card."

>> To read the microSD media on your computer, you'll need a microSD card adapter. This hardware comes with the microSD card, so don't lose it!

Adding a print service

Another form of file transfer is printing: The output device is a printer, not storage on another computer. Your Android deftly handles the printer task. Just ensure two things:

>> A printer is available to the same wireless network that the Android uses. It doesn't need to be a wireless printer — just available to the network.

>> The proper print service software is installed.

Printing is covered in the next section. Before you can print, however, your Android must have a print service installed. It probably does, but follow these steps to confirm:

1. **Open the Settings app.**

2. **Choose Connected Devices and then choose Printing.**

For older versions of the Android operating system, choose the Printing item located on the main Settings app screen.

On some Samsung devices, choose Connections, More, Printing.

You see a list of print services. You're looking for a service that matches the printer models on the Wi-Fi network — for example, the HP Print Service Plugin, which lets you print to any networked HP printer.

3. **If a print service is listed as Off, choose it and switch its master control to the On position.**

   You're done. Otherwise, if you don't see a print service for the network printer, continue with Step 4.

4. **Choose Add Service or Download Plug-In.**

   The Play Store app opens, listing available printing services.

5. **Select and install a print service.**

   For example, if you use Canon printers, choose and install the Canon Print service. Refer to Chapter 17 for details on installing apps. You do not need to open the service after it's installed.

After the service is installed, or if you confirm that the service is available, you can print from your Android. Keep reading in the next section.

Printing

As long as your Android is connected to a Wi-Fi network with an available printer and that printer's printing service is installed, printing works like this:

1. **View the material you want to print.**

   You can print a web page, photo, map, or any number of items.

2a. **Tap Action Overflow and choose the Print action, or:**

2b. **Tap the Share icon, or choose the Share action from the Action Overflow, then choose Print.**

   It's crazy, but both methods (Steps 2a and 2b) are used in different apps. Sometimes the Print action is on an Action Overflow; other times, you must choose Share and then tap a Print icon.

   If you can't find a Print action or icon on a Share menu, your Android lacks this feature, or the item cannot be printed.

3. **Choose a printer.**

   The current printer is shown on the action bar, as shown in Figure 19-5. To view additional printers, tap the action bar.

Select printer action bar.

Print

Show more details.

Print preview

FIGURE 19-5: Android printing.

4. **To change any print settings, tap the Show More Details chevron.**

   The items presented let you set which pages you want to print, change the number of copies, and make other common printer settings.

5. **Tap the PRINT button.**

   The item prints.

REMEMBER

Not every app supports printing. The only way to know is look for the Print action or icon. If you can't find it, you can't print.

Streaming your own media

When you desire to watch movies, look at your photos, or listen to music on a large-format screen, it's time to screencast: This technology takes the media presented on your Android (video or music) and sends it to an HDTV, monitor, or other compatible device.

You need several items prepared for streaming, or *screencasting*, to work properly:

>> An HDTV or a monitor with HDMI input

>> A screencasting dongle, such as Chromecast, attached to one of the HDMI ports

>> Access to the same Wi-Fi network for both the HDTV or monitor and your Android phone or tablet

After the Chromecast dongle is installed and configured on the HDTV, follow these steps to stream media:

1. Open the app that plays the media you want to watch or listen to.

Compatible apps include Play Music, Play Movies & TV, YouTube, Netflix, and so on.

2. Tune the HDTV or monitor to the proper HDMI input.

For example, if a Chromecast dongle is installed on HDMI Input 4, switch the TV to that input. The casting dongle must be awake and active.

 3. Tap the Chromecast icon.

The icon appears similar to the one shown in the margin. If you don't see this icon, either the Chromecast dongle isn't awake or the media cannot be cast to another device.

4. Choose the TV or monitor's Chromecast from the list.

5. Play the media.

The media appears or is heard from the other device.

You can still use your Android while it's casting. The app on the screen may offer you controls, such as Play and Pause, or it might display additional information about the media.

To stop streaming, tap the Chromecast icon and then tap the STOP CASTING or DISCONNECT button.

Android Storage Mysteries

Somewhere, nestled in your Android's bosom, lies a storage device. That storage works like the hard drive in a computer, and for the same purpose: to keep apps, music, videos, pictures, and a host of other information for the long term.

>> Android phones and tablets come with a given quantity of internal storage. The amount is preset by the manufacturer, usually given as an option at purchase time.

>> Typical quantities of internal storage include 16GB, 32GB, 64GB, and more.

>> Removable storage in the form of a microSD card is available on some Androids.

TECHNICAL STUFF

>> *GB* stands for gigabyte, or 1 billion bytes (characters) of storage. A typical 2-hour movie occupies about 4GB of storage, but most items that you store on your Android — music and pictures, for example — occupy only a sliver of storage.

Reviewing storage stats

To see how much storage space is available on your Android, follow these steps:

1. **Open the Settings app.**

2. **Choose the Storage item.**

This item might be titled Storage & USB on some devices. On some Samsung galactic gizmos, choose the Device Maintenance category and then choose Storage.

Figure 19-6 shows a typical storage screen. It details information about internal storage and, if available, the microSD card.

Tap the storage item or category to view details on how the storage is used or to launch an associated app. For example, tap the Photos and Videos item to see (and manage) photos and media storage on the device.

>> Things that consume the most storage space are videos, music, and pictures, in that order.

REMEMBER

>> Most media is stored in the cloud and streamed from the Internet to your Android. That's how music, videos, and books work, as described in Chapter 16. If you're keeping media on the device (described in Chapter 17), you can remove it to free storage.

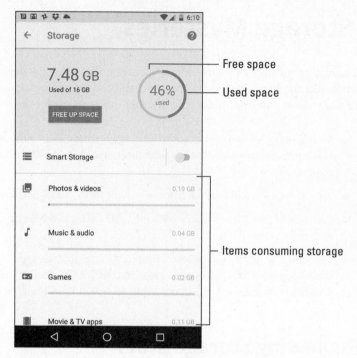

Free space

Used space

Items consuming storage

FIGURE 19-6:
Android storage details.

» If storage space is getting low, tap the FREE UP SPACE button, illustrated in Figure 19-6. This feature isn't available to every version of the Android operating system.

» The Smart Storage feature (refer to Figure 19-6) also frees up storage by automatically removing backups over 90 days old.

TECHNICAL STUFF

» Don't feel ripped-off if the Total Space value is far less than the stated capacity of your Android. For example, your device may have 32GB of storage but the Storage screen reports only 29.85GB of total space. The missing space is considered overhead, as are several gigabytes taken by the government for tax purposes.

Managing files

TECHNICAL STUFF

You probably didn't get a snazzy new phone or tablet because you enjoy managing files on a computer and you wanted another gizmo to hone your skills. Even so, you can practice the same type of file manipulation on the Android as you would on a computer. Is there a need to do so? Of course not! But if you want to get dirty with files, you can.

To view files and folders, attempt these steps:

1. **Open the Settings app.**

2. **Choose Storage.**

   This item might be titled Storage & USB. For some Samsung devices, choose Device Maintenance and then choose Storage.

3. **Swipe to the bottom of the screen and choose Files or Explore.**

   You see folders and files stored on your device.

Some Androids come with a file management app. It's called Files or My Files, and it's a traditional type of file manager, which means that if you detest managing files on your computer, you'll experience the same delightful frustration on your mobile gizmo.

TIP

>> If you want to peruse files you've downloaded from the Internet, open the Downloads app, found in the Apps drawer.

>> If your Android lacks a file management app, you can swiftly obtain one. An abundance of file management apps is available from Google Play. See Chapter 17.

Unmounting the microSD card

The microSD card provides removable storage on some Android devices. When the gizmo is turned off, you can insert or remove the microSD card at will; directions are provided in Chapter 1. The microSD card can also be removed when the Android is turned on, but you must first unmount the card. Obey these steps:

1. **Open the Settings app and choose Storage.**

   This item might be titled Storage & USB.

2. **Choose Unmount SD Card or tap the EJECT button.**

   The button may be located by the USB storage item shown on the Storage screen. Otherwise, the Unmount SD Card action is found near the bottom of the screen.

3. **Ignore the warning and tap the OK button.**

4. **Remove the microSD card.**

It's important that you follow these steps to safely remove the microSD card. If you don't, and you just pop out the card, it could damage the card and lose information.

You can insert a microSD card at any time. See Chapter 1 for details.

REMEMBER

Formatting microSD storage

Your Android instantly recognizes a microSD card after it's inserted. If not, you can try formatting the card to see if that fixes the problem.

All data on the microSD card is erased by the formatting process.

WARNING

To format a microSD card, follow these steps:

1. **Open the Settings app and choose Storage or Storage & USB.**

2. **Choose the action Format SD Card.**

   If necessary, tap the microSD cards item on the Storage screen to locate the Format action.

3. **Tap the FORMAT or FORMAT SD CARD button.**

4. **If prompted, tap the DELETE ALL button to confirm.**

   The microSD card is unmounted, formatted, and then mounted again and made ready for use.

After the card is formatted, you can use it to store information, music, apps, photos, and stuff like that.

WHY REMOVABLE STORAGE IS UNPOPULAR

When Android phones first appeared, one of their key features was removable storage. The iPhone lacked this feature, and users wanted it, which was a selling point. Android tablets echoed the trend, offering removable storage in the form of a microSD card.

Recently, however, fewer devices come with microSD cards. The primary reason is that many Androids now sport an abundance of internal storage. Further, removing the cards can alter the way the system behaves, which can make the Android experience clunky. So, although you can use a microSD card to expand the device's storage, I don't recommend using them. Instead, buy a device with plenty of storage.

Chapter **20**

Apps and Widgets

O f the gazillions of apps available for your Android, you probably want to keep a handful of your favorites ready and available. The best way to keep them accessible, neat, and tidy is to place their launcher icons on the Home screen. Indeed, the whole point of having a Home screen is to keep handy apps and widgets.

Apps and Widgets on the Home Screen

Your Android came with app launchers and perhaps some widgets affixed to the Home screen. You can keep those items, add your own, remove some, and change their locations. And when the Home screen brims with launchers like an overflowing teacup, you can build folders to further organize and keep your apps neat and tidy.

REMEMBER

App icons on the Home screen are called *launchers*.

Adding launchers to the Home screen

As you find yourself using an app frequently, consider slapping its launcher icon on the Home screen. Here's how that works:

1. **Visit the Home screen page on which you want to stick the launcher.**

The page must have room for the launcher icon. If it doesn't, swipe the screen left or right to hunt down a page with room.

If you're organizing Home screen pages by app type, visit the proper page. For example, on my Android gizmos, the second Home page is just for games.

2. **Tap the Apps icon to display the Apps drawer.**

3. **Long-press the app icon you want to add to the Home screen.**

After a moment, the Home screen page you chose in Step 1 appears, as shown in Figure 20-1.

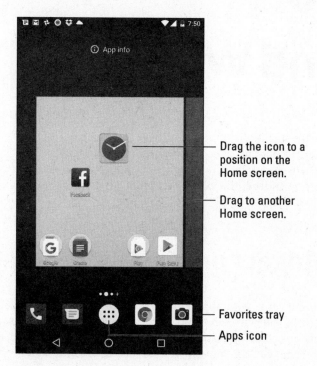

Drag the icon to a position on the Home screen.

Drag to another Home screen.

Favorites tray

Apps icon

FIGURE 20-1:
Placing an app icon on the Home screen.

On some Samsung devices, you may see a pop-up showing several actions for the app icon. You can choose Add Shortcut to Home, though if you wait a tick, you can proceed with Step 4.

4. **Drag the app to a position on the Home screen page.**

Launchers are aligned to a grid. Other launchers may wiggle and jiggle as you find a spot. That's okay.

5. **Lift your finger to place the app.**

The app hasn't moved: What you see is a launcher, which is like a copy or a short-cut. You can still find the app in the Apps drawer, but now the app is available — more conveniently — on the Home screen.

>> Newly installed apps often automatically affix a launcher to the Home screen. If you want to remove that launcher, see the later section "Removing an item from the Home screen."

>> Not every app needs a launcher on the Home screen. I recommend placing only those apps you use most frequently.

>> The top row of the Apps drawer may list frequently accessed apps. Review this list to consider adding a frequent app to the Home screen if its launcher isn't there already.

TIP

>> You can't cram more launchers on the Home screen than will fit in the grid. As an alternative, consider moving launchers to another Home screen page, as covered in the later section "Moving launchers and widgets." Also see the section "Working with folders" for another solution. Finally, if your Android allows you to add more Home screen pages, you can solve the problem that way; see Chapter 21.

Placing a launcher on the Favorites tray

The row of launcher icons at the bottom of the Home screen remains the same no matter which Home screen page you're viewing. It's called the *Favorites tray*, and it's an ideal spot for apps you use most frequently.

Launchers are added to the Favorites tray in one of two ways:

>> **Drag a launcher off the Favorites tray,** either to the Home screen page or to the Remove or Delete icon. This step makes room for a new icon on the Favorites tray.

>> **Drag a launcher from the Home screen to the Favorites tray,** in which case any existing icon swaps places with the icon that's already there.

Of these two methods, the second one may not work on all Androids. In fact, the second method may create a folder on the Favorites tray, which is probably not what you want. (See the later section "Working with folders.")

The best launchers to place on the Home screen are those that show notifications, as shown in the margin. The apps include Facebook, Twitter, Email, and others.

Using launcher shortcuts

Some apps feature shortcuts to common activities. These shortcuts let you do something with an app without opening it and then working through specific steps. As an example, in Figure 20-2 you see shortcuts for the Clock app.

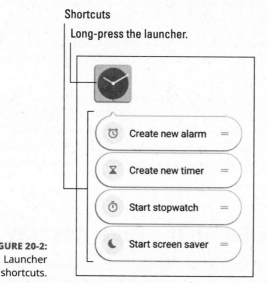

FIGURE 20-2:
Launcher
shortcuts.

To view the shortcuts, long-press the app. You can long-press a launcher on the Home screen or any app in the Apps drawer. Then choose an action from the cartoon bubbles displayed.

>> The Phone, Contacts, and text messaging apps pop up frequent contacts. Other apps pop up specific activities, such as the Twitter app, which lets you instantly create a new tweet.

>> Not every app features pop-up shortcuts.

Slapping down widgets

Beyond launchers, the Home screen is also where you'll find widgets. A *widget* works like a tiny, interactive or informative window, often providing a gateway into another app, or it displays information such as status updates, the current song that's playing, or the weather.

To add widgets to the Home screen, obey these steps:

1. **Switch to a Home screen page that has enough room for the new widget.**

   Widgets come in a variety of sizes. The size is measured by launcher dimensions: A 1x1 widget occupies the same space as a launcher. A 2x2 widget is twice as tall and twice as wide as a launcher.

2. **Long-press a blank part of the Home screen.**

   You see a Home screen overview, along with icons at the bottom of the screen.

3. **Tap the Widgets icon.**

   A list of widgets appears.

4. **Long-press the widget you want to add.**

   Swipe through the pages to find widgets, which are listed alphabetically and show preview images, just like apps. Also shown are the widget's dimensions.

5. **Drag the widget to the Home screen.**

   As you drag the widget, existing launcher icons and widgets jiggle to make room.

6. **Lift your finger.**

   If the widget grows a border, it can be resized. See the next section.

After adding some widgets, you may be prompted for additional information — for example, a location for a weather widget or a contact name for a contact widget.

>> The variety of available widgets depends on the apps installed. Some apps come with widgets, some don't, and some widgets are independent of any app.

>> Fret not if you change your mind about the widget's location. See the later section "Moving launchers and widgets" for obtaining the proper feng shui.

>> To remove a widget, see the later section "Removing an item from the Home screen."

Resizing a widget

Some widgets are resizable. You can change a widget's size immediately after plopping it down on the Home screen — or at any time, really: The secret is to long-press the widget. If it grows a box, as shown in Figure 20-3, you can change the widget's dimensions.

Drag to resize.

FIGURE 20-3:
Resizing a widget.

To resize, drag one of the resizing dots in or out. Tap elsewhere on the touch-screen when you're done.

Moving launchers and widgets

Launchers and widgets aren't fastened to the Home screen with anything stronger than masking tape. That's obvious because it's quite easy to pick up and move a launcher or widget, relocating it to a new position or removing it completely. To start, long-press an item, as illustrated in Figure 20-4.

Drag the item to another position on the Home screen. If you drag to the far left or far right of the screen, the icon or widget is sent to another Home screen page.

Long-press to "lift."

Remove from Home screen.

Uninstall app.

Drag to another page.

FIGURE 20-4:
Moving a
launcher.

Drag to another page.

REMEMBER

>> When you long-press some launchers, action shortcuts appear. Refer to the earlier section "Using launcher shortcuts." To move the launcher, ignore the shortcuts and drag your finger to relocate the launcher.

>> On some Samsung devices, long-pressing a launcher displays a pop-up of actions for the icon. As with the shortcuts, drag your finger to make the pop-up vanish.

Removing an item from the Home screen

To banish a launcher or widget from the Home screen, move the launcher or widget to the Remove icon located atop the Home screen.

For some Samsung devices, long-press the app to view its shortcut menu. Choose Remove Shortcut.

WARNING

>> The Remove icon may be an X or the word *Remove* (refer to Figure 20-4), though some devices show a Delete (trash) icon. Be careful because the Trash icon is often used for the Uninstall action, as illustrated in Figure 20-4.

>> Removing an app or widget from the Home screen doesn't uninstall the app or widget. See the later section "Uninstalling an app."

Working with folders

For further organization of the Home screen, consider gathering similar apps into folders. For example, I have a Listen folder that contains all my streaming music apps. Your Android may have come with a Google folder, which contains all the various apps provided by Google. These folders not only help organize your apps but also solve the problem of a crowded Home screen.

Folders are created in different ways, depending on the device. The stock Android method to create a folder is to drag one launcher on top of another. When the two launchers get close, a circle encloses them, which provides visual feedback that a folder is created.

Another technique is to look for a folder creation icon: Drag the launcher icon up to that icon, which creates a new folder. Or, perhaps, you long-press the Home screen and choose the Create Folder action. Drag icons into the new folder.

Examples of various folder icons are shown in Figure 20-5.

FIGURE 20-5:
Folder icon
varieties.

To open a folder, tap its icon. Tap a launcher to start the associated app. Or, if you don't find what you want, tap the Back navigation icon to close the folder.

>> To add more app launchers to the folder, drag in their icons.

>> Some folders may feature a Plus (+) icon or the ADD APPS button. Tap this icon or button to add more launchers.

» Folders are organized just like other items on the Home screen. You drag folder icons around or delete them. When you delete a folder, you remove the launcher icons from the folder; deleting the folder doesn't uninstall the apps.

» To change a folder's name, open the folder and tap the folder's name. Use the onscreen keyboard to type a new name.

» Some Androids may display a palette in a folder, from which you can set the folder's background color.

» To remove a launcher from a folder, open the folder and drag out the icon. When the second-to-last last icon is dragged out of a folder, the folder is removed. If not, drag the last icon out, and then remove the folder as you would any other item on the Home screen, as described in the preceding section.

App Management

The apps you install on your Android originate from the Play Store. And that's where you can return for basic app management. The task includes reviewing apps you've downloaded, updating apps, and removing apps that you no longer want or that you severely hate.

Additional app management is provided in the Settings app, though for most app chores, it's off to the Play Store.

Reviewing your apps

To peruse the apps you've downloaded from Google Play, follow these steps:

1. **Open the Play Store app.**

2. **Ensure that you're viewing the main screen.**

    Tap the Back navigation icon until you see the main screen.

3. **Tap the Side Menu icon.**

4. **Choose My Apps & Games from the navigation drawer.**

5. **Peruse your apps.**

Your apps are presented in three categories: Updates, Installed, and Library, shown in Figure 20-6. You might also see a Subscriptions tab, with recurring items, such as video subscriptions and magazine subscriptions.

Side Menu icon

Apps on the Android

All your Android apps

App(s) in need of an update

Update apps

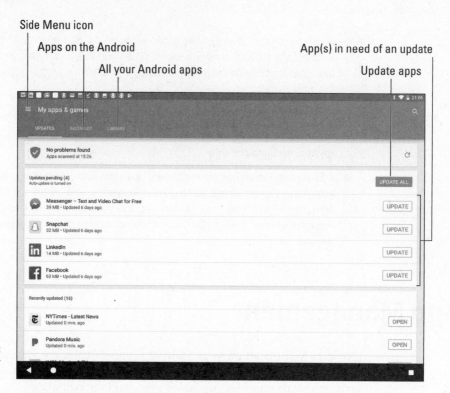

FIGURE 20-6:
Locating all your
Android's apps.

The difference between the Installed and Library tabs depends on the apps installed on the device. Only those apps appear on the Installed tab. Apps you've obtained, even on other Android gizmos, but not installed on the device, are listed on the Library tab.

» Tap an app in the list to view its details. Some of the options and settings on the app's details screen are discussed elsewhere in this chapter.

» Uninstalled apps remain on the Library tab because you did, at one time, download the app. To reinstall them (and without paying a second time for paid apps), choose the app from the Library tab's list and tap the INSTALL button.

Updating apps

New versions, or updates, of apps happen all the time. They're automatic. Occasionally, you're called upon to perform a manual update. How can you tell? The App Update notification appears, which is the generic Google Play notification, shown in the margin.

To deal with a manual update, open the Play Store app to view all your installed apps as presented in the preceding section. What you're looking for is the UPDATE ALL button, shown in Figure 20-6. Tap that button to apply necessary app updates. If prompted to accept the app's permissions, tap the ACCEPT button.

You can view the app update process in the Play Store app or wander off and do something else with your Android.

>> Yes, an Internet connection is required in order to update apps. If possible, try to use Wi-Fi so that you don't incur any data surcharges on your cellular bill. Android apps aren't super-huge in size, but why take the risk?

>> If the Internet connection is broken during an update, the update process continues once the connection is reestablished. Apps aren't messed up by the interruption.

Uninstalling an app

I can think of a few reasons to remove an app. It's with eager relish that I remove apps that don't work or that somehow annoy me. It's also perfectly okay to remove redundant apps, such as when you're trying to find a decent music-listening app and you end up with a dozen or so that you never use.

Whatever the reason, heed these steps to remove an app:

1. **Open the Play Store app.**

2. **Choose My Apps & Games from the navigation drawer.**

3. **Tap the Installed tab.**

4. **Choose the app that offends you.**

   Tap the app's card, not the OPEN button. You see the app's description from within the Play Store app.

5. **Tap the UNINSTALL button.**

6. **Tap the OK button to confirm.**

   The app is removed.

The app appears on the Library list even after the app has been removed. That's because you downloaded it once. That doesn't mean, however, that the app is installed.

>> You can always reinstall paid apps that you've uninstalled. For paid apps, you aren't charged twice for doing so.

>> It's possible to remove an app from the Home screen *and* uninstall the app. Refer to Figure 20-4: When you drag an icon off the Home screen, drag it to the Uninstall icon instead of Remove. The app is then uninstalled.

>> On some Samsung galactic gizmos, long-press an app in the Apps drawer. Choose the Uninstall action from the shortcuts pop-up.

WARNING

>> You can't remove apps that are preinstalled by either the manufacturer or cellular provider. I'm sure there's a technical way to uninstall such apps, but seriously: Just don't use the apps if you want to remove them and discover that you can't.

Controlling app notifications

The Android operating system now collects all app notification controls in a single location in the Settings app. This change is convenient in that formerly you changed notification settings within each app.

To set an app's notifications, heed these directions:

1. **Open the Settings app.**

2. **Choose Apps & Notifications.**

   If you don't see this item, your device is using an older version of the Android operating system that lacks this feature.

3. **Choose Notifications.**

4. **Tap the Notifications item.**

   You see a list of all apps on the device.

5. **Choose an app to set individual notification options.**

   For example, in Figure 20-7, notification options for the Gmail app appear. You can disable all notifications by switching the master control to the Off position. Or you can set individual notification options as offered by the specific app.

As an example, I disabled notifications on one app that kept bugging me all the time with trivial notices. The app still runs, albeit silently.

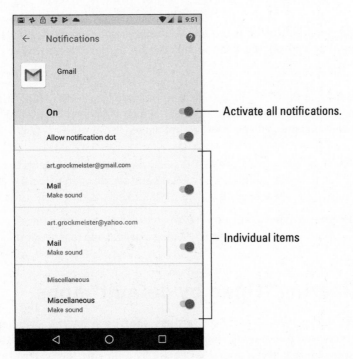

FIGURE 20-7:
App notifications.

Selecting an "Open by default" app

Every so often, you may see the Complete Action Using prompt, which may look like the one shown in Figure 20-8. Regardless of its appearance, you're prompted to choose an app to complete an action and then given the choice of JUST ONCE or ALWAYS.

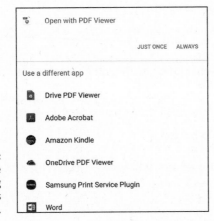

FIGURE 20-8:
The Complete
Action Using
question is
posed.

The app atop the list is the one you used previously, or the first installed app. To use that app all the time and never be bothered again with the prompt, tap ALWAYS.

To use the top app and see the prompt again, tap JUST ONCE. Otherwise, you can choose a different app from the list, which is opened "just once" for the current task. Next time, you see the prompt again.

TIP

>> My advice is to choose JUST ONCE until you get sick of seeing the Open With card. At that point, choose ALWAYS and set the open-by-default app. The fear, of course, is that you'll make a mistake. Keep reading in the next section.

>> The open-by-default app is different from what Android refers to as "default apps." See the later section "Setting a default app for specific duties."

Clearing "Open by default" apps

Fret not, gentle reader. The settings you chose for the Complete Action Using prompt can be undone. For example, if you select the PDF Viewer app from Figure 20-8, you can undo that choice by following these steps:

1. **Open the Settings app.**

2. **Choose Apps & Notifications.**

   This item is titled Apps in some releases of the Android operating system.

3. **Choose App info.**

   If you don't see this item, skip to Step 4.

4. **Choose the app that always opens.**

   This is the tough step because you must remember which app you chose to "always" open.

5. **On the app's screen, choose Open by Default or Set as Default.**

   If the item shows the text *Some Defaults Set,* you're on the right track. Apps that haven't been chosen as the default show the text *No Defaults Set.*

6. **Tap the CLEAR DEFAULTS button.**

After you clear the defaults for an app, you see the Open With card again. The next time you see it, however, make a better choice.

Setting a default app for specific duties

Adding confusion to the already befuddling term *default,* your Android features a set of default apps. These are the apps designated to control specific device features, such as

>> The app to place phone calls on an Android phone

>> The app to send and receive text messages on an Android phone

>> The web browser app

>> The camera app

>> The Home screen app

>> Other various duties

For example, if you want to use a different camera app or text messaging app, you can reset the default app by following these steps:

1. **Open the Settings app.**

2. **Choose Apps & Notifications.**

   On some devices, this item is titled Apps.

3. **Choose Default Apps.**

   You may need to expand the Advanced item: Tap the chevron to view the Default Apps item. On Samsung devices, tap the Action Overflow on the Apps screen to locate the Default Apps action.

4. **Select a default app to reset.**

   For example, choose Browser App to set a web browser other than Chrome.

5. **Choose the default app.**

   Available apps appear in the list.

If the list is empty, you can obtain alternative apps at Google Play; see Chapter 17.

>> The most common default app to change is the text messaging app. Usually, a phone has two: the stock Android version and one supplied by your device's manufacturer. See Chapter 8.

>> The Home screen app is the one you see when you tap the Home navigation icon. Yes, it can be changed. Many alternative Home screen apps are available, from those that display very basic uses to advanced and nerdy Home screen apps.

REMEMBER

>> I don't recommend resetting default apps until you become comfortable using your Android. Remember that the documentation and helpful resources such as this book assume that you're using the stock Android apps, such as Chrome for the web browser.

Reviewing app permissions

The Android operating system is completely open about which apps access which device features. That's the reason you see the various permission cards to allow or deny access. To review or reset those permissions, obey these directions:

1. **Open the Settings app.**

2. **Choose Apps or Apps & Notifications.**

3. **Choose App Permissions.**

   On Samsung phones and tablets, tap the Action Overflow to locate the App Permissions action.

   You see a list of hardware and software items an app can access on your Android. For example: Location, Microphone, Storage, and so on.

4. **Tap a category.**

   A list shows apps that can access the resource. Each app has a master control set to On or Off, indicating whether it has permission to use the resource.

5. **Reset the master control to allow or deny access to the specific app.**

Resetting the access permission doesn't prevent the app from asking again in the future. Some permission cards feature a Do Not Ask Again check box, which you can select to ensure that the question doesn't arise again. Still, some apps are persistent.

Shutting down an app run amok

Sometimes an app goofs up or crashes. You may see a warning message on the touchscreen, informing you that the app has been shut down. That's good. What's better is that you too can shut down apps that misbehave or those you cannot otherwise stop.

First, try dismissing the app from the Overview:

1. **Tap the Recent navigation icon.**

2. **Swipe away the miscreant app's thumbnail, or tap the X button.**

   The app is closed.

When these steps don't work, more drastic measures are required:

1. **Open the Settings app.**

2. **Tap the Apps or Apps & Notifications item.**

3. **If you don't see a list of apps, choose App Info.**

4. **Choose the errant app from the list.**

   For example, if the Annoying Sound app is bothering you, choose it from the list.

5. **Tap the FORCE STOP button.**

   The app is terminated.

If the FORCE STOP button isn't highlighted, the app isn't running.

WARNING

Use the FORCE STOP button only as a final act. Don't kill off any app or service unless the app is annoying or you are otherwise unable to stop it. Avoid killing off Google Services, which can change the device's behavior or make the Android operating system unstable.

Apps Drawer Organization

Some Androids offer tools for arranging apps in the Apps drawer. These tools allow you to present the apps in an order other than alphabetical, rearrange the apps, or even collect apps into folders.

The key to organizing the Apps drawer is to look for an Action Overflow or for specific icons or buttons on the screen. For example, some Samsung gizmos feature an EDIT button, which is used to arrange icons in the Apps drawer. The A–Z command arranges apps in alphabetical order.

You may find a FOLDER action that lets you build Apps drawer folders, or you might create folders by dragging icons over each other, similar to how folders work on the Home screen folder. Refer to the earlier section "Working with folders" for details.

- » Working with Home screen pages
- » Setting orientation
- » Changing the screen brightness
- » Putting shortcuts on the lock screen
- » Activating keyboard feedback
- » Checking predictive text
- » Setting sound options

Chapter **21**

Customize and Configure

ustomizing your Android doesn't involve sprucing up the case, so put away that Bedazzler™. The kind of customization this chapter refers to involves fine-tuning the way the Android operating system presents itself. You can modify the Home screen, adjust the display, customize the keyboard, and change sounds. The goal is to truly make the device your own.

It's Your Home Screen — and Lock Screen

The typical Android Home screen sports anywhere from three to nine pages and a specific background, or *wallpaper*, preset by the device's manufacturer or cellular provider. You are not stuck with this choice — the Home screen is yours to change at your whim.

Accessing Home screen actions

To start your Home screen decoration project, long-press a blank part of the Home screen. Don't long-press an icon or a widget. Upon success, you see Home screen management icons, as shown in Figure 21-1.

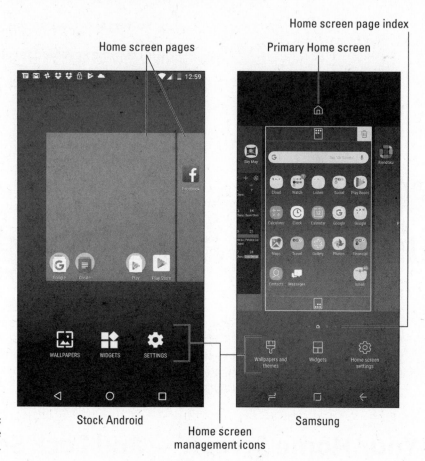

FIGURE 21-1:
The Home
screen menu.

The icons or options presented for Home screen management include some or all of the following:

Wallpaper: Change the background image on the Home screen.

Widgets: Add widgets to the Home screen.

Settings: Open the Settings app.

Folder: Create a Home screen folder.

Page: Add, remove, or manage Home screen pages.

These items might appear as icons (refer to Figure 21-1), or you may see a menu of options presented as a list. The most common items are the first three, illustrated in Figure 21-1.

Hanging new wallpaper

The Home screen background can be draped with two types of wallpaper: traditional and live. *Traditional* wallpaper can be any image, such as a picture you've taken or an image provided by the device's manufacturer. *Live* wallpaper is animated or interactive.

To set a new wallpaper for the Home screen, obey these steps:

1. **Long-press the Home screen.**

2. **Choose Wallpapers.**

The item might be titled Set Wallpapers.

3. **Tap a wallpaper to see a preview.**

Swipe the list left or right to peruse your options. You see the previous wallpaper images plus those provided by the manufacturer. On the far right, you'll find the live wallpapers.

To choose your own images, tap the MY PHOTOS button.

Some Androids may first prompt you to select a category: Wallpapers, Life Wallpapers, My Photos, and so on.

4. **Tap the SET WALLPAPER button to confirm your choice.**

5. **Choose to set the wallpaper for the Home screen, lock screen, or both.**

The new wallpaper takes over.

On some Androids, you might be given the opportunity to crop the image before setting the wallpaper. Unlike cropping a photo (covered in Chapter 14), you may see two rectangles for cropping in both landscape and portrait orientations.

>> Live wallpapers can be obtained from Google Play. See Chapter 17.

>> Some live wallpapers may interfere with certain features. If so, you see a warning, which lets you choose between using the live wallpaper or the specific feature.

>> Yes, some wallpapers come with advertising. You're not required to use them.

>> The Zedge app is an über-repository of wallpaper images, collected from Android users all over the world. Zedge is a free app.

TIP

» Google also offers a wallpapers app, called Google Wallpapers.

» Another way to set wallpaper is to view an image in the Photos app. Select the image and tap Action Overflow. Choose the Use As action and then Wallpaper.

Managing Home screen pages

The number of pages on the Home screen isn't fixed. You can add pages. You can remove pages. You can even rearrange pages. This feature might not be available to all Androids and, sadly, it isn't implemented in exactly the same way.

The stock Android method of adding a Home screen page is to drag an icon left or right, just as though you were positioning that icon on another Home screen page. When a page to the left or right doesn't exist, a new page is added automatically.

Some Androids may be more specific in how pages are added. For example, you can choose a Page command from the Home screen menu.

Samsung devices present a Home page overview, as shown in Figure 21-2. To edit Home screen pages, pinch the Home screen: Touch the screen with two fingers and drag them together. You can then manage Home screen pages as illustrated in the figure.

To move a page, long-press and drag it to a new spot. When you're done, tap the Back or Home navigation icon.

» The maximum number of Home screen pages may be three, five, seven, or nine, depending on your device. The minimum is one.

» On some Androids, the far left Home screen page is the Google Assistant app.

» Samsung places its Bixby assistant on the far left Home screen page.

» Some devices let you reset the primary Home screen page, which doesn't necessarily have to be the center Home screen page. I've seen different ways to accomplish this task. The most common one is to tap the Home icon in a thumbnail's preview, which is illustrated in Figure 21-2.

Adding lock screen launchers

Most Androids feature a Camera launcher in the lower right corner of the lock screen. Swipe that icon to run the Camera app without fully unlocking the device. It's a quick way to take a picture.

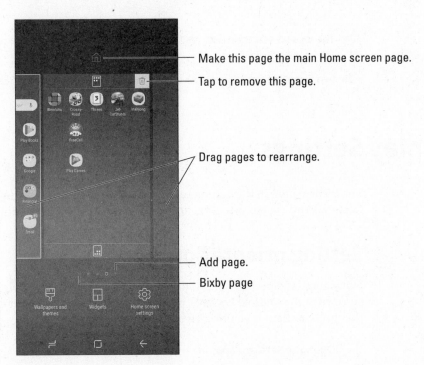

Make this page the main Home screen page.

Tap to remove this page.

Drag pages to rearrange.

Add page.

Bixby page

FIGURE 21-2:
Manipulating
Home screen
pages.

To see whether your Android lets you customize or add lock screen launchers, heed these steps:

1. **Open the Settings app.**

2. **Choose Lock Screen or Lock Screen and Security.**

   If you can't find a Lock Screen item, your Android lacks the capability to modify lock screen launchers.

3. **Choose Apps Shortcuts.**

   This item might be titled Info and Apps Shortcuts. If so, choose Apps Shortcuts on the next screen.

4. **Select the apps to place on the lock screen.**

You may see one or more app screen shortcuts for launchers along with the Camera app. I've seen devices that let you line up five launchers at the bottom of the lock screen. Because this feature isn't a part of stock Android, it can vary.

REMEMBER

>> When you use a lock screen launcher (shortcut) to start an app, the device isn't fully unlocked. To access other features, you must work the screen lock.

>> The lock screen shortcuts might not be available if you've not set a screen lock for your Android.

>> See Chapter 22 for details on screen locks and lock screen notifications.

Display Settings

The Display item in the Settings app deals with touchscreen settings. Two popular items worthy of your attention are the Brightness and Screen Timeout options.

Setting orientation

Many apps, and perhaps the Home screen itself, can change their presentation as you switch the Android between portrait and horizontal orientations. You can lock that presentation, if you like. Heed the directions:

1. Open the Settings app.

2. Choose Display.

3. Choose Device Rotation.

If necessary, tap the chevron by the Advanced item to locate the Device Rotation item.

4. Select an option.

The options might include two or more of the following:

Rotate the contents of the screen. The device orients the screen to match whichever direction is "up."

Stay in Portrait view. The device stays in Portrait view, the standard presentation on an Android phone.

Stay in Landscape view. The device holds to landscape presentation, which is standard for an Android tablet.

Stay in current orientation. The device remains in its current orientation.

If you don't see any of these options, look to the Quick Settings drawer. A Rotation icon is found there, which lets you switch between freely rotating the touchscreen and locking it into one position or the other.

TIP

The Play Books app offers its own screen orientation controls, which make it easier (and more predictable) to read an eBook. See Chapter 16.

Adjusting display brightness

The touchscreen can be too bright, too dim, or just right. Which setting is best? That's up to you. Follow these steps:

1. Open the Settings app.

2. Choose Display.

3. Choose Brightness Level.

This item might not appear in some Settings apps. Instead, you immediately see the Brightness slider.

4. Adjust the slider to set the touchscreen's intensity.

If you'd rather have the Android's brain and secret eyeball adjust the brightness for you, set the master control by the Adaptive Brightness item to the On position, or tap to place a check mark in the Auto box.

TIP

» The Adaptive Brightness setting might be called Auto Brightness or Automatic Brightness.

» You also find a Brightness setting in the Quick Settings drawer. See Chapter 3.

Setting the screen lock time-out

You can press the Power/Lock key lock your phone or tablet anytime. When you don't, the touchscreen automatically locks itself after a given period of inactivity. To adjust that period, obey these steps:

1. Open the Settings app.

2. Choose Display.

3. Choose Sleep.

This item might be titled Screen Timeout.

4. Select a time-out value from the list.

The standard value is 1 minute.

The sleep timer measures inactivity; when you don't touch the screen, the timer starts ticking. About 5 seconds before the touchscreen locks, the screen dims. Then the touchscreen turns off and the device locks. If you tap the screen before then, the timer is reset.

TECHNICAL STUFF

The lock screen has its own time-out. If you unlock the Android but don't work the screen lock, the device locks itself automatically after about ten seconds. This time-out is not adjustable.

Configuring the always-on touchscreen

Many Androids feature an always-on or wake-up display. This feature shows the current time and perhaps a few notifications, even when the device is locked. This convenience doesn't affect battery life, but the settings can be disabled, if you prefer. Obey these steps:

1. **In the Settings app, choose Display.**

2. **Set the master control by Ambient Display.**

   The On setting keeps the screen on or wakes it up; the Off option keeps the touchscreen dark while the device is locked.

For Samsung devices, work through these steps:

1. **Open the Settings app.**

2. **Choose Lock Screen and Security.**

3. **Set the master control by Always On Display.**

Keyboard Settings

Quite a few options are available for the Google keyboard, the *Gboard.* Some of these settings enable special features, and others supposedly make the onscreen typing experience more enjoyable. I'll leave it up to you to determine whether that's true.

Generating keyboard feedback

The onscreen keyboard can assist your typing by generating haptic feedback. This feedback is in the form of either a pleasing click sound or the vibrating of the device. To check these settings, follow these steps:

1. **Open the Settings app.**

2. **Choose System and then choose Language & Input.**

   On some Androids, the Language & Input item is on the main Settings app screen.

3. **Choose Virtual Keyboard.**

4. **Choose Gboard.**

5. **Choose Preferences.**

6. **Set the master controls by the items Sound on Keypress and Vibrate on Keypress.**

   Some Android tablets lack a vibration feature, so that setting is missing.

Samsung galactic gizmos may follow a different set of steps:

1. **Open the Settings app.**

2. **Choose General Management and then choose Language and Input.**

   The Language and Input item might be located on the main Settings app screen.

3. **Choose Onscreen keyboard and then choose Samsung Keyboard.**

4. **Choose Key-Tap Feedback.**

5. **Set the master control by the Sound and Vibration items.**

REMEMBER

Not every Android tablet features vibration.

Ensuring that predictive text is active

Predictive text is on all the time when you use the Gboard. To ensure that the feature is active, follow these steps:

1. **Open the Settings app.**

2. **Choose System and then choose Language & Input.**

   The Language & Input item might appear on the main Settings app screen.

3. **Choose Virtual Keyboard and then choose Gboard.**

   The Gboard Keyboard Settings screen appears.

4. **Choose Text Correction.**

5. **Ensure that all the master controls are set to the On position.**

Some of these items you might consider disabling. For example, Auto-Correction is the bane of folks who enjoy texting. If so, disable that option; slide the master control to the Off position.

On a Samsung device, follow these steps:

1. **Open the Settings app.**

2. **Choose General Management and then choose Language and Input.**

   You might find the Language and Input item on the main Settings app screen.

3. **Choose Onscreen Keyboard and then choose Samsung Keyboard.**

4. **Ensure that the master control by Predictive Text is on.**

Refer to Chapter 4 for details on using the predictive text feature.

Activating glide typing

Once known as *gesture* typing, *glide* typing allows you to swipe your finger over the onscreen keyboard to create text. Chapter 4 explains the details, although this feature may not be active on your phone or tablet. To ensure that it is, follow these steps:

1. **Open the Settings app.**

2. **Choose System and then choose Language & Input.**

3. **Choose Virtual Keyboard and then choose Gboard.**

4. **Choose Google Keyboard and then choose Glide Typing.**

5. **Ensure that the item Enable Glide Typing is active.**

   Set its master control to the On position.

Only the Enable Glide Typing item needs to be enabled, although activating the other items does enhance the experience.

For some Samsung gizmos, follow these steps:

1. **Open the Settings app.**

2. **Choose General Management and then choose Language and Input.**

   The Language and Input item might be located on the main Settings app screen.

3. **Choose Onscreen keyboard and then choose Samsung Keyboard.**

4. **Choose Keyboard Swipe Controls.**

5. **Ensure that the option Swipe to Type is chosen.**

Audio Adjustments

Yes, your Android makes noise. Incoming calls ring; you hear music, alarms sound; and games go "beep," "bleep," and "blort." The Settings app is the place to go when the sound needs fine-tuning.

Setting the volume

The Volume key on the side of your Android sets the volume as sound is generated. To preset the sound levels, follow these steps:

1. **Open the Settings app.**

2. **Choose Sound or Sound & Notification.**

   Samsung devices may label this category Sounds and Vibration. Also, on your Samsung gizmo, choose Volume to see the sound sliders mentioned in the next step.

3. **Adjust the sliders to set the volume for various noise sources.**

   The common volume sliders are:

   Media volume controls the sound for movies, videos, audio in the web browser, and so on.

   Alarm volume sets the intensity used for the Clock app's alarm.

   Ring volume sets an Android phone's ringtone volume. This category includes incoming calls and notifications, although some phones may feature a separate slider for notifications.

   Notification volume sets an Android tablet's volume for notifications.

   Other sliders may appear, such as System to adjust any volume not covered by the other categories.

4. **Slide the gizmo to the left to make a sound quieter; slide to the right to make a sound louder.**

   When you lift your finger, you hear a sound preview.

TIP

If you'd like your phone to vibrate on an incoming call, enable the Also Vibrate for Calls setting. This item might be titled Vibrate When Ringing, and it may be found on a separate Vibrations item on the Sound & Notification screen.

Selecting a ringtone

The term *ringtone* applies to any sound an Android uses for certain activities. Yes, on an Android phone, the ringtone sounds for an incoming call. The device also features a notification ringtone. The Clock app also uses a ringtone for various alarms.

To review and set the various ringtones, follow these steps:

1. **Open the Settings app.**

2. **Choose Sound or Sound & Notification.**

   The item may be titled Sounds and Vibration.

3. **Choose Phone Ringtone or Ringtone.**

   You may be confronted with a Complete Action Using card. Choose an app, such as Media Storage. Also refer to Chapter 20 for details on "open by default" apps.

4. **Select a ringtone from the list.**

   You hear the ringtone's preview.

5. **Tap OK to set the new ringtone, or tap CANCEL or the Back navigation icon to retain the current ringtone.**

Repeat Steps 4 and 5 for the Default Notification Sound and Default Alarm Sound items. You may need to tap the Advanced item (tap the chevron) to view these two items. On Samsung devices, choose Notification Sounds instead.

» Various apps may set their own ringtones, such as text messaging ringtones and alert sounds for Facebook. These ringtones are set within the given app: Look for a Settings action in the app, either found on the navigation drawer or accessed by tapping the Action Overflow icon. The ringtones might also be set from the Settings app, as covered in Chapter 20.

TIP

» To disable a ringtone, choose None in Step 4. Do keep in mind that it's possible to temporarily disable sound on your Android. Refer to Chapter 3.

Chapter **22**

Android Security

As more and more of your life is surrendered to the digital realm, the topic of security grows in importance. This concern extends directly to your Android mobile device, which is often home to your email, social networking, and other online accounts — including, potentially, important files and financial information. Don't take Android security lightly.

Lock Your Android

The first line of defense for your Android is the screen lock. It can be simple, complex, or nonexistent. The choice is up to you.

Finding the screen locks

All screen locks on your Android are found in the Settings app, on the Choose Screen Lock screen. Heed these steps to visit that screen:

1. **Open the Settings app.**

2. **Choose Security & Location.**

This item may have another name, such as Security or Lock Screen and Security. If you see both items in the Settings app, choose Lock Screen.

On some Samsung gizmos, choose the Lock Screen item on the Device tab in the Settings app.

3. **Choose Screen Lock.**

The item might also be titled Screen Lock Type, Set Up Screen Lock, or Change Screen Lock.

4. **Work any existing secure screen lock to continue.**

Eventually, you see the Choose Screen Lock screen, which might instead be called Select Screen Lock.

The Choose Screen Lock screen lists several types of screen locks. Some are unique to your device, and others are common Android screen locks, which include

None: This choice is no screen lock at all. You unlock the device by pressing the Power/Lock key or swiping the screen.

Swipe: Unlock the device by swiping your finger across the touchscreen. This item might also be titled Slide.

Pattern: Trace a pattern on the touchscreen to unlock.

PIN: Type a personal identification number (PIN) to unlock the touchscreen.

Password: Type a password to unlock.

Some devices feature additional lock types, including face unlock, signature, and so on. Also see the later section "Using a fingerprint lock."

REMEMBER

>> The most secure lock types are the PIN and password. Either screen lock type is required if the Android has multiple users, has a kid's account, or accesses a secure email server.

>> The fingerprint lock is also considered secure, though it often uses a secondary lock as a backup.

>> The screen lock doesn't appear on an Android phone when you answer an incoming call. You're prompted, however, to unlock the phone if you want to use its features while you're on a call.

>> The screen lock appears when you first power-on the device or after an update to the Android operating system.

>> If you're in a panic, you can tap the EMERGENCY CALL button on the phone's lock screen to bypass the screen lock and dial 911 or another emergency number.

WARNING

>> I know of no recovery method available should you forget your Android's PIN or password screen locks. If you use either one, write it down in an inconspicuous spot, just in case.

Removing a screen lock

You don't remove the screen lock on your Android. Instead, you replace it with a non-lock, such as Swipe or None. Follow the directions in the preceding section to get to the Choose Screen Lock screen. Then switch from the Pattern, PIN, or Password screen lock to Swipe or None.

>> You may be prompted for confirmation if you're opting to reset a secure screen lock to one that's less secure.

>> You're prohibited from removing a secure screen lock if the device is encrypted or accesses secure email or when other security features are enabled.

Setting a PIN

The PIN lock assigns a 4- to 16-digit code to the lock screen. You must type the PIN, or personal identification number, to gain access to the device. This type of screen lock is also employed as a backup for the less secure screen-unlocking methods, such as the pattern lock.

>> To set the PIN lock, follow the directions in the earlier section "Finding the screen locks" to reach the Choose Screen Lock screen. Select PIN from the list of locks.

TIP

>> The Android requires you type the PIN twice — once to set it and again to confirm. I also recommend that you write down the PIN elsewhere in a secure location.

Applying a password

The most secure way to lock an Android is to apply a full-on password. Unlike a PIN, a password contains more than digits, including a combination of numbers, symbols, and uppercase and lowercase letters.

Choose Password from the Choose Screen Lock screen to set the password; refer to the earlier section "Finding the screen locks." The password must be at least four characters long, though keep in mind that longer passwords are more secure.

You're prompted to type the password whenever you unlock your Android, initially turn on the device, restart, or try to change the screen lock. Tap the OK button to accept the password and use your gizmo.

Creating an unlock pattern

Perhaps the most popular, and certainly the most unconventional, screen lock is the Pattern lock. You must trace a pattern on the touchscreen to unlock the device. To create a Pattern lock, follow these steps:

1. **Summon the Choose Screen Lock screen.**

   Refer to the earlier section "Finding the screen locks."

2. **Choose Pattern.**

   If you haven't yet set a pattern, you may see the tutorial describing the process; tap the NEXT button to skip merrily through the dreary directions.

3. **If you're prompted for Secure Start-up, tap the YES button.**

   I strongly recommend using the Secure Start-up feature.

4. **Trace an unlock pattern.**

   Use Figure 22-1 as your guide. You can trace over the dots in any order, but you can trace over a dot only once. The pattern must cover at least four dots.

5. **Tap the CONTINUE button.**

6. **Redraw the pattern.**

7. **Tap the CONFIRM button.**

   You may be required to type a PIN or password as a backup to the Pattern lock. If so, follow the onscreen directions to set that lock as well.

TIP

After the Pattern screen lock is set, you see it shown as selected on the Security & Location screen in the Settings app. A Settings icon appears to the right of the Screen Lock option. Tap that icon and ensure that the setting Make Pattern Visible is chosen. For even more security, you can disable this option, but you must remember how — and where — the pattern goes.

Also: Clean the touchscreen! Smudge marks can betray your pattern.

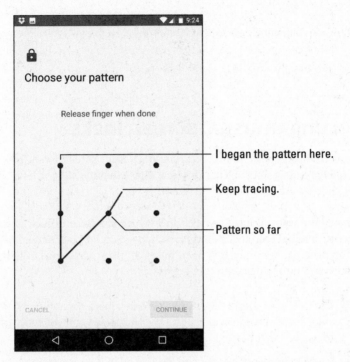

I began the pattern here.

Keep tracing.

Pattern so far

FIGURE 22-1:
Set the unlock
pattern.

Using a fingerprint lock

It's trendy for a smartphone to feature a fingerprint scanner. Usually found on the back of the device, right near where you can smudge the rear camera lens, you tap the scanner to instantly unlock the phone. Android tablets lack this handy feature, probably due to their larger size.

The fingerprint scanner is usually configured when you first set up the device. As part of the initial setup, you're prompted to tap the fingerprint scanner a few times to register a specific digit.

With some Androids, you can register additional fingers: Open the Settings app and choose Security & Location or the Lock Screen item to peruse options. For example, on the Nexus 5 phone, the feature is called Nexus Imprint. Samsung refers to the feature as Fingerprint Scanner, located on the Lock Screen and Security item's screen.

» To work the fingerprint scanner, tap your finger. Sometimes, you may need to do it twice to fully register input.

» Backup security is required for the fingerprint scanner, such as a pattern, PIN, or password.

REMEMBER

>> Older Samsung devices used the physical Home button as the fingerprint scanner.

>> The Fingerprint screen lock is *not* considered secure.

Setting unusual screen locks

Many Android device manufacturers offer other screen locks, beyond the conventional locks described in this chapter. These include silly or fancy locks — perhaps not that secure but fun and different.

Among the more unusual screen lock types are Face Unlock and Signature Lock. Choose these screen locks from the Choose Screen Lock screen. Work through the setup process. You may also need to set a PIN or password as a backup to the less secure and unusual screen lock types.

>> The face unlock uses the Android's front camera. To unlock the device, you stare at the screen. So long as it's not Halloween and you're wearing zombie makeup, the device unlocks.

>> The Signature lock is unique to the Samsung Galaxy Note line of phones and tablets. Use the S Pen to scribble your John Hancock on the touchscreen. The device unlocks.

Eschewing the lock screen

Your Android has a few tricks to keep security applied to the device, but avoid the screen lock under certain circumstances. This utility is called Smart Lock, and it includes several features:

On Body Detection: After initially unlocking the Android, it stays unlocked while you're moving. Once you stop, the device locks again.

Trusted Places: The screen lock isn't applied while the Android is near one of the locations listed as a trusted place; you swipe the screen to unlock the device.

Trusted Devices: While connected with a specific Bluetooth device, such as a smartwatch or your car, the phone or tablet stays unlocked.

Trusted Face: This item activates the face unlock, covered in the preceding section.

Trusted Voice: When this one is active, you can utter "OK, Google" to unlock your Android and perform certain actions.

To set one or more of these items, follow these steps:

1. **Open the Settings app.**

2. **Choose Security & Location.**

3. **Choose Smart Lock.**

   If this item isn't listed, your Android may lack these features, though they could be found under a different heading.

4. **Work any existing screen lock.**

5. **Select a Smart Lock feature to activate.**

   For example, Trusted Places.

Follow the directions onscreen to set up the Smart Lock feature. For example, add a trusted place such as your home or office or choose a trusted Bluetooth device.

Even with a Smart Lock feature enabled, a screen lock still appears whenever you haven't used your Android for a while.

Other Security Features

Beyond locking the screen, other tools are available to help you thwart the Bad Guys and keep safe the information in your phone or tablet. Tools are also available to help locate a lost or stolen device and to wipe your personal data, should you ever need to depart with your Android.

Controlling lock screen notifications

Lock screen notifications can be handy — unless you're haggling over the price of a used car and the seller sees a notification from your bank showing how much you can spend. Some notices are innocent, but some are sensitive. To control how all notifications appear on the lock screen, follow these steps:

1. **Open the Settings app.**

2. **Choose Apps & Notification.**

   Some devices may title this item Sound & Notification or something similar.

3. **Choose Notifications.**

4. **Choose On the Lock Screen.**

This item may be titled When Device Is Locked or Notifications on Lock Screen.

5. **Select a Lock screen notification level.**

Up to three settings are available:

- Don't Show Notifications at All
- Show All Notification Content
- Hide Sensitive Notification Content

The names of these settings may be subtly different on your device.

6. **Choose a notification level.**

On some Samsung devices, lock screen notifications are set by the app: In the Settings app, choose Notifications. Then choose an app and select On Lock Screen to set notification preferences.

» The Hide Sensitive Notification Content option (refer to Step 5) appears only when a secure screen lock is chosen.

» Double-tap a lock screen notification to open its related app and view more details. You must unlock the screen first, and then the app opens.

Adding owner info text

Suppose that you lose your phone or tablet. A kind person finds it, and they look on the touchscreen to see whether they can determine who owns the device. How would they know? Because you followed these steps to set the owner info text on the lock screen:

1. **Open the Settings app.**

2. **Choose Security & Location.**

This item might be titled Security. On Samsung devices, choose the Lock Screen and Security category. Also look for a Lock Screen category.

3. **Tap the Settings icon by the Screen Lock item.**

If you don't see a Settings icon, skip to Step 4.

On Samsung devices, choose Information and FaceWidgets.

4. **Choose Lock Screen Message.**

This item might also be titled Contact Information, Owner Info, or Owner Information.

5. **Type text in the box.**

For example, type **This phone belongs to Arius Sterling** — if your name is Arius Sterling.

You can type more than one line of text, though the information is displayed on the lock screen as a single line.

6. **Tap the SAVE or DONE button.**

TIP

Whatever text you type in the box appears on the lock screen. Therefore, I recommend typing something useful: your name, address, another phone number, an email address, or similar vital information. This way, should someone find your Android, he or she can easily contact you.

The owner info may not show up when None is selected as a screen lock.

Finding a lost device

Someday, you may lose your beloved Android. It might be for a few panic-filled seconds, or it might be for forever. The hardware solution is to weld a heavy object to the phone or tablet, such as an anvil. Alas, that strategy kind of defeats the entire mobile/wireless paradigm.

To quickly locate your Android, follow these steps while using a computer:

1. **Open a web browser, such as Google Chrome.**

2. **Visit the main Google search page:** www.google.com

3. **Type** find my phone **or** find my tablet **and press the Enter key.**

4. **If prompted, sign in to your Google (Gmail) account.**

Your phone or tablet's location appears on the screen.

To ensure that this system works best, complete these steps on your phone or tablet:

1. **Open the Settings app.**

2. **Choose Security & Location.**

3. **Choose Find My Device.**

4. **Ensure that both master controls are set to the On position.**

    The first item activates the remote-locate feature; the second allows you to remotely lock and erase the device.

Other locator services are available, through your cellular provider or Android manufacturer or as a third–party app. Look for such apps in the Apps drawer or search on Google Play. One that I recommend is Lookout Mobile Security.

Encrypting storage

I find the step of encrypting an Android's storage to be drastic, but it's highly secure. The process ensures that if someone finds your phone or tablet, and some–how manages to bypass all the device's security features, he still can't access any information.

WARNING

It's not currently possible to remove encryption. After encryption is applied, it's stuck forever like a regrettable, drunken tattoo.

To start the encryption process, follow these steps:

1. **Ensure that the device has a secure screen lock — a PIN or password.**

    Refer to the first part of this chapter for details.

2. **Connect the Android to a power source, or ensure that it's fully charged.**

    Encryption can take as long as several hours if your device's storage is rather full.

3. **Open the Settings app and choose Security & Location.**

4. **Look below the heading Encryption & Credentials.**

    If the text reads *Device encrypted,* you're done; the device is already encrypted. Otherwise, continue with Step 5.

5. **Choose Encryption & Credentials.**

6. **Choose Encrypt Phone or Encrypt Tablet.**

    This item may be titled Protect Encrypted Data.

7. **Tap the ENCRYPT PHONE or ENCRYPT TABLET button.**

8. **Wait.**

On Samsung devices, choose the Lock Screen and Security item in the Settings app. Then choose Secure Folder. Follow the directions presented.

Performing a factory data reset

The most secure thing you can do with the information on your Android is to erase it all. The procedure, known as a *factory data reset*, effectively restores the device to its original state, fresh out of the box.

A factory data reset is a drastic thing. It not only removes all information from storage but also erases all your accounts. Don't take this step lightly! In fact, if you're using this procedure to cure an ill, I recommend first getting support. See Chapter 24.

When you're ready to erase all the device's data, follow these steps:

1. **Open the Settings app.**

2. **Choose System.**

    On older devices, choose Backup & Reset.

    On Samsung devices, choose the General Management item in the Settings app.

3. **Choose Reset.**

    If you don't see this item, skip to Step 4.

4. **Choose Factory Data Reset.**

5. **Review the data presented.**

    Everything gets wiped, so the reminder screen reinforces the extreme measures taken in a factory data reset.

6. **Tap the button RESET PHONE or RESET TABLET.**

7. **If prompted, work the screen lock.**

    This level of security prevents others from idly messing with your beloved gizmo.

8. **Tap the ERASE EVERYTHING or DELETE ALL button to confirm.**

    All the information you've set or stored on the device is purged, including all your accounts, any apps you've downloaded, music — everything.

Practical instances when this action is necessary include selling your Android, giving it to someone else to use, and upgrading to a new phone or tablet.

This process doesn't erase removable storage data. You must reformat the microSD card or otherwise subject it to some form of erasure. Refer to Chapter 19 for details on formatting external storage.

Erasing all the data from an Android phone doesn't reset the phone number. You must remove the SIM card to disassociate the phone number from that phone. Or you can replace the SIM card to add another phone number to the phone.

Chapter **23**

On the Road Again

You're in a land far, far away. The sun shines warmly upon your face. A gentle breeze wafts over crashing waves. You wiggle your toes in the soft, grainy sand. And the number-one thought on your mind is, "Can my Android phone get a signal?"

For an Android tablet, the question is the same: "Do they have Wi-Fi on this beach?" Funny as it sounds, they probably do.

As a mobile device, your Android is designed to go wherever you go. And if you give the thing a good throw, it can go beyond where you go, but that's not my point. Because it is wireless and has a generous battery, an Android mobile device is built to go on the road. Where can you take it? How can it survive? What if it runs off by itself? Does it need wheels? These are some of the issues regarding taking your tablet elsewhere.

Where the Android Roams

The word *roam* takes on an entirely new meaning when applied to an Android phone or LTE tablet. It means that your device receives a cell signal whenever you're outside the service provider's operating area. In that case, your Android is roaming.

Roaming sounds handy, but there's a catch: It almost always involves a surcharge for using another cellular service — an unpleasant surcharge.

Detecting phone service roaming

Relax: Your Android alerts you whenever it's roaming. The Roaming icon appears at the top of the screen, in the status area, whenever you're outside your cellular provider's signal area. The icon differs from device to device, but generally the letter *R* figures in it somewhere, as in the margin.

On an Android phone, you might even see the alien cellular provider's name appear on the lock screen.

There's little you can do to avoid roaming surcharges when making phone calls. Well, yes: You can wait until you're back in an area serviced by your primary cellular provider.

TIP

If you're concerned about roaming while overseas, place the phone into Airplane mode, as discussed elsewhere in this chapter.

Stopping MMS when roaming

Another network service you might want to disable while roaming has to do with multimedia, or MMS, text messages. To avoid surcharges from another cellular network for downloading an MMS message, follow these steps:

1. **Open the phone's text messaging app.**

2. **Ensure that you're viewing the main screen, not an individual message thread.**

3. **Tap the Action Overflow icon or the MORE button.**

   On Samsung's Message+ app, tap the Side Menu icon to display the navigation drawer.

4. **Choose Settings.**

5. **Choose Advanced or More Settings.**

   On Samsung's Message+ app, choose When Roaming. Ensure that each item is unchecked. Tap OK. You're done.

6. **Ensure that the Auto-Download MMS setting is off or disabled.**

   This item might also be called Auto-Retrieve or Roaming Auto Retrieve.

Disabling data roaming

One feature you want to disable on your Android phone or LTE tablet is data roaming. As with cellular service, the mobile data network also roams when you're outside the provider's operating area. To ensure that this service is disabled, work through these steps:

1. **Open the Settings app.**

2. **Choose Network and Internet.**

   On some Androids, choose the More item located in the Wireless & Networks area.

3. **Choose Mobile Network or Cellular Networks.**

4. **Ensure that the Data Roaming setting is disabled or denied.**

On some Samsung gizmos, follow these steps:

1. **Open the Settings app.**

2. **Choose Connections.**

   If you don't see this item, skip to Step 3.

3. **Choose Mobile Networks.**

4. **Choose Data Roaming Access.**

5. **Select the option Deny Data Roaming Access.**

6. **Tap OK.**

REMEMBER

Your Android can still access the Internet over the Wi-Fi connection when it roams. Setting up a Wi-Fi connection doesn't affect the mobile data network connection, because the device prefers to use Wi-Fi. See Chapter 18 for more information about Wi-Fi.

International Calling

A phone is a bell that anyone in the world can ring. To prove it, all you need is the phone number of anyone in the world. Use your Android phone to dial that number and, as long as you both speak the same language, you're talking!

To make an international call with your Android phone, you must know the foreign phone number. The number includes the international country-code prefix, followed by the number. For example:

01-234-56-789

Before dialing the international country-code prefix (01, in this example), you must first type a plus (+). The + symbol is the country exit code, which must be dialed in order to flee the national phone system and access the international phone system. For example, to dial Finland on your phone, type +358 and then the number in Finland. The +358 is the exit code (+) plus the international code for Finland (358).

To type the + character, press and hold down the 0 key on the Phone app's dialpad. Then type the country prefix and the phone number. Tap the Dial icon to place the call.

>> Dialing internationally involves surcharges, unless your cellular plan provides for international calling.

>> International calls fail for several reasons. One of the most common is that the recipient's phone service blocks incoming international calls.

>> Another reason that international calls fail is the zero reason: Oftentimes, you must leave out any zero in the phone number that follows the country code. So, if the country code is 254 for Kenya and the phone number starts with 012, you dial +254 for Kenya and then 12 and the rest of the number. Omit the leading zero.

>> Know which type of phone you're calling internationally — cell phone or landline. The reason is that an international call to a cell phone might involve a surcharge that doesn't apply to a landline.

WARNING

>> The + character isn't a number separator. When you see an international number listed as 011+20+xxxxxxx, do not insert the + character in the number. Instead, type +20 and then the rest of the international phone number.

>> Most cellular providers add a surcharge when sending a text message abroad. Contact your cellular provider to confirm the text message rates. Generally, you find two rates: one for sending and another for receiving text messages.

>> If texting charges vex you, remember that email has no associated per-message charge. You also have alternative ways to chat, such as Google Hangouts and Skype; Skype can also be used to place cheap international calls. See Chapter 11.

>> In most cases, dialing an international number involves a time zone difference. Before you dial, be aware of what time it is in the country or location you're calling. The Clock app can handle that job for you: Summon a clock for the location you're calling and place it on the Clock app's screen.

You Can Take It with You

You can take your Android with you anywhere you like. How it functions may change depending on your environment, and you can do a few things to prepare before you go. Add these items to your other travel checklists, such as taking cash, bringing an ID, and preparing to wait in inspection lines.

Preparing to leave

Unless you're being unexpectedly abducted, you should prepare several things before leaving on a trip with your Android phone or tablet.

First and most important, of course, is to charge the thing. I plug in my Android overnight before I leave the next day. The device's battery is nice and robust, so power should last until well after you reach your destination.

Second, consider loading up on some media, plus a few new apps before you go: eBooks, movies, music, saved web pages, games. The more stuff, the more you'll have to occupy your time.

Finally, don't forget your tickets! Many airlines offer apps. The apps may make traveling easy because they generate notifications for your schedule and provide timely gate changes or flight delays — plus, you can use the touchscreen as your e-ticket. Search Google Play to see whether your preferred airline offers an app.

>> If you plan to read books, listen to music, or watch a video while on the road, consider downloading that media to your Android before you leave. See Chapter 16 for information.

>> I save a few of my regular morning web pages for offline reading before I go. See Chapter 10 for details on saving web pages in the Chrome app. To access saved web pages, tap the Action Overflow and choose Downloads.

>> For entertainment, consider getting some eBooks for the road. I prefer to sit and stew over Google Play's online library before I leave, as opposed to wandering aimlessly in some airport sundry store, trying hard to focus on the good books rather than on the salty snacks. Chapter 17 covers reading eBooks.

>> Picking up some music might be a good idea as well. Visit Chapter 15.

>> I usually reward myself with a new game before I go on a trip. Visit Google Play and see what's hot or recommended. A good puzzle game can make a nice, long international flight go by a lot quicker.

Arriving at the airport

I'm not a frequent flier, but I am a nerd. The most amount of junk I've carried with me on a flight is two laptop computers and three cell phones. I know that's not a record, but it's enough to warrant the following list of travel tips, all of which apply to taking an Android phone or tablet with you on an extended journey:

>> Take the Android's AC adapter and USB cable with you. Put them in your carry-on luggage or backpack.

>> Nearly all major airports feature USB chargers, so you can charge the Android in an airport, if you need to. Even though you need only the cable to charge, bring along the AC adapter anyway.

>> At the security checkpoint, place your Android phone or tablet in a bin by itself or with other electronics. You might be able to get away with leaving the tablet inside a pouch or backpack, though first confirm that possibility with the security personnel.

>> You can never walk through the metal detector or scanner wearing a cell phone. Well, you can, but you'll be directed to secondary search and get dirty looks from others waiting in line. (Yeah, I've done that.)

TIP

>> Use the Calendar app to keep track of your flights. The event title serves as the airline and flight number. For the event time, use the take-off and landing schedules. For the location, list the origin and destination airport codes. And, in the Description field, put the flight reservation number. If you're using separate calendars (categories), specify the Travel calendar for your flight. See Chapter 16 for more information on the Calendar app.

>> If you ordered your tickets online and use your Gmail account, the Calendar app automatically grabs the flight information from the confirmation email message. Pretty cool.

>> Scan for the airport's Wi-Fi service. Most airports don't charge for the service, though you may have to use the web browser app to agree to terms before getting full access.

Flying with an Android

Readers of the future: The title of this section applies to mobile Android devices, popular in the first part of the 21st century. What you probably want is the title *Personal Robots For Dummies*, first published in 2049.

It truly is the trendiest of things to be aloft with the latest mobile gizmo. Still, you must follow some rules:

1. **Obey the flight crew.**

    When they say to turn off your mobile device, do so. They might also ask you to unplug the device from the in-cabin power. And do pay attention to the safety instructions.

2. **Place your device into Airplane mode.**

    This direction applies to both phones and tablets. The easy way is to use the quick settings and tap the Airplane Mode icon. See Chapter 3 for details on using the quick settings.

3. **If you want to use the in-flight Wi-Fi, turn on Wi-Fi after the service is available.**

    Yes, it's possible to have the device's Wi-Fi radio on while Airplane mode is active.

4. **During descent, or whenever asked to, turn off or lock your Android.**

When the Android is in Airplane mode, a special icon appears in the status area, similar to the one shown in the margin.

>> To exit Airplane mode, tap the Airplane Mode icon on the Quick Settings drawer.

>> Airplane mode disables the device's cellular, GPS, and Bluetooth radios. You are admonished not to use these radios while flying. That means you can't effectively use the Maps app to confirm that you see Greenland down there.

Getting to your destination

After you arrive at your destination, the Android may update the date and time according to your new location. One additional step you may want to take is to set the time zone. By doing so, you ensure that your schedule adapts properly to your new location.

To change or confirm the device's time zone, follow these steps:

1. **Open the Settings app.**

2. **Choose System and then choose Date and Time.**

On some Androids, the Date and Time item appears on the main Settings app screen. On Samsung devices, choose General Management, where you'll find the Date and Time item.

3. **If you find an Automatic Date & Time setting, ensure that it's active.**

If so, you're done; the Android automatically updates its time references. Otherwise, continue with Step 4.

4. **Choose Select Time Zone.**

5. **Pluck the current time zone from the list.**

If you've set appointments for your new location, visit the Calendar app to ensure that their start and end times have been properly adjusted. If you're prompted to update appointment times based on the new zone, do so.

REMEMBER

When you're done traveling or you change your time zone again, make sure that the Android is updated as well. When the Automatic Time Zone setting isn't available, follow the steps in this section to reset the time zone.

The Android Goes Abroad

Yes, your Android works overseas. The two resources you need to consider are how to recharge the battery and how to access Wi-Fi. As long as you have both, you're pretty much set. You also must be careful about mobile data (cellular) roaming surcharges when using an Android phone or LTE tablet.

Calling with your Android phone overseas

The easiest way to use a cell phone abroad is to rent or buy one in the country where you plan to stay. I'm serious: Often, international roaming charges are so high that it's cheaper to simply buy a temporary cell phone wherever you go, especially if you plan to stay there for a while.

When you opt to use your own phone rather than buy a local phone, things should run smoothly — if a compatible cellular service is in your location. Not every Android phone uses the same network type and, of course, not every foreign country uses the same cellular network. Things must match before the phone can work. Plus, you may have to deal with foreign carrier roaming charges.

The key to determining whether your phone is usable in a foreign country is to turn it on. The name of that country's compatible cellular service shows up on the phone's lock screen. So, where your phone once said *Verizon Wireless*, it may say *Wambooli Telcom* when you're overseas.

REMEMBER

>> You receive calls on your cell phone internationally if the phone can access the network. Your friends need only dial your cell phone number as they normally do; the phone system automatically forwards your calls to wherever you are in the world.

>> The person calling you pays nothing extra when you're off romping the globe with your Android phone. Nope — *you* pay extra for the call.

>> While you're abroad, you must dial internationally. When calling home (for example, the United States), you need to use a 10-digit number (phone number plus area code). You may also be required to type the country exit code when you dial. See the earlier section "International Calling."

>> When in doubt, contact your cellular provider for tips and other information specific to whatever country you're visiting.

Using overseas power

You can easily attach a foreign AC power adapter to your Android's AC power plug. You don't need a voltage converter — just an adapter. After it's attached, you can plug your phone or tablet into those weirdo overseas power sockets without facing the risk of blowing up anything. I charged my Android nightly while I spent time in France, and it worked like a charm.

Accessing Wi-Fi in foreign lands

Wi-Fi is universal. The same protocols and standards are used everywhere, so if your Android can access Wi-Fi at your local Starbucks, it can access Wi-Fi at the Malted Yak Blood Café in Wamboolistan. As long as Wi-Fi is available, your Android can use it.

» Internet cafés are more popular overseas than in the United States. They're the best locations for connecting to the Internet and catching up on life back home.

» Many overseas hotels offer free Wi-Fi service, although the signal may not reach into every room. Don't be surprised if you can use the Wi-Fi network only while you're in the lobby.

TIP

» Obtain Skype Credit to use your Android to place phone calls overseas. Skype's international rates are quite reasonable. The calls are made over the Internet, so when the Android has Wi-Fi access, you're good to go. See Chapter 11 for more information on making Skype calls.

Chapter **24**

Maintenance, Troubleshooting, and Help

Maintenance is that thing you were supposed to remember to do but you didn't do, and that's why you need help and troubleshooting advice.

Don't blame yourself; no one likes to do maintenance. Okay, well, I like maintaining my stuff. I even change the belt on my vacuum cleaner every six months. Did you know that the vacuum cleaner manual tells you to do so? Probably not. I read that in *Vacuum Cleaners For Dummies*. This book is *Android Phones & Tablets For Dummies*, which is why it contains topics on maintenance, troubleshooting, and help for Android mobile devices, which lack belts that you should change every six months.

The Maintenance Chore

Relax. Unlike draining the lawnmower's oil once a year, regular maintenance of an Android phone or tablet doesn't require a drip pan or a permit from the EPA. In fact, an Android requires only two basic regular maintenance tasks: cleaning and backing up.

Keeping it clean

You probably already keep your Android clean. Perhaps you're one of those people who uses their sleeves to wipe the touchscreen. Of course, better than your sleeve is something called a *microfiber* cloth. This item can be found at any computer or office–supply store.

WARNING

>> Never use ammonia or alcohol to clean the touchscreen. These substances damage the device. If you must use a cleaning solution, select something specifically designed for touchscreens.

>> Touchscreen-safe screen cleaners are available for those times when your sleeve or even a microfiber cloth won't cut it. Ensure that you get a screen cleaner designed for a touchscreen.

>> If the touchscreen keeps getting dirty, consider adding a screen protector: This specially designed cover prevents the glass from getting scratched or dirty but still allows you to use your finger on the touchscreen. Be sure that the screen protector is designed for use with the specific brand and model of your phone or tablet.

>> For an Android phone, consider a phone case, belt clip, or another protector, which can help keep the phone looking spiffy. Be aware that these items are mostly for decorative or fashion purposes and don't even prevent serious damage should you drop the phone.

>> Android tablets offer special cases or folios. Some are even combination case-keyboards, which eases the frustration of typing with the onscreen keyboard.

Backing up your stuff

For a majority of the information on your Android, backup is automatic. Your Google account takes care of Gmail, the calendar, and your contacts, music, eBooks, movies, and apps. This stuff is synchronized and backed up automatically.

To confirm that your account's media is synchronized and other information is backed up, heed these steps:

1. **Open the Settings app.**
2. **Choose Users & Accounts.**
3. **Ensure that the master control by Automatically Sync Data is on.**
4. **Tap your Google account in the list.**
5. **Choose Account Sync.**
6. **Ensure that the master control by each item is on.**

   These are the items that synchronize between the device and your Google account on the Internet.

7. **Tap the Back navigation icon until you see the main Settings app screen.**
8. **Choose System.**
9. **Choose Backup.**
10. **Ensure that the master control by Back Up to Google Drive is on.**

    You can review each item in the list to confirm that a recent backup was made.

The steps to confirm sync and backup settings are different for older versions of the Android operating system. If you don't see the User & Accounts item (see Step 2 in the preceding steps), follow these steps instead:

1. **Open the Settings app and choose Accounts.**
2. **Choose Google to access your Google account settings.**
3. **Ensure that the master control by each item in the list is enabled.**
4. **Back at the main Settings app screen, choose Backup & Reset.**
5. **Ensure that the item Back Up My Data is enabled.**

Specific items from your device can be backed up manually. For example, if you download a PDF and want to keep a backup, copy that file from the device to a computer. Chapter 19 covers options for getting files out of your Android.

Updating the system

Every so often, your Android signals that a system update is available. Android operating system security updates occur about once a month. The device's manufacturer may release an update. And Google occasionally releases a new version of the Android operating system.

 When an update is available, you see the System Update notification icon, as shown in the margin. Choose that notification to apply the update.

You might also see a pop-up message, or "toast," appear on the screen when an update is available. Your options are to immediately update or postpone. My advice is to apply the update immediately, as long as the Android has sufficient battery life left (or you can connect to a power supply) and you're not expecting to do anything major with the phone or tablet during the next few minutes.

You can also manually check for an update. Heed these directions:

1. **Open the Settings app.**

2. **Choose System.**

3. **Choose System Updates.**

4. **Tap Check for Update.**

   If an update is pending, you'll see it listed.

In older versions of the Android operating system, choose About Phone or About Tablet in Step 2. The System Updates item is located on that screen.

>> Android version 8.0 "Oreo" fetches an update if one is pending. Older versions of the Android operating system allow updates by quota. So, manually checking for an update, even when one is pending, may not result in updating the device.

 >> Connect your device to a power source during a software update. You don't want the battery to die in the middle of the operation.

REMEMBER

Battery Care and Feeding

Perhaps the most important item you can monitor and maintain on your Android is its battery. The battery supplies the necessary electrical juice by which the device operates. Without battery power, your gizmo is basically an expensive drink coaster or trivet. Keep an eye on the battery.

Monitoring the battery

Your Android displays its current battery status at the top of the screen, in the status area, next to the time. The icons used are similar to those shown in Figure 24-1. They can appear white-on-black or use a charming color scheme, as illustrated in the figure.

Fully charged   Starting to drain   Low — charge soon   Very low — stop using and charge at once!   Charging

You might also see an icon for a dead battery, but for some reason I can't get my Android to turn on and display that icon.

TIP

>> Heed those low-battery warnings! You hear a warning sound and see a notification whenever the battery power gets low. Another sound chimes whenever the battery gets very low.

>> When the battery level is too low, the device shuts itself off.

>> The best way to deal with low battery power is to connect the Android to a power source: Either plug it into a wall socket or use the USB cable to connect it to a computer. The phone or tablet begins charging itself immediately; plus, you can use the device while it's charging.

>> Android devices charge more efficiently when plugged into a wall socket rather than a computer.

>> You aren't required to fully charge the battery. For example, if you have only 20 minutes before the next flight, and you get only a 70 percent battery level, that's great. Well, it's not great, but it's far better than a lower battery level.

TECHNICAL STUFF

>> Battery percentage values are best-guess estimates. Just because you get 8 hours of use from the device and the battery meter shows 20 percent remaining doesn't imply that 20 percent equals 2 more hours of use. In practice, the amount of time you have left is much less than that. As a rule, when the battery percentage value gets low, the battery appears to drain faster.

Determining what is drawing power

The Battery screen in the Settings app informs you of the device's battery usage over time, as well as which apps have been consuming power, as illustrated in Figure 24-2.

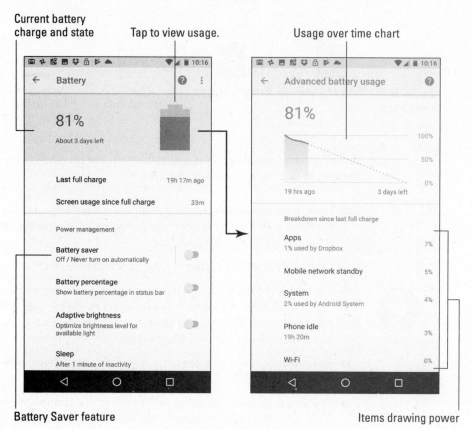

FIGURE 24-2: Power consumption details.

To view the battery usage, follow these steps:

1. **Open the Settings app.**

2. **Choose Battery.**

   On Samsung devices, choose the Device Maintenance category, and then choose Battery.

   You see general information about battery usage, plus some power-saving tools, shown on the left in Figure 24-2. At the bottom of the screen (swipe down), you see which apps are using power.

3. **Tap the Battery icon at the top of the screen (refer to Figure 24-2).**

You see a charge illustrating battery power over time, plus which apps are using the most power.

The number and variety of items shown on the battery usage screen depend on what you've been doing with your Android between charges. Don't be surprised if an item doesn't show up in the list; not every app consumes a lot of battery power.

Extending battery life

A surefire way to make a battery last a good, long time is to never turn on the device in the first place. That's kind of impractical. So instead, I offer a smattering of suggestions you can follow to help prolong battery life:

Dim the screen: The touchscreen display draws quite a lot of battery power. Although a dim screen can be more difficult to see, especially outdoors, it saves on battery life.

Lower the volume: Consider lowering the volume for the various noises the Android makes, especially notifications.

Disable the vibration options: Vibration is caused by a teensy motor. Though you don't see much battery savings by disabling the vibration options, it's better than no savings.

Turn off Bluetooth: When you're not using Bluetooth, turn it off. The fastest way to do that is to use the Bluetooth quick action.

TIP

Rather than fuss with these individual settings, consider activating your Android's battery-saver feature. Illustrated in Figure 24-2, switch on the master control by Battery Saver. When the power gets low, the actions listed earlier are all taken: The screen is dimmed, and services are disabled. The result is more battery life without fully affecting overall device performance.

» Samsung devices feature an "ultra" battery-saving mode. In this mode, the screen dims and color is disabled. The Home screen is replaced by a special interface that lists only necessary features. I've used this mode when my phone's battery level dipped below 30%, and it helped extend the battery life for hours.

» The Wi-Fi radio can drain the battery quickly, even when you're not using it. When driving long distances, I disable Wi-Fi on my Android. If I don't, it seems that the device tries to connect with every Wi-Fi signal available. Especially in highly populated areas, this activity can quickly — and surprisingly — drain the battery.

Help and Troubleshooting

Getting help with technology today isn't as bad as it was years back. I remember only two sources for help: the atrocious manual that came with your electronic device and a phone call to the guy who wrote the atrocious manual. It was unpleasant. Today, the situation is better. You have many resources for solving issues with your gizmos, including your Android.

Fixing random and annoying problems

Aren't all problems annoying? A welcome problem doesn't exist, unless the problem is welcome because it diverts attention from another, preexisting problem. And random problems? If problems were predictable, they would serve in office.

General trouble

For just about any problem or minor quirk, consider restarting the phone or tablet: Long-press the Power/Lock key. The device options menu may feature a Restart action. If so, use it. Otherwise, turn it off, and then turn it on again. This procedure fixes most of the annoying problems you encounter.

See Chapter 2 for basic Android on–off instructions.

Connection woes

As you move about, the cellular signal can change. In fact, you may observe the status icon change from 4G LTE to 3G to even the dreaded 1X or — worse — nothing, depending on the strength and availability of the mobile data network.

My advice for random signal weirdness is to wait. Oftentimes, the signal comes back after a few minutes. If it doesn't, the mobile data network might be down, or you may just be in an area with lousy service. Consider changing your location.

For Wi-Fi connections, ensure that Wi-Fi is set up properly and working. This process involves pestering the person who configured the Wi-Fi router or, in a coffee shop, bothering the cheerful person with the tattoos and piercings who serves you coffee.

WARNING

Be aware that some Wi-Fi networks have a "lease time" after which your device is disconnected. If so, follow the directions in Chapter 19 for turning off the Wi-Fi radio and then turn it on again. That often solves the issue. Also refer to Chapter 19 for details on metered Wi-Fi connections.

Another problem I've heard about is that the Wi-Fi router doesn't recognize your Android. In this case, the router might use older technology and it needs to be replaced.

Music is playing and you want it to stop

It's awesome that your Android continues to play music while you do other things. Getting the music to stop quickly, however, requires some skill. You can access the Play controls for the Play Music app from a number of locations. They're found on the Lock screen, for example. You can also find them in the notifications drawer.

An app has run amok

Sometimes, apps that misbehave let you know. You see a warning on the screen announcing the app's stubborn disposition. When that happens, tap the FORCE QUIT button to shut down the app. Then say, "Whew!"

To manually shut down an app, refer to Chapter 20.

You've reached your wit's end

When all else fails, you can do the drastic thing and perform a factory data reset on your device. Before committing to this step, you should contact support as described in the next section.

Refer to Chapter 22 for details on the factory data reset.

Getting help and support

Never discount your Android device's manufacturer for assistance when you need it. If you have an Android phone or LTE tablet, consider contacting the cellular provider. Between the two, I recommend contacting the cellular provider first, no matter what the problem. Beyond these resources, you can read the information I've presented in this section.

The Help app

Some manufacturers include a Help or Getting Started app with their devices. They may offer pop-up toasts, which present tips as you explore new features on your phone or tablet.

Google Support is available in the Settings app, though this feature was added only with newer releases of the Android operating system. Follow these steps:

1. **Open the Settings app.**

2. **Choose Support.**

The options on the Support screen include phoning or chatting with a Google support person, as well as searching online Help. An option for reviewing tips and tricks is also presented.

>> Also look for a Help eBook in the Play Books app.

>> The Settings app features the Search icon, which helps you locate specific settings without knowing exactly under which category the item might be found.

Cellular support

Contact information for both the cellular provider and device manufacturer is found in the material you received with your Android. In Chapter 1, I recommend that you save those random pieces of paper. You obviously have read that chapter and followed my advice, so you can easily find that information.

Okay, so you don't want to go find the box, or you didn't heed my admonition and you threw out the box. Table 24-1 lists contact information for U.S. cellular providers. The From Cell column lists the number you can call by using your Android phone; otherwise, you can use the toll-free number from any phone.

TABLE 24-1 ## U.S. Cellular Providers

Provider	From Cell	Toll-free	Website
AT&T	611	800-331-0500	www.att.com/esupport
Sprint Nextel	*2	800-211-4727	sprint.com
T-Mobile	611	877-453-1304	www.t-mobile.com/Contact.aspx
Verizon	611	800-922-0204	verizonwireless.com/support

Manufacturer support

Another source of support for your device, or only source if you have a Wi-Fi-only tablet, is the manufacturer, such as Samsung or LG. Information about support can be found in those random papers and pamphlets included in the device's box. If not, refer to Table 24-2 for contact information.

TABLE 24-2   **Android Manufacturers**

Manufacturer	Website
HTC	www.htc.com/us/support
LG	www.lg.com/us/support
Motorola	www.motorola.com
Samsung	samsung.com/us/mobile/phones or samsung.com/us/mobile/tablets

App support

For app issues, contact the developer. Follow these steps:

1. **Open the Play Store app.**

2. **Tap the Side Menu icon to display the navigation drawer.**

3. **Choose My Apps & Games.**

4. **Tap the Installed tab.**

5. **Tap the entry for the specific app, the one that's bothering you.**

6. **Choose the Send Email item.**

   Swipe the screen bottom-to-top to scroll down the app's Info screen and find the Send Email item. It's usually one of the last items on the screen.

REMEMBER

Contacting the developer is no guarantee that they'll respond.

Google Play support

For issues with Google Play itself, contact Google at

support.google.com/googleplay

Valuable Android Q&A

I love Q&A! Not only is it an effective way to express certain problems and solutions, but some of the questions might also cover things I've been wanting to ask.

"I can't turn the thing on (or off)!"

Sometimes an Android locks up. It's frustrating, but I've discovered that if you press and hold the Power/Lock key for about 8 seconds, the device turns either off or on, depending on which state it's in.

If waiting 8 seconds doesn't work, let the phone or tablet sit for 10 minutes or so. Try again.

"The touchscreen doesn't work!"

A touchscreen requires a human finger for proper interaction. The screen interprets the static potential between the human finger and the device to determine where the touchscreen is being touched. The touchscreen will not work if the screen is damaged. It will not work when you're wearing gloves, unless they're specially designed touchscreen gloves. The touchscreen might fail also when the battery power is low.

"The screen is too dark!"

Android device's feature a teensy light sensor on the front. If the Adaptive Brightness or Auto Brightness feature is active, the sensor adjusts the touchscreen's brightness based on the amount of ambient light at your location. If the sensor is covered, the screen can get very, very dark.

Ensure that you don't unintentionally block the light sensor. Avoid buying a case or screen protector that obscures the sensor.

The automatic brightness setting might also be vexing you. See Chapter 21 for information on setting screen brightness.

"The battery doesn't charge!"

Start from the source: Is the wall socket providing power? Is the cord plugged in? The cable may be damaged, so try another cable.

When charging from a USB port on a computer, ensure that the computer is turned on. Most computers don't provide USB power when they're turned off. Also, some USB ports may not supply enough power to charge the battery. If possible, use a port on the computer console (the box) instead of a USB hub.

Some Android tablets charge from a special cord, not the USB cable. Check to confirm that your tablet is able to take a charge from the USB cable.

"The gizmo gets so hot that it turns itself off!"

Yikes! An overheating gadget can be a nasty problem. Can you hold the Android in your hand, or is it too hot to hold? When it's too hot to hold, turn off the power. Disconnect it from the power supply. Let it cool.

If the overheating problem continues, have the Android looked at for potential repair. The battery might need to be replaced. Some phones may have removable batteries, but most Android phones and tablets are sealed units where you cannot replace the battery yourself.

>> It's normal for a phone to get warm (not hot) as you use it. If you blab for an hour or so, the phone will seem warmer than normal. That's just the battery doing its job.

>> It's also normal for an Android to be warm as it's charging. If the device is too hot to hold, you need to disconnect the power cord and let the gizmo cool down.

>> Do not continue to use any device that's too hot! The heat damages the electronics. It can also start a fire.

WARNING

"The screen doesn't do Landscape mode!"

Not every app can change its orientation between Portrait and Landscape modes — or even Upside-Down mode. For example, many games present themselves in one orientation only. Some Androids don't rotate their Home screens. So, just because the app doesn't go into Horizontal or Vertical mode doesn't mean that anything is broken.

Confirm that the orientation lock isn't on: Check the quick settings. Ensure that the Auto-Rotate or Screen Rotation item is properly set. Also, some eBook reader apps sport their own screen rotation lock feature. Tap the Action Overflow to determine whether it's enabled.

5
The Part of Tens

» Flipping on the flashlight

» Creating a panoramic shot

» Monitoring data usage

» Watching the Android dream

» Making an account for a kid

» Spicing up your dictation

» Building the dictionary

» Adding useful Home screen widgets

» Creating a screen shot

Chapter **25**

Ten Tips, Tricks, and Shortcuts

A *tip* is a small suggestion, a word of advice often spoken from bruising experience or knowledge passed along from someone with bruising experience. A *trick*, which is something not many know about, usually causes amusement or surprise. A *shortcut* is a quick way to get home, even though it crosses the old graveyard and you never quite know whether Old Man Witherspoon is the groundskeeper or a zombie.

I'd like to think that just about everything in this book is a tip, trick, or shortcut for using an Android mobile gizmo. Even so, I've distilled items in this chapter into a list that is definitely worthy of note.

Switch Apps Quickly

REMEMBER

Android apps don't quit. Sure, some of them have a Quit action or Sign Out option, but most apps loiter in the device's guts while you do other things. The Android operating system may eventually kill off a stale app. Before that happens, you can deftly and quickly switch between all running apps.

The key to making the switch is to use the Recent navigation icon, found at the bottom of the touchscreen. Tap this icon and choose an app from the list. Swipe the list up or down to peruse what's available. To dismiss the list, tap the Back or Home navigation icons.

>> Variations on the Recent icon are shown in Chapter 3.

>> On older devices that lack the Recent icon, long-press the Home navigation icon.

>> To remove an app from the list of recent apps, swipe it left or right. This is effectively the same thing as quitting an app.

TIP

>> Double-tap the Recent icon to switch between the two most recently used apps.

>> Some Androids may feature a Task Manager. It's usually a more technical representation of the items you find on the list of recent apps, with the addition of internal apps and services.

TECHNICAL STUFF

>> The list of recent apps is called the *Overview,* though everyone I know calls it the List of Recent Apps.

Deploy the Flashlight

One of the first "killer apps" on mobile devices was the flashlight. It used the camera's LED flash to help you see in the dark. For a while, everyone had to get a flashlight app, but today the flashlight feature is frequently found on the Quick Actions drawer.

Use two fingers to swipe down the screen and display the quick settings. If one of the icons looks like a flashlight (see the margin), tap it to activate the flashlight feature. Tap again to turn off the flashlight.

» The flashlight feature might also appear as a lock screen app, or you can place it on the lock screen as an option. Refer to Chapter 21.

» Be aware that keeping the LED lamp on for extended durations drains the battery.

» Over time it was discovered that the seemingly innocent flashlight apps spied on their users. The apps collected data and beamed it back to a remote server somewhere. Such malicious apps were purged from Google Play long ago. In any event, the availability of the Quick Actions feature has rendered such apps unnecessary.

Shoot a Panorama

Most variations of the Camera app sport a panoramic shooting mode. The *panorama* is a wide shot — it works by panning the camera across a scene. The Camera app then stitches together several images to build the panoramic image.

To shoot a panoramic shot, follow these steps in the Camera app:

1. **Choose the Camera app's Panorama mode.**

    For the stock Android Camera app, tap the Side Menu icon (in the upper left corner of the screen) and then tap the Panorama icon, shown in the margin.

    With the current flavor of the Samsung Camera app, swipe in from the left edge of the screen to find the Panorama shooting mode.

2. **Hold the device steady, and then tap the Shutter icon.**

3. **Pivot in one direction as shown on the screen, following along with the animation.**

    Watch as the image is rendered and saved.

You can stop the panorama at any time. Look for a Done icon or tap the Shutter icon again. You don't have to twist all the way around and rupture something just to capture a panoramic shot.

TIP

Panoramas work best for vistas, wide shots, or perhaps family gatherings where not everyone likes each other.

Avoid Data Surcharges

An important issue for anyone using an Android phone or LTE tablet is whether you're about to burst through your monthly data quota. Mobile data surcharges can pinch the wallet, but your Android has a handy tool to help you avoid data overages. It's the data usage screen, shown in Figure 25-1.

To access the data usage screen, follow these steps:

1. **Open the Settings app.**

2. **Choose Network & Internet or Connections.**

   Some Androids don't feature this item, in which case you skip to Step 3.

3. **Choose Data Usage.**

The data usage screen shows how much data your device has used for both mobile data and Wi-Fi connections. Tap Mobile Data Usage or Wi-Fi Data Usage to see the consumption charts, as well as those apps that access the Internet, as illustrated in Figure 25-1.

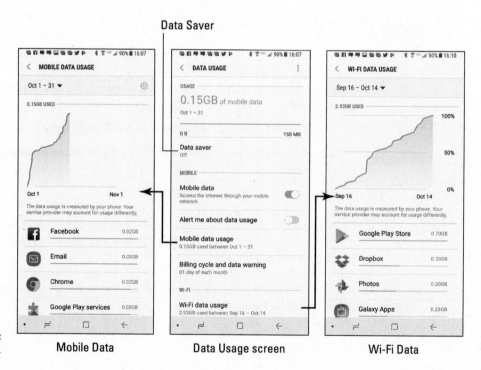

FIGURE 25-1: Data usage.

Data Saver

Mobile Data   Data Usage screen   Wi-Fi Data

Showing the details is interesting, but where the data usage screen is most useful is when setting warnings and limits on mobile data. Follow these steps:

1. **On the mobile data usage screen (on the left in Figure 25-1), tap the Settings (gear) icon.**

2. **Ensure that the master control by Set Data Warning is in the On position.**

3. **Tap Data Warning and set when the warning appears.**

   Say your plan allows for 3.0GB (gigabytes) of mobile data per billing cycle. Set the warning at 2.5GB. Tap the SET button.

4. **Ensure that the master control by Set Data Limit is in the On position.**

   You may see a warning. When the data limit option is set, your device is no longer permitted to send or receive information over the mobile data network. You can still use Wi-Fi, but mobile data is cut off to save you from a data surcharge.

5. **Tap Data Limit and set a limit.**

   This value should be just below your allowed usage — say, 2.8GB for a plan that allows 3.0GB per month.

REMEMBER

It's important to remember that your device and the cellular provider monitor data usage differently. For example, your monthly quota may be 5GB but if you set the limit (when the device stops using the mobile data network, in Step 5) to 5GB, you may still be surcharged. That's why I recommend (in Step 5) to set a limit below your maximum allowed monthly usage.

TIP

You can also use the Data Saver, illustrated in Figure 25-1. When this option is activated, the Android limits network access to only two apps maximum. Other apps must wait, which cuts down on data usage.

Watch Your Android Dream

Does your Android lock itself to sleep? After the touchscreen time-out kicks in, the apps keep running and activity goes on, but does the device dream?

Well, of course it does! You can even see the dreams, if you activate the Daydream feature — and if you keep a power source connected. Heed these steps:

1. **Start the Settings app.**

2. **Choose Display.**

3. **Choose Screen Saver.**

   This item is titled Daydream on older devices.

4. **Ensure that the master control is in the On position.**

5. **Choose which type of daydream you want displayed.**

   The Clock is a popular item, though I'm fond of Colors.

 Some daydream options feature a Settings icon, which customizes the daydream's appearance.

6. **On the Screen Saver (or Daydream) screen, tap the Action Overflow.**

7. **Choose When to Daydream.**

8. **Choose Either.**

The daydreaming begins when the screen would normally time-out and lock, though the device must be receiving power.

›› To disrupt the dream, swipe the screen.

›› The Android doesn't lock when it daydreams. To lock the device, press the Power/Lock key.

›› Not every Android offers the Daydream feature.

Create a Kid's Account

All Androids have the capability to host multiple users. It's my observation, however, that this feature goes widely unused. It's just easier to hand a phone or tablet to another person or, as is the case with most devices, to get your own gizmo. Especially with phones, multiple users on a single device is silly.

One useful reason to have another account, however, is to create a kid's account. You can customize which apps Junior can use and rest easy knowing that your tot won't irrevocably change things or mess up your existence.

To add a kid's account, you must ensure that your own account is protected with a secure screen lock. See Chapter 22. Once a secure screen lock is applied, heed these directions:

1. **Open the Settings app.**

2. **Choose Users and Accounts.**

   If you don't see this item, skip to Step 3.

3. **Choose Users.**

4. **Choose Add User or Profile.**

5. **Choose Restricted Profile.**

   The new, restricted profile appears on the App & Content Access screen.

6. **Set controls and determine access.**

   Your job is to review items on the list. Set the master control to the On position to enable an item as a game or another app.

    Some apps, such as Netflix, may have a Settings icon. Tap that icon to further control access or set restrictions.

7. **Tap the New Profile item at the top of the screen and set a name for the account.**

If it is your desire to have separate accounts on an Android, in Step 5 choose User instead of Restricted Profile. Tap OK, and then tap SET UP NOW, and then hand the device over to the other user so that they may continue setting up and configuring their own account.

To switch accounts, lock the screen. When you unlock the screen, tap the user icon in the upper right corner, as illustrated in Figure 25-2. Choose another account from the list.

The other user's account takes over: Their screen lock appears (if applied) and then their Home screen, apps, and other customizations.

>> You can also access other user accounts from the bottom of the Quick Settings drawer. See Chapter 3.

>> To remove another user's account, follow Steps 1 through 3 in this section. Tap the Delete (trash) icon next to an account name. Tap the DELETE button to confirm.

>> To remove a restricted user's (kid's) account, tap the Settings icon by the account name, and then tap the Delete icon. Tap the DELETE button to confirm.

>> You can reset the app permission for a restricted account at any time: Tap the Settings icon next to the account name on the Users screen.

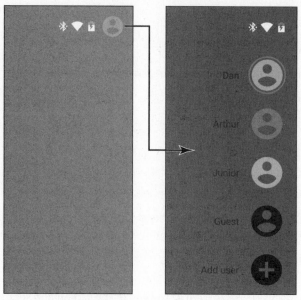

FIGURE 25-2:
User accounts on
the lock screen.

Current account

All accounts

Add Spice to Dictation

If you've used dictation, you might notice that it occasionally censors some of the words you utter. Perhaps you're the kind of person who doesn't put up with that kind of s***.

Relax. You can follow these steps to lift the vocal censorship ban:

1. **Start the Settings app.**

2. **Choose System and then choose Language & Input.**

   The Language & Input item might appear on the main Settings app screen.

   On Samsung devices, choose General Management and then choose Language & Input.

3. **Choose Virtual Keyboard and then choose Google Voice Typing.**

   The Google Voice Typing item might appear on the main Languages & Input screen.

   On Samsung devices, choose On-Screen Keyboard and then choose Google Voice Typing.

4. **Disable the option Block Offensive Words.**

And just what are offensive words? I would think that *censorship* is an offensive word. But no — apparently, only a few choice words fall into this category. I won't print them here.

Visit the Dictionary

Betcha didn't know that your Android sports a dictionary. The dictionary keeps track of words you type — words that may not be recognized as being spelled properly.

Unrecognized words are highlighted on the screen. Sometimes the word is shown in a different color or on a different background, and sometimes it's underlined in red. To add that word to the internal dictionary, tap it. Choose ADD TO DICTIONARY.

To review or edit the dictionary, follow these steps:

1. **Start the Settings app.**

2. **Choose System and then Language & Input.**

   Look for Language & Input item on the main Settings app screen in some versions of Android.

3. **Choose Virtual Keyboard or On-Screen Keyboard.**

4. **Choose Gboard.**

5. **Choose Dictionary.**

6. **Choose Personal Dictionary.**

7. **Choose English.**

   Behold your added words, if any.

With the dictionary visible, you can review words, edit them, remove them, or manually add new ones. Tap a word to edit or delete.

 To add a new word to the list, tap the Add icon.

As this book goes to press, current Samsung devices lack an editable dictionary. This situation may change in the future.

Add Useful Widgets

Your Android features a wide assortment of widgets with which to festoon the Home screen. They can be exceedingly handy, although you may not realize it because the sample widgets that are preset on the Home screen are weak and unimpressive.

Good widgets to add include navigation, contact info, eBook, and web page favorites. Adding any of these widgets starts out the same. Here are the brief directions:

1. **Long-press a Home screen page that has room for a widget.**
2. **Choose Widgets.**
3. **Drag a widget to the Home screen.**
4. **Complete the process.**

   The process is specific for each type of widget suggestion in this section.

Refer to Chapter 20 for specifics on managing widgets.

Direct Dial widget

Use the Contacts/Direct Dial widget on an Android phone to access those numbers you dial all the time. After adding the widget, choose a contact from the address book. Tap this widget to dial the contact's default number instantly.

Directions widget

The Maps/Directions widget allows you to quickly summon directions to a specific location from wherever you happen to be. After you add the widget to the Home screen, select a traveling method and destination. You can type a contact name, an address, a business name, and so on. Add a shortcut name, which is a brief description to fit under the widget on the Home screen. Tap the SAVE button.

Tap the Directions widget to use it. Instantly, the Maps app starts and enters Navigation mode, steering you from wherever you are to the location referenced by the widget.

eBook widget

When you're mired in the middle of that latest potboiler, put a Google Play Books/ Book widget on the Home screen: Choose the Book widget, and then select which eBooks in your digital library you want to access. Tap the widget to open the Play Books app and jump right into the book at the spot where you were last reading.

Web bookmark widget

If you collect bookmarks in the Chrome app, add their list to the Home screen. Choose the Chrome/Chrome Bookmarks widget. For a specific web page, however, open the Chrome app and visit the page. Tap the Action Overflow and choose Add to Home Screen, edit the web page name (if necessary), and then tap the ADD button. A widget is created to access that specific page.

Take a Screen Shot

A *screen shot*, also called a *screen cap* (for *cap*ture), is a picture of your Android's touchscreen. If you see something interesting on the screen or you just want to take a quick pic of your digital life, you take a screen shot.

The stock Android method of shooting the screen is to press and hold both the Volume Down and Power/Lock keys at the same time. Upon success, the touchscreen image reduces in size, you may hear a shutter sound, and the screen shot is saved.

>> Screen shots are accessed through the Photos app or from a Screenshot notification. In the Photos app, the images appear along with any photos you've snapped from the camera.

>> Some Samsung galactic gizmos use a Motion command to capture the screen: Hold your hand perpendicular to the touchscreen, like you're giving it a karate chop. Swipe the edge of your palm over the screen, right-to-left or left-to-right. Upon success, you hear a shutter sound.

TECHNICAL STUFF

>> Internally, screen shots are stored in the Pictures/Screenshots folder. They're created in the PNG graphics file format.

Chapter **26**

Ten Things to Remember

Have you ever tried to tie a string around your finger to remember something? I've not attempted that technique just yet. The main reason is that I keep forgetting to buy string and I have no way to remind myself.

For your Android, some things are definitely worth remembering. From that long, long list, I've come up with ten good ones.

Dictate Text

Dictation is such a handy feature — don't forget to use it! You can dictate most text instead of typing it. Especially for text messaging on an Android phone, it's just so quick and handy.

Just about any time you see the onscreen keyboard, you can dictate instead of typing: Tap the Dictation icon (shown in the margin) and begin speaking. Your utterances are translated to text. In most cases, the translation is instantaneous.

See Chapter 4 for more information on dictation.

Change the Orientation

The natural orientation of the Android phone is vertical — its *portrait* orientation. Larger-format Android tablets have a natural horizontal orientation. Smaller tablets beg to be held vertically. No matter what's natural, you won't break any law by changing the device's orientation.

Apps such as Chrome and Gmail can look much better in the horizontal orientation, whereas apps such as Play Books and Play Music can look much better in the vertical orientation. The key to changing orientation is to rotate the device to view the app the way you like best.

TIP

>> If you prefer a specific orientation, use the Quick Settings item that locks the orientation. See Chapter 3.

>> Not every app changes its orientation. Some apps — specifically, games — present themselves in one orientation only: landscape or portrait.

REMEMBER

>> eBook reader apps have screen rotation settings that let you lock the orientation to the way you want, regardless of what the Android is doing. Refer to Chapter 16.

Work the Quick Settings

Many Android controls are available at a single, handy location: the Quick Settings drawer: Use two fingers to swipe from the top of the screen downward, and behold the Quick Settings drawer.

Many common features sport Quick Settings icons: Wi-Fi, Bluetooth, screen orientation, and more. Using the Quick Settings drawer is far more expedient than visiting the Settings app.

Employ Keyboard Suggestions

Don't forget to take advantage of the predictive text suggestions that appear above the onscreen keyboard while you're typing text. Tap a word suggestion to "type" that word. Plus, the predictive text feature may instantly display the next logical word for you.

When predictive text fails you, keep in mind that you can use glide typing instead of the old hunt-and-peck. Dragging your finger over the keyboard and then choosing a word suggestion works quickly — when you remember to do it.

Avoid the Battery Hogs

Three items can suck down battery power on your mobile device faster than a massive alien fleet is defeated by a plucky antihero who just wants the girl:

» The display

» Navigation

» Wireless radios

The display is obviously a most necessary part of your Android — but it's also a tremendous power hog. The Adaptive Brightness (also called Auto Brightness) setting is your best friend for saving power with the display. See Chapter 21.

Navigation is certainly handy, but the battery drains rapidly because the touchscreen is on the entire time and the speaker is dictating your directions. If possible, plug the Android into the car's power socket when you're navigating.

Wireless radios include Wi-Fi networking, Bluetooth, and GPS. Though they require extra power, they aren't true power hogs, like navigation and the display. Still, when power is getting low, consider disabling these items.

See Chapter 24 for more tips on managing the battery.

Unlock and Launch Apps

The most common unlock-and-launch feature is the Camera app. Swipe this icon across the locked touchscreen to quickly snap a picture or record a video. Many

Androids let you add other lock screen launchers in addition to the Camera app. See Chapter 21 for the possibilities.

>> To unlock and launch an app, swipe the icon across the screen. That app instantly runs.

>> Depending on the screen lock that's installed, the app may run but the Android won't unlock. To do anything other than run the app, you must work the screen lock.

>> Lock screen launchers may not be available when the None or swipe screen lock is set.

Enjoy Phone Tricks

Most Androids sold are phones. They predate tablets by a few years. Still, it's possible to place phone calls on an Android tablet. That's just one of many phone tricks.

Locking the phone on a call

Whether you dialed out or someone dialed in, after you start talking, lock your phone. Press the Power/Lock key. By doing so, you disable the touchscreen and ensure that the call isn't unintentionally disconnected.

Of course, the call can still be disconnected by a dropped signal or by the other party getting all huffy and hanging up on you. But by locking the phone, you prevent a stray finger or your pocket from disconnecting (or muting) the phone.

TIP

If you like to talk with your hands, or just use your hands while you're on the phone (I sweep the floor, for example), get a good set of earbuds with a microphone. Using a headset lets you avoid trying to hold the phone between your ear and shoulder, which could unlock the phone or cause you to drop it or perhaps do something more perilous.

Making calls on a tablet

Yeah, I know: It's not a phone. Even Android tablets that use the mobile data network can't make phone calls. Why let that stop you?

Both the Hangouts and Skype apps let you place phone calls and video-chat with your friends. Boost your Skype account with some coinage and you can even dial into real phones. See Chapter 11 for details.

Avoiding roaming

Roaming can be expensive. The last non-smartphone (dumbphone?) I owned racked up $180 in roaming charges the month before I switched to a better cellular plan. Even though you might have a good phone plan, keep an eye on the phone's status bar to ensure that you don't see the Roaming status icon when you're making a call.

Well, yes, it's okay to make a call when your phone is roaming. My advice is to remember to check for the icon, not to avoid it. If possible, try to make your phone calls when you're back in your cellular service's coverage area. If you can't, make the phone call but keep in mind that you will be charged roaming fees. They ain't cheap.

Use the plus (+) symbol when dialing internationally

That phone number may look like it needs the + symbol, and the Phone app's dialpad features a + key, shared with the 0 key, but don't use it unless you're dialing an international number. The + symbol prefix is the first part of any international phone number.

Refer to Chapter 23 for more information on international dialing.

Check Your Schedule

The Calendar app reminds you of upcoming dates and generally keeps you on schedule. A great way to augment the calendar is to employ the Calendar Widget on the Home screen.

The Calendar Widget lists the current date and then a long list of upcoming appointments. It's a helpful way to check your schedule, especially when you use your Android all the time. I recommend sticking the Calendar Widget right on the main, or center, Home screen panel.

>> See Chapter 20 for information on adding widgets to the Home screen; Chapter 16 covers the Calendar app.

TIP

>> As long as I'm handing out tips, remember to specify location information when you set up an appointment in the Calendar app. Type the information as though you were searching in the Maps app. You can then quickly navigate to your next appointment by touching the location item when you review the event.

Snap a Pic of That Contact

Here's something I always forget: Whenever you're near one of your contacts, take the person's picture. Sure, some people are bashful, but most folks are flattered. The idea is to build up entries in the address book so that all your contacts have photos.

REMEMBER

When taking a picture, be sure to show it to the person before you assign it to the contact. Let them decide whether it's good enough.

>> Receiving a call on an Android phone is then much more interesting when you see the caller's picture, especially a silly or an embarrassing one.

>> Refer to Chapter 13 for more information on using the Camera app; Chapter 7 covers the address book.

Use Google Assistant

Google is known worldwide for its searching capabilities and its popular website. By gum, the word *Google* is synonymous with searching. So please don't forget that your Android, which uses the Google Android operating system, has a powerful search, nay, knowledge companion. It's called the Google Assistant.

>> On many Androids, you access Google Now from the far left Home screen page.

>> The Google Search widget on the Home screen provides a shortcut to your Google Assistant.

>> The Google Assistant app is titled Google.

>> Review Chapter 16 for details on various Google Now commands.

>> Next to the Google Assistant, you can take advantage of the various Search icons found in just about every app. Use this icon to search for information, locations, people — you name it. It's handy.

Index

About the Author

Dan Gookin has been writing about technology for way too long. He combines his love of writing with his gizmo fascination to create books that are informative, entertaining, and not boring. Having written over 160 titles, with 12 million copies in print and translated into over 30 languages, Dan can attest that his method of crafting computer tomes seems to work.

Perhaps his most famous title is the original *DOS For Dummies* (Wiley), published in 1991. It became the world's fastest-selling computer book, at one time moving more copies per week than the *New York Times* number-one bestseller (though, as a reference, it could not be listed on the *Times'* Best Sellers list). That book spawned the entire line of *For Dummies* books, which remains a publishing phenomenon to this day.

Dan's most popular titles include *PCs For Dummies, Word For Dummies, Laptops For Dummies,* and *Troubleshooting & Maintaining Your PC All-in-One For Dummies*. He also maintains the vast and helpful website www.wambooli.com.

Dan holds a degree in Communications/Visual Arts from the University of California, San Diego. He lives in the Pacific Northwest.

Publisher's Acknowledgments

Acquisitions Editor: Katie Mohr

Senior Project Editor: Paul Levesque

Copy Editor: Rebecca Whitney

Production Editor: Siddique Shaik

Cover Image: © Can Yesil/Shutterstock,
© Marc Bruxelle RF/Alamy Stock Photo